ALAN SINFIELD

THE LANGUAGE OF TENNYSON'S *IN MEMORIAM*

BASIL BLACKWELL
OXFORD
1971

ISBN 0 631 12980 4
Library of Congress Catalogue Card No. 76–129586

PRINTED IN GREAT BRITAIN BY
WESTERN PRINTING SERVICES LTD, BRISTOL
AND BOUND BY KEMP HALL BINDERY

CONTENTS

ACKNOWLEDGMENTS

MORE friends and colleagues than I can mention have been generous with help and encouragement. They have contributed valuable suggestions and saved me from a number of errors and follies—for those that remain I alone am responsible.

Mr. John Spencer and Dr. Ruqaiya Hasan have given their expert advice on parts of the typescript; Dr. Cedric Watts and Mr. Peter Hay have read it all through and their observations have been of very great assistance. My brother, Mark Sinfield, has been with the project since it was in its earliest form, and his astute and sympathetic criticism has supported me throughout. Finally, I am most grateful for the guidance of Dr. Isobel Armstrong, who has placed her knowledge, experience and insight completely at my disposal.

Pleasure at acknowledging indebtedness is qualified only by the realization of one's inability to express it adequately.

ALAN SINFIELD

University of Sussex

I

POETRY AND THE LANGUAGE

THIS study began simply with the belief that *In Memoriam* was rather a good poem and that the key to its quality lay in its language. Apart from this, there were very few preconceptions and, indeed, very few critical tools, either literary or linguistic. I found that it was widely accepted that Tennyson was 'a great stylist', but somehow this opinion was always touched with a tone of deprecation. Those who admired certain short passages did not seem to penetrate to the sources of his power, and the prevailing view implied that Tennyson's art was all too frequently a matter merely of pretty decoration.

Many of the techniques developed by literary criticism seemed to be of little assistance, even though they had been designed for close analysis of texts. They had been discovered along with seventeenth-century poetry and did not seem to work very well for the Romantics and their successors. Here is section xi of *In Memoriam*:[1]

> Calm is the morn without a sound,
>   Calm as to suit a calmer grief,
>   And only thro' the faded leaf
> The chestnut pattering to the ground:
>
> Calm and deep peace on this high wold,
>   And on these dews that drench the furze,
>   And all the silvery gossamers
> That twinkle into green and gold:
>
> Calm and still light on yon great plain
>   That sweeps with all its autumn bowers,
>   And crowded farms and lessening towers,
> To mingle with the bounding main:
>
> Calm and deep peace in this wide air,
>   These leaves that redden to the fall;
>   And in my heart, if calm at all,
> If any calm, a calm despair:

[1] All quotations from Tennyson's poems are from *Poetical Works of Alfred Lord Tennyson* (London, 1899). *In Memoriam* as a whole will be referred to as 'the poem', the 131 subdivisions as 'sections'.

Calm on the seas, and silver sleep,
And waves that sway themselves in rest,
And dead calm in that noble breast
Which heaves but with the heaving deep.

I must confess to thinking these lines very good indeed. But where is the irony, the paradox, the extravagant metaphor, the tough reasonableness, the rough, colloquial rhythm? These are the qualities twentieth century criticism has taught us to respect in poetry, and yet their absence did not make me feel able to relinquish my opinion of the section.

Where does the strength of section xi lie? Is it just a beautiful scene with nice sentiments, or is the poet carefully controlling our response by his deployment of the language? Should we relax and let the poetry sweep over us or does it reward close attention? Is Tennyson's art just a matter of euphony of sound or does he exploit to the full the vast potential of the language? What concepts do we need to identify the sources of the power of this poetry?

There is a further problem. *In Memoriam* is a long poem—some 3,000 lines. This raises the question of what we are to do with the parts which are not as exciting as section xi. The tendency has been to assume that we must abandon the poem as a whole and salvage just the intense fragments. Moreover, the analytical approaches which have been developed by literary critics have hardly been applied to long poems, and the linguists, though claiming much, have as yet supplied few valuable hints. Nevertheless, this is a problem which must not be evaded, for the context of section xi makes a great deal of difference to how we understand it. When we look carefully at the scenic description here we notice that it is doing more than evoking a mood, for the poet's eye is moving steadily over the countryside until it comes to the sea. It is only in the light of the two preceding sections, which are about the poet's concern for the safe return of the body of his dead friend, Hallam, in a ship, that the principle underlying the selection of descriptive items is evident. Their significance is psychological, for they exhibit the movement of the poet's mind out to his dead friend. Our awareness of the rest of *In Memoriam* influences the smallest details. We might identify 'deep' in the last line as 'poetic diction', but its effect on the reader will be modified by the fact that he will already have realized that Tennyson is liable to use such words. Again, there is little point in saying that the section has few transitive verbs, or that syntax, sound and metre combine to produce a slow, meditative rhythm, if these things occur throughout *In Memoriam* (actually, the latter does, the former does not). Every line of *In Memoriam* has 3,000 other lines bearing upon it to a greater or lesser degree, and this makes our task very different from the analysis of a sonnet.

My aim in this chapter is to clarify some of these problems in the study of poetic language in long poems, to discuss the efficacy of various approaches (and specially the claims of literary criticism and linguistics) and to describe the procedures adopted in this book.

It is possible to do several different things when talking about poetry and language:

1. One may discuss the forms of language which poetry tends to employ. Studies of metaphor, metre, and other linguistic forms which are of special importance to the poet can make the reader more aware of the variety and subtlety of poetic language and provide him with concepts and categories which will assist his own thinking.

2. One may describe the forms of language used habitually and distinctively (the two are *not* the same) by a poet or group of poets, or in a poem or group of poems. Thus one will produce an account of the *style* of the poet, or the poem, etc.[2] If style describes distinctive uses, then it must be defined in opposition to the practice of other poets or in other poems.[3] I do not see that the style of a poet or poem can be usefully defined against the more general norm of the language as a whole, for such an attempt would mostly reveal factors which are shared by a great many poets and poems—rhyme, metre, inversion of subject and verb, unusual imagery, a lot of adjectives. Nevertheless, the norms of ordinary language must be taken into account *en route*, for if we wish to say that Tennyson uses more poetic diction than Browning then we must first be able to identify poetic diction, and we could never do this by considering only poetry.

3. The habitual and distinctive forms which constitute style are not necessarily those which will feature most in a discussion of a poem as a work of art. Quite often they will not be, for the very fact

<hr/>

[2] 'Style' is a much disputed topic. See Nils Erik Enkvist, John Spencer and Michael J. Gregory, *Linguistics and Style* (London, 1964), pp. 10–27; Richard Ohmann, 'Generative Grammars and the Concept of Literary Style', *Word*, XX (1964), 423–39; Graham Hough, *Style and Stylistics* (London, 1969), pp. 1–19.

[3] Cf. Michael A. K. Halliday, 'The Linguistic Study of Literary Texts', *Proceedings of the Ninth International Congress of Linguists* (The Hague, 1964), 302–7.

that an image or construction is rare in the poet or poem is liable to mean that it is important in its context. Conversely, a prominent stylistic factor (for example, the use, distinctive to a group of modern poets, of lower case letters at the beginnings of lines) may be of little real interest in the poem. The third possibility, then, is that one may study the poetically significant uses of language in a body of work. This kind of discussion deals with the *language* of the poet or poem.

The first of these three activities is obvious enough, but the confusion of the second two can be very troublesome and misleading. In this book I shall be attempting the last of the three: a study of the language of *In Memoriam*. At some points, therefore, I shall be discussing effects which I consider habitual and distinctive, at others just trying to explain the way the language works in a few lines. The criterion will be poetic significance.

One further major point about the three approaches I have listed. In all of them there may be great variation in the extent to which language is related to other aspects of the poetry. The investigator may or may not attempt to correlate his observations on language with biographical, philosophical, psychological or historical knowledge or theories which he believes to be relevant, or even with the structure or meaning of the text. Occasionally the student whose background is in linguistics will disclaim any purpose other than the description of the language of a poem in terms of the sounds and syntactic structures it contains.[4] It does not seem too difficult or extravagant to connect the relative absence of transitive verbs in section xi to the calm which is evoked in the landscape. However, all three approaches and all degrees of explicit relating of language to meaning can be valuable for certain purposes when pursued with sensitivity.

My own feeling is that we can only hope to account for the power of Tennyson's language in *In Memoriam* if we take into consideration all its manifold relationships with other aspects of the poem. The psychological state of the poet in the sections around xi—his obsession with the return of the ship—is extra-linguistic, but surely the force of the language in the section cannot be explained without it. We need to know of the poet's fears in order to confirm our suspicion that there is something sinister in the autonomy with which the waves 'sway themselves': they have a life which Hallam has not,

---

[4] E.g. Sol Saporta, 'The Application of Linguistics to the Study of Poetic Language', in *Style in Language*, ed. Thomas A. Sebeok (Cambridge, Mass., 1960), pp. 88–90.

and they could threaten the ship. Again, it is important, as I hope to show, to appreciate how Tennyson's use of poetic diction is related to other aspects of his thought and practice in *In Memoriam*. Poetic language is so complex in its manifold inter-relations that we cannot afford to ignore any potentially helpful approach. Only thus will we begin to comprehend the fulness of Tennyson's use of the resources of language.

The principal remaining question concerns how we know which are 'the poetically significant uses of language' in a poem. I have a linguist and a literary critic to support my view:

> Literary utterances can be assumed to differ from other utterances by having characteristics of heightened symmetry and structure over and above the symmetry and structure inherent in all uses of language.

> ... in my own opinion the chief difference between language in poems and language outside poems is that the one is more highly structured than the other, and the more complex organisation set up in poems makes it possible for the poet both to redress and to exploit various characteristics of language at large.[5]

Poetry is more densely structured than ordinary language; simply to follow the sequence of the argument is not to exhaust the meaning of the lines. The elements of poetic language are so presented as to invite us to perceive further relationships between them such that the whole poem becomes a complex web of inter-connecting meanings working almost simultaneously.

Poetically significant uses of language are those which contribute to patterns—semantic, syntactical and phonological—which go beyond our normal expectations that an utterance will remain within the rules of syntax and that its subject matter will follow in a fairly coherent manner. A word in a poem is not dispensable once we have grasped its relations with the words on either side. We must hold it in our minds and be prepared to find its significance not merely persisting, but actually expanding, over several lines, or even pages. This is poetic structure. It is not necessary to assume that the poet 'intended' each detail to work in such a complex way, or even that he was properly conscious of the full organization of his poem. He writes a line and thinks, That's rather good, I'll keep that

[5] Archibald A. Hill, 'Towards a Literary Analysis', *English Studies in Honour of James Southall Wilson* (Virginia, 1951), p. 151; Winifred Nowottny, *The Language Poets Use* (London, 1962), p. 72—the whole chapter is very relevant.

one; whereas we are observing exactly what it is about the line that makes it special. The creation of such involved correspondences— where words, phrases, images, syntactic constructions, sounds and rhythms enter into a simultaneous mutual interplay adding vastly to the meanings of each—is the unique characteristic of poetic language.

The ultimate structure is the entire poem in all its manifold complexity, but within it may be distinguished, for critical convenience, smaller, contributory structures of all kinds and sizes. Thus section xi is part of the totality of *In Memoriam* and, specially in its use of the images of the sea and countryside, is intricately related to many other sections, often very far distant from it. It has more immediate connections to section xv, which describes a contrary mood, and section xvi, where the poet considers the implications of these violent extremes of feeling. Within the section we find a low proportion of transitive verbs, which seems to suggest the calm of the morning, and that the description, as well as evoking a mood, embodies a movement across the landscape which is consonant with the poet's state of mind. The repetition of 'calm', pointed up by parallel syntax and stanza structure, does not only emphasize the stillness of the day. It has, in fact, three applications: to the scenery, the poet and the dead Hallam.

> And in my heart, if calm at all,
> If any calm, a calm despair:
>
> Calm on the seas, and silver sleep,
>   And waves that sway themselves in rest,
>   And dead calm in that noble breast
> Which heaves but with the heaving deep.

Only for external nature can 'calm' be used in an unqualified form: the poet has only 'calm despair' and Hallam is 'dead calm' (the point is in this line stressed by a rhythmic structure very unusual in the poem). The use of the one word with appropriate qualifications brings out the respects in which the three are similar and different, but ultimately expresses the disjunction between them. The poet is out of sympathy with nature and his friend has even less life than the sea. The repetitions of 'calm' declare the poet's predicament by creating a structure of meaning over and above that which we normally expect in language.

It seems to be a fact about the way in which we perceive structures that once having discerned elements of a pattern we will naturally proceed to assimilate into it all relevant items in the context. Hence features which are in themselves quite unexceptional will be drawn inevitably into relationships with each other once the initial hint is taken. Thus in section xi we notice further the connection between 'in my heart' and 'in that noble breast'. The same organ is involved, but in the one case it is regarded as the seat of the emotions, in the other merely as the means by which one breathes. Breathing is the most basic human activity, but Hallam cannot even do that, let alone experience emotions. Once again the disjunction between the human being and the corpse is insisted upon through the use of words whose meanings are similar in some ways, but ultimately horribly different. It is the sea which has movement and, moreover, this is expressed in terms of sleeping and resting, activities literally performed by people. Once again we see the contrast with the dead Hallam. There is yet a further complication: 'sleep' and 'rest' are common euphemisms for death—the sea is calm and at rest, but Hallam is dead calm and his sleep is the sleep of death. Thus we have yet another structure of similarities and oppositions, bringing out the awful facts of the disharmony between nature, the poet and his dead friend.

The last six lines of section xi are richly overlaid with complex correspondences, and I have hardly begun to consider the contributions of syntax, sound and rhythm. The poet achieves his most fundamental effects through this pattern-making propensity of the human mind. It is this density of structure which is the special feature of poetic language, and which should be our overriding concern.

I had better say a little about some other concepts which have been suggested as criteria for identifying significant uses of language in poetry. 'Choice' and 'deviation' have been widely discussed, and they evidently express something which happens in poetic language. The poet, like the rest of us, may choose at various points between alternative forms (for instance, an active or passive construction), and he may, moreover, violate the rules which most of us observe.[6]

[6] On choice, see H. A. Gleason, Jr., *Linguistics and English Grammar* (New York, 1965), pp. 425–39; Stephen Ullmann, *Language and Style* (Oxford, 1964), p. 102. On deviation, see Ullmann, op. cit., p. 154; *Style in Language*, ed. Sebeok, pp. 101, 293–6, 330–5; Walter A. Koch, *Recurrence and a Three-Modal Approach to Poetry* (The Hague, 1966), p. 44; Samuel R. Levin, 'Deviation—Statistical and Determinate—in Poetic Language', *Lingua*, XII (1963), 276–90.

Obviously it is necessary for the reader of poetry to be aware of when these things are occurring, for only thus can he appreciate the full implications of the poet's selection of language. If one did not sense that the relative absence of transitive verbs in section xi was unusual, one could not claim a special relationship between it and the calm of the morning.

The notion of choice is most helpful in relation to syntax and metre, where there is a limited number of alternatives. Deviation is much more flexible, but there are several reasons against making it the principal focus of attention in a discussion of poetic language (though it will be more important in a study of style). Firstly, it is in practice difficult to decide which norm one should consider poetic language as deviating from, since it is probable that the reader is in fact conscious of several norms simultaneously—the norm of ordinary language, of language in poetry, of the relevant poetic convention, and the norm established within the poem itself. Secondly, as Michael Riffaterre has argued,[7] the immediate context must be a very important influence on the reader's response, and it is within this range that he is most aware of an occurrence as remarkable or otherwise. It becomes silly to speak of deviation within such a small frame of reference. And thirdly, deviation tends to lead us to the odd, and it is noticeable that proponents of the term have tended to make most of their case from highly inventive poets like Dylan Thomas and e. e. cummings. Concentrating on the peculiar seems undesirable in any event, but with nineteenth century poems one would often have difficulty in identifying other than trivial deviations. The concept could hardly account for the relationship in section xi between 'in my heart' and 'in that noble breast': these phrases are really only deviant in so far as we feel encouraged to relate them to each other—that is, in so far as they form a structure more complex than we normally find in language. We therefore find ourselves trapped in a circle unless we make structure our dominant concern. Choice and deviation will often be essential to the understanding of the detailed workings of poetic language, but they cannot finally be the key factors.

We should also observe that simply to note an item as deviant or chosen from several possibilities is not to attempt any kind of

---

[7] There are four articles by Riffaterre: review in *Word*, XII (1956), 324–7; 'Criteria for Style Analysis', *Word*, XV (1959), 154–74; 'Stylistic Context', *Word*, XVI (1960), 207–18; 'The Stylistic Function', *Proceedings of the Ninth International Congress*, 316–22.

decision as to its appropriateness in the poem. This must be a matter of structure.[8] This fact is evidently appreciated by those who employ the related concept of 'foregrounding'. This term refers to the way in which some items of language in poetry stand out from their context (or background) and demand the reader's attention in their own right. Foregrounding also occurs in less formal expressive language, but the special feature of poetry is the consistency and systematic character of its deployment. Hence one may demonstrate the 'cohesion' of foregrounded items in a poem.[9] It will be seen at once that this insight is ultimately similar to the concept of structure, but it is not identical with it. Cohesion of foregrounding, like deviancy, leads us into confusion if we attempt to see it as the fundamental principle of poetic language. It will work for 'deep' which, as a poetic diction word for ocean, stands out because it is unusual in the language, but there is little out of the ordinary in the waves sleeping and resting other than the correspondence with the condition of the poet's dead friend. In other words, in this latter instance it is almost entirely the structure (or cohesion) which foregrounds the phrase. Cohesion of foregrounding here becomes a circular and redundant way of describing what happens, since it assumes that we first perceive foregrounded items and then their cohesion, whereas in fact the process is the other way about.

Finally, the frustration or fulfilment of expectations has been proposed as the major principle of poetic language.[10] Again this is certainly important, but is best thought of as subsumed under the concept of structure. As we first read a poem we may indeed be startled by what happens, and we may then find that what looked like a frustration is in fact a more complex fulfilment (this second step is essential: there is little point in simply surprising the reader). But it is generally recognized that it is worthwhile to read a poem more than once, and when we do this our experience is not of expectations frustrated or fulfilled, but of a structure which is both the cause and the result of these expectations. On the first time through section xi we may be taken aback by the new application of 'calm'

[8] This point is taken by Gleason, *Linguistics and English Grammar*, and by Roger Fowler in *Essays on Style and Language*, ed. Fowler (London, 1966), p. 25.

[9] Cf. Paul L. Garvin (ed. and trans.), *A Prague School Reader on Esthetics, Literary Structure and Style* (Georgetown, 1964), pp. 9–16, 19–22; Gleason, *Linguistics and English Grammar*, pp. 435–9; Geoffrey Leech, ' "This Bread I Break"—Language and Interpretation', *REL*, VI (1965), 66–75, and in *Essays on Style and Language*, ed. Fowler, p. 145.

[10] See the Riffaterre articles in note 7 above; Koch, *Recurrence and a Three-Modal Approach*, pp. 44–7; *Style in Language*, ed. Sebeok, pp. 99–103.

B

to the poet's friend as 'dead calm', but on subsequent readings we will be conscious of this feature primarily as an aspect of the total structure of the section. Expectation and structure are intimately connected, for without structure there could be no expectation, but the end result for the reader is an awareness of structure, and this is the most useful concept for an understanding and appreciation of poetic language.

I have discussed the kind of examination I wish to make of Tennyson's language in *In Memoriam* and the way in which I believe attention should be focussed. It remains to consider the methods and approaches which are best suited to the task. Although I believe firmly in the usefulness of linguistic techniques to this kind of work, I fear that my methodology would displease some linguists. As I see it, the qualities they tend to admire most are rigorous objectivity, simplicity and explicitness, and the establishment of clear rules. It may already be apparent that, given my view of poetic structure, these qualities would be very difficult, and probably impossible, to attain. Linguistics operates for much of the time at a fairly high level of generality, but poetry achieves significance through its uniqueness; only very limited progress can be made without abandoning preconceived rules and submitting to the highly individual creation of the literary artist. Poetic structure is so vastly complex and so dependent upon semantic nuances that objectivity, simplicity and explicitness could only be gained by paying a very high price in terms of any pretence of giving a reasonably full account of one's response. Linguists, of course, have their own various purposes in their treatment of poetry, and no one would wish to hinder them— though a literary critic would be horrified to find Walter A. Koch trying to discover 'a basis for the determination of the portion of poetry a particular text contains' and the 'degree of poeticalness' possessed by any instance of discourse.[11] My argument here concerns the kinds of statement I wish to make about poetic language.

Some of the analyses of English poems made by linguists are, however, very interesting. Archibald A. Hill, one of the first in the field, has published notable discussions of the song 'Tell me where is fancie bred' from *The Merchant of Venice* and of Browning's Pippa's Song, though unfortunately he misunderstands Tennyson's 'Now sleeps the crimson petal, now the white', wrongly supposing that it

[11] *Recurrence and a Three-Modal Approach*, p. 9.

is addressed to a man (it is spoken by a woman in *The Princess*, but she is reading from a book and immediately afterwards goes on to quote 'Come down, O maid, from yonder mountain height').[12] John Spencer and Michael Gregory are impeccable on syntactical ambiguity in Donne's 'A Hymn to God the Father',[13] and J. McH. Sinclair gives a full and easily comprehensible account of the syntax of Philip Larkin's 'First Sight', though he evidently has no interest in pushing his analysis beyond simple description at the syntactic level.[14] Geoffrey Leech is more inclusive, though rather cumbersome, on Thomas' 'This bread I Break',[15] and Michael A. K. Halliday demonstrates the high proportion of nominal groups in Yeats' 'Leda and the Swan', though without attempting to discuss their significance.[16]

All these essays are suggestive in their different ways, though the literary critic is liable to find them somewhat cumbersome and unwieldy. The linguistic approach has certain more disabling tendencies, though these need not be endemic. The drive towards simplicity may lead to a fatal smoothing out of ambiguities and nuances, as we find in Hill's interpretation of 'The Windhover'[17] and Sumner Ives' analysis of 'You, Andrew Marvell' by MacLeish.[18] In the latter poem it is at several points unclear whether one should understand the verbs 'to be' or 'to feel'. The uncertainty about what actually exists and what the poet feels seems to be relevant to the state of mind described, but Ives always chooses one and excludes the other—and without even explaining why.

Yet more alarming is the way in which some linguists treat the semantic level. Sinclair says of 'First Sight', 'there is little to say about the vocabulary of such a short text when we have no proper description of English vocabulary patterns to use as a basis'—

---

[12] Three articles by Hill: 'Towards a Literary Analysis', pp. 160–5; 'Pippa's Song: Two Attempts at Structural Criticism', *Introductory Readings in Language*, ed. Wallace L. Anderson and Norman C. Stageberg, rev. edn. (New York, 1966), pp. 266–71; 'A Sample Literary Analysis', in *Report of the Fourth Annual Round Table Meeting on Linguistics and Language Teaching*, ed. Hill (Washington, 1953), pp. 87–93.

[13] *Linguistics and Style*, pp. 97–8.

[14] In *Essays on Style and Language*, ed. Fowler.

[15] *REL*, VI (1965), 66–75.

[16] 'The Linguistic Study of Literary Texts' and *Patterns of Language, Papers in General, Descriptive and Applied Linguistics*, ed. Halliday and Angus McIntosh (London, 1966), pp. 55–61.

[17] 'An analysis of *The Windhover*, an Experiment in Structural Method', *PMLA*, LXX (1955), 968–78.

[18] 'Grammatical Analysis and Literary Criticism', *Introductory Readings on Language*, ed. Anderson and Stageburg, pp. 260–5.

though Larkin says, for instance, of lambs, that 'their bleating clouds the air.'[19] There certainly are things that can be said of diction without a description of patterns in the language; indeed, it may be doubted whether any such description could be constructed which would be sufficiently sensitive to be of any real value to the reader of poetry. Nevertheless, we find Koch setting out 'to measure the informational content' of poems[20] and Samuel R. Levin attempting to envisage *grammatical* rules which will allow for expressions like 'A grief ago'.[21] The desire to disqualify a 'sentence' like 'Argumentative windows cook with their destinies' from English through absolute rules like those which govern syntax is surely misguided, and fortunately is rather discouraged by Noam Chomsky in his more recent writings.[22] But whether any system of rules for vocabulary could ever approach the experienced reader's intuitive sensitivity to the slender nuances of meaning upon which poetry depends is to my mind extremely doubtful. I believe that we should pluck up courage and manage with our own impressionistic responses, checking them as best we can. The achievements of literary criticism have not been negligible.

The aim of reducing semantics to a precise set of rules is expressed mainly by the group of linguists called transformationalists (foremost among whom is Chomsky). Their approach can, in my opinion, also be highly misleading in terms of the syntactic structure of a poem. The transformationalist is distinguished by his attempt to reduce the rules of syntax to a basic core by regarding, for instance, the passive construction as a 'transform' or 'rewrite' of the active construction. As a system of rules for grammar this may be excellent, but when lines of poetry are 'rewritten' so that the form selected by the poet is entirely disregarded, the student is removed from all possibility of appreciating the poet's chosen structure. Shakespeare wrote, 'But if the while I think on thee, dear friend, / All losses are restored and sorrows end' (Sonnet 30), but Levin 'rewrites' the last line as 'Then you restore all losses and you end all sorrows'.[23] This

---

[19] *Essays on Style and Language*, ed. Fowler, p. 68; cf. McIntosh, *Patterns of Language*, pp. 94–5.
[20] *Recurrence and a Three-Modal Approach*, pp. 27–9.
[21] 'Poetry and Grammaticalness', *Proceedings of the Ninth International Congress*, pp. 308–14; cf. the ensuing discussion, and Saporta in *Style and Language*, ed. Sebeok, pp. 84–5.
[22] *Aspects of the Theory of Syntax* (Cambridge, Mass., 1965), pp. 75ff., 120–3, 148–50. and specially 153–60 and 192. Cf. Ullmann, *Language and Style*, pp. 3–16.
[23] Samual R. Levin, *Linguistic Structures in Poetry* ('S-Gravenage, 1962), pp. 53–4.

is *not* the same. Shakespeare does not say that his friend does anything; indeed, at various points in the sequence he accuses the other
man of ignoring his feelings, and these lines only say definitely that
thinking of the friend is restorative. If he were to put in an appearance the whole sonnet would be rendered unnecessary. The 'rewrite' irons out this undertone. Levin wishes to demonstrate the
importance of parallelism, but the whole point must surely be that
Shakespeare does *not* choose an active construction here as he does
in the rest of the sonnet.

Koch undertakes an even more startling reduction of Shelley's
poem 'Night' to a point where it can be quantified.[24] Thus the first
six lines are 'rearranged' to read 'Author likes night', so that a
scheme can be imposed whereby 'When I arose and saw the dawn /
I sigh'd for thee' can be listed as consisting of Author likes night and
Author dislikes dawn. Such an approach must take the investigator
so far from the poem as to disconnect utterly any statement based
on it from the reality of a reader's experience. The essential feature
of poetry is that it does not operate at that level of generality.
Fortunately, Chomsky has disowned this kind of procedure[25] which,
though it may be useful to linguists for certain purposes, can
certainly not be said to take us closer to the intrinsic nature of
poetic structure.

I should repeat that I think linguistics has much to offer the student
of poetic language. One could easily produce a number of ill-
advised literary approaches, and one can still find people claiming
that Tennyson replaced the word 'glassy' with 'placid' in section ix
because he disliked having too many sibilants in his verse. The
contribution we might expect from linguistics is basically threefold.
Firstly, it can offer us theories of how language functions, both in
general and in particular, providing a greater understanding of the
medium in which literature works. Secondly, linguistics aims to
make available methods for the description of texts which have been
tested for their accuracy and their completeness. Using such methods
makes it possible to explain more clearly what one means and, moreover, to do so in relation to an existing system whose validation is
known.[26] Acquaintance with a complete description of the language

[24] *Recurrence and a Three-Modal Approach*, pp. 27–9.
[25] *Aspects of the Theory of Syntax*, pp. 126–7.
[26] Cf. Halliday, 'The Linguistic Study of Literary Texts', and *Patterns of Language*,
pp. 45–7, 64–7; and R. Hasan, 'Linguistics and the Study of Literary Texts', *Études de
Linguistique Appliquée*, V (1967), 106–21.

should also add to the student's consciousness of the potential range of usage, thereby decreasing the chances of the effect of a poem being only partially (or even wrongly) explained through ignorance of some of the operative linguistic devices. This is especially true of syntax, where intuition, misguided by school-taught grammar, seems to be particularly inadequate. Finally, linguistics is helpful simply in inducing a greater general awareness of language, not just in terms of its variety, but with a corresponding sensitivity to its systematic nature. The linguist can offer a critical frame of mind, making us ready to appreciate the full range of functions within language but alert to the dangers of ill-founded assumptions.[27]

What, then, has the literary critic to add? Is it the case that the linguist must first 'describe' the text and then the function of the critic is to come along behind and 'evaluate'?[28] The critic has to know about all kinds of things which, although they must have their bearing on the interpretation of the language of a poem, do not much interest the linguist. I am thinking of things like attitudes to the language and to poetic language at various times in history, literary genres, conventions and forms (e.g. the special kind of signal transmitted when we glance down a page and find that a poem has fourteen lines), literary figures, allusion. The literary critic also takes it upon himself to gather relevant information about literary history, philosophy, history, religious beliefs, current notions in the sciences and the effects of foreign influences. I say again, all these things are liable to have an important part in our understanding of a text.

Linguistics admits, moreover, to major inadequacies which may be temporary or permanent. One of these, as I have suggested, concerns the difficulty of formulating rules to cope with minute details of semantics; another is the problem of what to do with sequences longer than the sentence. In both cases the choices open to a user of the language are so vast and the implications of these choices so complex, that they may well continue to defy any codi-fication which will be sufficiently sensitive to account for the most highly patterned utterances, namely those we call poetry. In these

[27] For other moderate discussions of the role of linguistics, see Hough, *Style and Stylistics*; Edward Stankiewitz, 'Linguistics and the Study of Poetic Language', in *Style and Language*, ed. Sebeok, pp. 69–81; Roger Fowler, 'Linguistics, Stylistics; Criticism?', *Lingua*, XVI (1966), 153–65; and Fowler, P. J. Wexler and A. L. Binns in *Essays on Style and Language*, ed. Fowler.

[28] Cf. Sumner Ives, 'Grammatical Analysis and Literary Criticism', p. 261.

areas the literary critic must bring to bear such experience and expertise as he can, hoping for hardly more objective confirmation than the agreement of others similarly qualified.

But my main point, as the reader may have anticipated, is that poetic structure is only to be appreciated by working, as some scholars manage to do, on all these levels simultaneously. The skills and habits of mind which I have attributed to linguists and literary critics must all be brought to bear on a poem if one wishes to comprehend the fulness of the creative use of language. The whole point about a poem is the inter-relation of all these aspects: a total approach is essential. The uncharitable may regard this as an arrogant claim for my own competence; of course, it is always easier to see what should be done than to do it, but the attempt should nevertheless be made.

There is no method except to familiarize oneself with the techniques and concepts which others have found useful and to read and re-read the poem until ideas begin to crystallize. Weeks of frustration will usually precede the emergence of an apparently viable way of regarding the language of the poem, and this way will often have to be disregarded as its insufficiencies subsequently become evident. Counting selected features (a method so despised by many literary critics) can be an aid to focussing attention; the difficulty, of course, is which things to count. Comparison with other texts can also help from this point of view, though once again we have the problem of *which* other texts. I have omitted most of this exploratory detail from this study partly because it can be very tiresome for the reader, and partly because I believe that if an aspect of the language is not reasonably apparent when pointed out then it is almost certainly not having very much effect.[29] Moreover, my emphasis on poetic structure means that inter-relationships within the text are ultimately more significant than whether an isolated aspect of its language is exploited or ignored by other poets.

One further approach which has been found useful in this case is comparison of the text with known manuscript variants. Christopher Ricks' edition of *The Poems of Tennyson* now makes most of this material generally available (though my own work was largely completed before its publication),[30] as well as providing a full

[29] Cf. W. K. Wimsatt, Jr., *The Prose Style of Samuel Johnson*, 2nd edn. (New Haven and London, 1963), p. 24.
[30] See Philip Lovin Elliott, Jr., 'A textual study of *In Memoriam*', unpubl. diss. (Georgia, 1963) for the Harvard, Huntington, Yale and Heath manuscripts, the Trial

account of the scholarly issues involved. Almost no certain con-
clusions can be drawn from this kind of evidence though it is often
interesting to propose theories about Tennyson's motivation.
Variant readings can be very instructive, however, in demonstrating
by contrast important features of the final version.

The bulk of this book is divided into chapters on diction, syntax,
imagery, sound and rhythm. On a number of occasions it has been
difficult to decide under which heading to make a point; such
divisions are ultimately arbitrary, but some kind of form had to be
chosen. The closing chapter ambitiously sets out to make a few
suggestions about the relationship of Tennyson's language in *In
Memoriam* to that of other nineteenth-century and modern poetry,
though its ideas are necessarily very tentative since they lack the
weight of full close analysis. I should emphasize that the shape of
the book was not imposed until a great deal of its substance had
begun to emerge. This is equally true of the second chapter, which
seeks to lay down some large, general concepts which will recur
throughout the study. They are placed at the beginning in order that
the reader shall have some sense of direction, but in no sense did
they precede the examination of the language: they followed from it.

This chapter may perhaps best conclude with a cautionary word
about style from John Middleton Murry:

> The manifest dangers of talking about style are two: the danger of
> talking about the accidentals and not the essentials; and, in the
> endeavour to avoid this, the danger of vague generalisation.[31]

and subsequent early editions. The authorities of the Usher Gallery, Lincoln, and Lord
Tennyson and the Master and Fellows of Trinity College, Cambridge, have kindly
allowed me to inspect and quote the Lincoln and Trinity manuscripts.

[31] *The Problem of Style* (London, 1960), p. 32.

II

IN MEMORIAM:
THE LINNET AND THE ARTIFACT

> All, as in some piece of art,
> Is toil cöoperant to an end. (cxxviii)

> I do but sing because I must,
> And pipe but as the linnets sing. (xxi)

THESE two comments on the nature of poetry from *In Memoriam* illustrate the twin attitudes behind the poem. The first suggests that a work of art is an artifact, finished and perfected with all its parts carefully designed so as to contribute to a meaningful whole, perhaps with a moral purpose. The second shows the poet as writing because he cannot help himself, because he has to express his feelings. In this account the poet has little conscious control: his emotional state governs his mind, and he can write only what he feels. There is no thought of an end to be achieved, no suggestion of a pre-arranged scheme to which every part must contribute.

These quotations pick out precisely the duality in *In Memoriam* and in its language. Like most of Tennyson's work, it does not fit easily into pre-existing categories of literary criticism. In particular, it is a mixture of attributes generally associated with the neo-classical writers of the eighteenth-century Enlightenment and with the early nineteenth-century Romantic movement. Thus on the one hand we have the familiar picture of Tennyson as the black-blooded melancholic, brooding over the Lincolnshire Wolds, writing 'Byron is dead' in the chalk and presenting in *In Memoriam* the intimate diary of a man confessing himself.[1] On the other hand we find the Poet Laureate, associated by F. L. Lucas with Theocritus and Callimachus, Virgil and Horace, Pope and Gray in 'their mellowed learning, their chiselled style, their pleasure in remoulding the brave tales of older days into a more perfectly polished form'.[2] One view of Tennyson's poetry finds him personal, subjective and

---

[1] See Sir Harold G. Nicolson, *Tennyson: Aspects of his Life, Character and Poetry* (London, 1923), pp. 9–10; and T. S. Eliot, *Selected Prose* (paperback, London, 1963), p. 170.
[2] F. L. Lucas, ed., *Tennyson: Poetry and Prose* (London, 1947), p. ix.

impressionistic, the other sees him as a public writer, the mouthpiece of his age, using a highly stylized mode of poetic language to give classical form and order to his utterances. The duality is observed by a recent critic, who remarks, 'He is a romantic and an idealist and a sentimentalist; but he is also a realist, a Classicist and a satirist'.[3]

I am well aware of the dangers involved in describing Tennyson in these terms. A. O. Lovejoy has claimed that one cannot meaningfully speak of 'Romanticism', but only of several 'Romanticisms',[4] and Geoffrey Clive has declared that 'The ruptures and divisions in modern consciousness which often continue to be associated with nineteenth-century Romanticism were just as characteristic of the eighteenth century, although differently expressed'.[5]

However, the majority of students of the history of ideas accept that there are two distinct clusters of attributes which can be labelled 'Enlightenment' and 'Romanticism'. Whether they were successively or simultaneously present, and whether or not they can be seen as self-conscious movements where we can meaningfully enrol all the writers who have been marshalled under their banners, does not matter for my purposes. Perhaps the most important aspect of these terms for a study of Tennyson is that they exist in critics' minds, where they provide neat pigeon-holes into which he can be tidily fitted. Tennyson cannot be fully comprehended without some understanding of the modes of thought which characterized his immediate predecessors, the Romantics; but, at the same time, there are elements in his art which derive from impulses more often associated with the eighteenth century. The attempt to Tennyson in terms solely of the one or the other results in a devaluing of his achievement: he becomes a victim of literary history.

Before going further I must describe what I take to be the Enlightenment and Romantic characteristics. Such a brief account as can be given here will obviously simplify the issues, but a fairly bald polarization of the two positions should have the advantage of making plain the radical differences in attitude.

The eighteenth-century Enlightenment saw a universe where everything was in its place. Newtonian science had strengthened the

---

[3] Edward Elton Smith, *The Two Voices: A Tennysonian Study* (Lincoln Nebraska, 1964), p. 55.
[4] Arthur O. Lovejoy, 'On the Discrimination of Romanticisms', in *Essays in the History of Ideas* (Baltimore, 1948). For a reply see René Wellek, 'The Concept of "Romanticism" in Literary History', *Comparative Literature*, I (1949), 1–23 and 147–72.
[5] Geoffrey Clive, *The Romantic Enlightenment* (paperback, New York, 1960), p. 20.

belief in a great chain of being in which every created thing was a
link. The machine was in order, and though man's position was the
uncomfortable one of the bridge between thinking and non-thinking
creatures, this was as it was meant to be.[6] Nature was unchanging
and knowable through scientific method, and neither was threatening: they worked together in a demonstration of God's control over
his universe. As this scheme was reasonable, appreciation of it was
denied to no man, for all were endowed with reason.[7] Since this
faculty was deemed to be available to everyone, it could clearly not
involve anything very complicated: it provided a simple frame of
reference by which all things could be determined by all men who
opened themselves freely to it.[8] The principal distraction was liable
to be too much subjectivity—too much reliance upon personal
intuition at the expense of what was evident to all men. The emphasis was not on the individual, but on society.[9] Lovejoy calls the
dominant creed 'uniformitarianism':

> in nearly all the provinces of thought in the Enlightenment the
> ruling assumption was that Reason—usually conceived as summed
> up in the knowledge of a few simple and self-evident truths—is
> the same in all men and equally possessed by all; that this common
> reason should be the guide of life; and therefore that universal
> and equal intelligibility, universal acceptability, and even universal
> familiarity, to all normal members of the human species, regardless
> of differences of time, place, race, and individual propensities and
> endowments, constitute the decisive criterion of validity or of
> worth in all matters of vital human concernment.[10]

These attitudes extended to works of art, which should be
similarly accessible to all men. This conformity to a universal standard
was manifested in an adherence to rules which, it was claimed,
derived from the ancients. True achievement consisted in displaying

[6] Arthur O. Lovejoy, *The Great Chain of Being* (Cambridge, Mass., 1936), especially
pp. 183–200, 208–26; Wellek, 'The Concept of "Romanticism" in Literary History',
p. 161; Alfred North Whitehead, *Science and the Modern World*, in *Alfred North
Whitehead, An Anthology* (ed. F. S. C. Northrop and Mason W. Gross) (London, 1953).
[7] Lovejoy, *The Great Chain of Being*, pp. 227–32; Whitehead, *Science and the Modern
World*, p. 414; Sir Isaiah Berlin, 'Some Sources of Romanticism', six lectures in the
National Gallery of Art in Washington (1965) sponsored by the Bollingen Foundation,
recorded at the time for the B.B.C. Third Programme and broadcast in August and
September 1966.
[8] Lovejoy, *The Great Chain of Being*, p. 292; R. A. Foakes, *The Romantic Assertion*
(London, 1958), p. 12.
[9] Clive, *The Romantic Enlightenment*, p. 23; Edmund Wilson, *Axel's Castle* (paperback,
London, 1961), p. 10; Graham Hough, *The Romantic Poets*, 2nd edn. (London, 1957), p. 8.
[10] Lovejoy, *The Great Chain of Being*, pp. 288–9.

excellence within established forms, for they provided a standard of what was fitting.[11] The artist imitated nature, and this meant showing the proportionate sanity, order and design which were seen as existing in the universe. God's world was complete, and so the rules for poetic achievement were laid down for all time and the aim was to render objectively the design which was evident to any man's unbiased gaze.[12] The poem was judged as an artifact, something which had been made and whose qualities could be rationally assessed.[13] Originality was not prized, but a just representation of what was generally understood to be the case; this meant that innovation in poetic language was not in itself a virtue. Style was supposed to ornament thought and to present it in a pleasing form:

> According to the most fundamental neo-classic frame of reference, language is the 'dress' of thought, and figures are the 'ornaments' of language, for the sake of the pleasurable emotion which distinguishes a poetic from a merely didactic discourse. These elements must be joined to form a consistent whole according to the basic neo-classic unifying principle of the decorum or proportionableness of parts—a complex requirement, involving adjustment to the poetic kind, and the matter signified, as well as the character and emotional state of the speaker depicted.[14]

For the Romantics, the Enlightenment system was unsatisfactory because it excluded too many aspects of experience: they *knew*, inside themselves, that it was not true. Moreover, the rational questioning of dogma which had seemed so promising began to undercut the very scheme on which it was based, for the answers did not always prove compatible with each other.[15] According to Whitehead, Western man had long held (and still holds) two inconsistent attitudes: scientific realism based on mechanism, and a belief in man as a self-determining organism.[16] Partly, perhaps, because of the increasing claims made by science, the Romantics found themselves compelled to recognize this split. Their response was to declare that poetry proclaimed a more vital form of truth than science, and to opt for a view of the universe as an organism

---

[11] Berlin, 'Some Sources of Romanticism'; Foakes, *The Romantic Assertion*, p. 12.
[12] Lovejoy, *The Great Chain of Being*, pp. 290–5.
[13] Berlin, 'Some Sources of Romanticism'; Wilson, *Axel's Castle*, p. 10.
[14] M. H. Abrams, *The Mirror and the Lamp* (paperback, London, 1960), p. 290; and see W. K. Wimsatt, Jr., *The Prose Style of Samuel Johnson*, 2nd ed. (New Haven and London, 1963), pp. 103–6.
[15] Clive, *The Romantic Enlightenment*, p. 31; Berlin, 'Some Sources of Romanticism'.
[16] Whitehead, *Science and the Modern World*, p. 431.

rather than a mechanism.[17] Thus the possibility of change and individual growth was included. Whitehead's main contentions are that 'the nature-poetry of the romantic revival was a protest on behalf of the organic view of nature, and also a protest against the exclusion of value from the essence of matter of fact'.[18] Several Romantics anticipated the scientists by hitting upon the evolutionary theory of the universe which Tennyson was to adopt in *In Memoriam* —indeed, already in the eighteenth century poet Akenside we find the notion that the Creator,

> From the mute shell-fish gasping on the shore,
> To men, to angels, to celestial minds,
> Forever leads the generations on
> To higher scenes of being.

Nature was now seen not as static but as progressing upwards. Thus value was incorporated into the system, for mankind was envisaged as ever aspiring towards a perhaps unattainable ideal.[19]

Whether he adopted an evolutionary world view or not, the Romantic found that the undermining of dogma and reason forced him to become his own authority. He had to attend to the inner promptings of his own mind, for these were the only sources upon whose integrity he could rely.[20] The imagination was no longer seen as an associative power passively receiving and arranging impressions, but as involved in a creative interchange with its objective surroundings, and it became the principal organ of truth.[21] Men became far less confident that all important questions could be answered; the external and objective sanctions with which faith had been supported became doubtful and any major assertion had to be qualified with a degree of caution.[22]

In poetry, this shift in outlook dictated a change in subject matter:

[17] Abrams, *The Mirror and the Lamp*, pp. 310–12; D. G. James, *Matthew Arnold and the Decline of English Romanticism* (London, 1961), pp. 32–3.

[18] Whitehead, *Science and the Modern World*, p. 449.

[19] Lovejoy, *The Great Chain of Being*, pp. 262–5, 316–26; Wellek, 'The Concept of "Romanticism" in Literary History', p. 150.

[20] Foakes, *The Romantic Assertion*, p. 42; Joseph Warren Beach, *The Concept of Nature in Nineteenth-Century English Poetry* (New York, 1936), p. 20; Walter E. Houghton, *The Victorian Frame of Mind* (New Haven and London, 1957), pp. 94–6, 150–1.

[21] Wellek, 'The Concept of "Romanticism" in Literary History', pp. 159–65; Stephen Prickett, *Coleridge and Wordsworth: The Poetry of Growth* (London, 1970). Dr. Prickett kindly allowed me to read his book whilst it was in the press.

[22] Berlin, 'Some Sources of Romanticism'; Whitehead, *Science and the Modern World*, p. 439; Robert Langbaum, *The Poetry of Experience* (paperback, New York, 1963), p. 35.

It is always, as in Wordsworth, the individual sensibility, or, as in Byron, the individual will, with which the Romantic poet is preoccupied; and he has invented a new language for the expression of its mystery, its conflict and confusion. The arena of literature has been transferred from the universe conceived as a machine, from society conceived as an organisation, to the individual soul.[23]

Poetry became the study of the individual mind, usually the poet's own mind, for that was where the truth was to be found. Universality came to be seen as unattainable, but could be best approached through the inclusion of the marvellous diversity in humanity, not through conformity to what was known to be common to all.[24] The poet's experience was his evidence, and assessment of a poem became a matter of whether it seemed to be a pure expression of his emotional state; even if recollected in tranquillity, it had to bear the marks of a spontaneous overflow of powerful feeling. Poetry was no longer judged primarily as something which had been made, but as the expression of an individual. Criticism began to make the quest for the man behind the poem its main activity and to value the sincere and genuine above all else; originality was highly praised.[25] Thus we find an opposition to rigid forms, an antipathy towards standardization—the only appropriate form was that which the emotion actually took. Self-conscious artifice was devalued as a falsification of the poet's experience. Abrams describes as widely accepted Wordsworth's view that the language of poetry should be:

> the spontaneous and genuine, not the contrived and simulated, expression of the emotional state of the poet. On this thesis . . . . depends also the general romantic use of spontaneity, sincerity, and integral unity of thought and feeling as the essential criteria of poetry, in place of their neo-classic counterparts: judgment, truth, and the appropriateness with which diction is matched to the speaker, the subject matter, and the literary kind.[26]

These two accounts of the Romantic and Enlightenment outlooks represent radical positions and their presence in a writer is rarely a matter of unswerving commitment. My point is that *In Memoriam* displays the extremes of both attitudes. On the one hand the poet pipes but as the linnets sing, on the other we find that all is toil

---

[23] Wilson, *Axel's Castle*, pp. 11–12.
[24] Lovejoy, *The Great Chain of Being*, pp. 306–7.
[25] Abrams, *The Mirror and the Lamp*, pp. 318–20; Foakes, *The Romantic Assertion*, p. 13.
[26] Abrams, *The Mirror and the Lamp*, pp. 101–2; see also Lovejoy, *The Great Chain of Being*, p. 300; Berlin, 'Some Sources of Romanticism'.

cöoperant to a carefully devised and executed end. Tennyson's approach to the problems of love and death, morality and faith created by the death of Arthur Hallam is in many ways subjective, personal, individualistic. The poet is shown creating his own values from his own imaginative resources in the Romantic manner. Though *In Memoriam* has been widely thought of as propounding a philosophy for its times, this view will not account for the greater part of the poem, which is devoted to presenting the poet's developing *experience*. The poet himself says that this is so:

> If these brief lays, of Sorrow born,
>   Were taken to be such as closed
>   Grave doubts and answers here proposed,
> Then these were such as men might scorn.   (xlviii)

In Memoriam presents us with the successive thoughts and feelings of a person; it is not, until the end, the ideas put forward that count, but the attitudes which the poet adopts towards those ideas. We do not find an argument, but something much more like the growth of the poet's mind (the subtitle of *The Prelude*). We do not watch the expounding of a philosophy, but the changes in the poet's outlook.

The crucial section in the poet's development is xcv, for it is here that he experiences a vision which puts him in touch with a suprarational reality. As the poet reads Hallam's letters,

> So word by word, and line by line,
>   The dead man touch'd me from the past,
>   And all at once it seem'd at last
> The living soul was flash'd on mine,
>
> And mine in this was wound, and whirl'd
>   About empyreal heights of thought,
>   And came on that which is, and caught
> And deep pulsations of the world.

In the second line quoted Hallam is 'The dead man', but by the fourth he has become 'The living soul'. Most of *In Memoriam* has been taken up with the poet's various thoughts, but none of them has more authority than another. The vision of section xcv (which alludes plainly to Dante's Paradise) has a unique significance because it provides the poet with a sanction for belief other than mere speculation or wishful thinking. Throughout the poem his main desire has been for renewed contact with Hallam; the vision supplies this. The poet is encouraged to believe that there is something more than physical life and final death, and his other problems disappear. As a result of this experience he knows that there is something other than impotent mankind and indifferent nature, that Hallam does still exist, that they will be reunited one day and that Hallam can still be with him in his present life. The poet had considered all these possibilities and many others, but only the supra-rational experience could give him authority for believing in what his fantasies and dreams had always represented to him as desirable. At the beginning the poet lost touch with Hallam: in section xcv he regains it, and the optimistic conclusion of the poem becomes possible.[27]

All this shows a strong dependence on subjective experience as a way of reaching truth, and is fully consonant with Romantic ways of thinking. It is impossible for the poet's claims to be verified: the experience was in his mind and he believes it. Tennyson's son tells us that he exclaimed:

> Yet God *is* love, transcendent, all pervading! We do not get *this* faith from Nature or the world. If we look at Nature alone, full of perfection and imperfection, she tells us that God is disease, murder and rapine. We get this faith from ourselves, from what is highest within us, which recognizes that there is not one fruitless pang, just as there is not one lost good.[28]

This is just what happens in *In Memoriam*: the poet gets his faith from within himself, and the poem is a record of his experience. He began by speaking of the *loss* of a philosophy: 'I held it truth'

> That men may rise on stepping-stones
> Of their dead selves to higher things.

By the end of the poem he has at last arrived at a settled way of looking at life. Because he is sure that 'I shall not lose thee tho' I die' (cxxx) he can also believe that man can be 'The herald of a higher race' (cxviii). Human existence is not purposeless for, whatever setbacks there may be, man is seen as striving ever upwards to God. This evolutionary theory of the universe is already apparent in the

[27] For a detailed discussion of section xcv see my article in *The Major Victorian Poets: Reconsiderations*, ed. Isobel Armstrong (London, 1969). It is seen as the turning point also by J. L. Kendall, 'A Neglected Theme in Tennyson's *In Memoriam*', *MLN*, LXXVI (1961), 414-20; M. J. Svaglic, 'A Framework for Tennyson's *In Memoriam*', *JEGP*, LXI (1962), 810-25; and Carlisle Moore, 'Faith, Doubt and Mystical Experience in *In Memoriam*', *VS*, VII (1963), 155-69.

[28] *Works, The Eversley Edition*, ed. Hallam Lord Tennyson (London, 1908), III, 214.

lines I have just quoted from section i; the point is whether the poet
can accept it. Hallam's apparently meaningless death shattered his
faith, but the vision of section xcv gives him the authority he needs
for an optimistic outlook.

Tennyson is very explicit in his dependence upon personal experience, and exhibits just that distrust of scientific method and
reasonable arguments for a mechanistic universe which I have
described as characteristic of the reaction against the Enlightenment.

> Let Science prove we are, and then
> What matters Science unto men,
> At least to me? I would not stay.   (cxx)

He tells us in section cxxiv that he has his faith because 'the heart /
Stood up and answer'd "I have felt" '; he almost despises attempts
to reason out a belief based on the argument from design:

> I found Him not in world or sun,
>   Or eagle's wing, or insect's eye;
>   Nor thro' the questions men may try,
> The petty cobwebs we have spun.   (cxxiv)

Hume had long ago pointed out that the mechanistic universe presupposes only the kind of God who would make that mechanism.[29]
For Tennyson, a mechanic God was not good enough, for He could
not guarantee that love would endure, that there was a point to
Hallam's death and the poet's deprivation, that the two men might
meet again at some time. Only a vision where 'The living soul was
flash'd on mine' could underwrite these desires. Thus he declares
that Knowledge is 'earthly of the mind', whereas Wisdom is 'heavenly of the soul' (cxiv). Science, for Tennyson, deals with the
material world and tries to understand it by rational processes, but
for him the most important truths are to be discovered through a
personal experience in which the mind is freed by a vision from the
restraints of both matter and reason. And this attitude Tennyson
held to the end of his life—'Nothing worthy proving can be proven',
he is still writing in 'The Ancient Sage'.

When critics charge Tennyson with stupidity or romantic vagueness they may well have these aspects of *In Memoriam* in mind. It
should be clear, however, that his subjective mode of arriving at
beliefs is not his alone, but is entirely in accord with the reaction

[29] Whitehead, *Science and the Modern World*, pp. 432–3.

C

against the Enlightenment. For Robert Langbaum, 'The essential idea of romanticism' is:

> the doctrine that the imaginative apprehension gained through immediate experience is primary and certain, whereas the analytic reflection that follows it is secondary and problematical. The poetry of the nineteenth and twentieth centuries can thus be seen in connection as a poetry of experience—a poetry constructed upon the deliberate disequilibrium between experience and idea, a poetry which makes its statement not as an idea but as an experience from which one or more ideas can be abstracted as problematical rationalisations.[30]

Milton and Pope set out to explain the ways of God to men: they are secure in the case they wish to make from the start, and their concern is to present it clearly and convincingly. Tennyson starts by saying how he has lost his faith, and it is only after describing the experience of three years that he can state a coherent set of beliefs. Jung declared that this is the only procedure which seems viable in the twentieth century: 'The modern man abhors dogmatic postulates taken on faith and the religions based upon them. He holds them valid only in so far as their knowledge-content seems to accord with his own experience of the deeps of psychic life'.[31] As for certain of the Romantic poets, this operation pivots for Tennyson upon a moment of mystical awareness. Seen from this point of view, the familiar charge that the Victorians always constructed a dream world into which they could escape becomes quite untenable. In *In Memoriam* at least it is nearer the truth to claim that Tennyson is tapping psychic depths in order to frame a world view that is in harmony with his profoundest experience of reality. The implications of this process for a study of the poem's language must not be ignored; its effects will be seen in many aspects of the rest of this book.

A principal corollary of the Romantic side of *In Memoriam* is that the poem should *look like* the poet's experience. This is the function of the realistic background detail—both the scenic description and the poet's family setting. The character of the poem as an evolving experience is also evident in the sequence of short sections, each relatively self-contained, which makes up the totality. Each section encapsulates a moment in the poet's development, a thought or an

[30] Robert Langbaum, *The Poetry of Experience* (paperback, New York, 1963), p. 35.
[31] C. G. Jung, *Modern Man in Search of a Soul* (paperback, London, 1961), p. 239.

incident, and the flexibility of length allows just the amount of elaboration the subject requires. A more rigid form would falsify the experience. In some ways, in fact, we can think of *In Memoriam* as rather like a novel. It opens with the central character musing to himself about his loss, then he strolls down to the graveyard (as an impressionable young man might). More of his meditations follow (iii); he goes to bed, and the reader sees how his loss affects his sleep (iv). Later on he thinks about his art (v), and then he receives a letter from a friend, which sets off a further train of thought (vi). Very early in the morning he goes for a walk to the dead man's house (vii). These events are such as might appear in a novel, but there is no novel like this in the nineteenth century. The poem lacks all the linking passages we expect in a novel. We are not told how or why the poet visits the graveyard in section ii or Hallam's house in vii: we are given no information that is not immediately relevant to his inner emotions. All extraneous matter is excluded so that we are made to concentrate on the poet's most personal thoughts and feelings. The focus is on his internal development, but there is sufficient background to give the sequence credibility.

The short sections make this economy and intensity possible. Each is a moment in the continuum of the poet's changing attitudes, with other parts of his life cut neatly away. T. S. Eliot had the point precisely when he declared that *In Memoriam* has 'the unity and continuity of a diary, the concentrated diary of a man confessing himself'.[32] It has been objected that the sections are not presented in the order in which they were composed. Study of the manuscripts shows that this is certainly true, but we are concerned with the poem, not Tennyson's life. It may well be that *In Memoriam* consists largely of things that happened to Tennyson and it may be that it does not; it is mostly impossible to decide, and in my view fairly unimportant. In order to keep clear the distinction between biography and poem I propose always in this study to use 'Tennyson' of the man who historically wrote *In Memoriam*, and 'the poet' of the 'I' in the poem. The facts of composition do not affect the diary-like appearance of the poem, which is a major cause of the reader's impression that what he has before him has the validity of an actual experience.

The section-sequence structure, so faithful to Romantic modes of thought, has troubled critics by its lack of obvious overall form. Almost all have tried to divide the poem up into fairly self-contained

[32] *Selected Prose*, p. 170.

parts—what Nicolson called 'its three arbitrary divisions of Despair, Regret and Hope, ticked off symmetrically by the successive Christmas Odes'.[33] These divisions are indeed arbitrary, but not, I believe, to be found in the poem. It will be objected that Tennyson mentioned parts, but he suggested two quite different schemes and it seems likely that it was pressure of questioning that elicited the 'parts' rather than anything inherent in the poem.[34] There is no need of divisions; the movement from grief to acceptance is not smooth and regular, but then, neither is life. Like the Romantics, Tennyson avoids predetermined forms which would cramp the expression of an individual experience. The poet tends to take three steps forward and two back, and it is this process of gradual, moment by moment development, visible only if we stand off a little from the text, which creates a sense of the reality of the poet's experience.

The typical movement of the poem does not follow a pattern of logic, or even of simple thought association. The governing factor is the rise and fall in the poet's feelings; the poem moves in waves from one high point of emotional intensity to the next, with the passages in between building up to and leading away from these points. At the first Christmas, for instance, we have two sections of anxiety and mundane preparations before the climax of section xxx, where the family hopefully sings 'They do not die'. The moment of deep feeling is the crest of a relatively mundane wave, even as the family's excitement arose out of their commonplace preparations for Christmas. Leading away from section xxx is a series taking up on a more prosaic level the question of the continuing existence of Hallam. Can the family's optimism be justified, the poet asks: the wave falls back again after the moment of intensity.

The poet on several occasions uses this very metaphor for his changing emotions—in section xix, for example, he compares the movement of his grief to the tide of the river Wye. *In Memoriam* proceeds in waves: a subject is taken up, gathers to a head, breaks in a climax, and then sinks back again, though occasionally a heavy swell comes unexpectedly. The section-sequence structure embodies a kind of rhythm of experience which it is difficult to define further.

[33] Nicolson, *Tennyson*, p. 297; cf. J. C. C. Mays, '*In Memoriam*: An Aspect of Form,' *University of Toronto Quarterly*, XXXV (1965-6), pp. 22-46.
[34] See Hallam Lord Tennyson, *Alfred Lord Tennyson, A Memoir* (London, 1897) (cited hereafter as *Memoir*), I, 305, and James Knowles, 'Aspects of Tennyson II', *Nineteenth Century*, XXXIII (1893), 182.

The form of *In Memoriam* recreates the shapes of the life of the emotions.

The final aspect of the Romantic side of *In Memoriam* which I wish to bring forward here is again related to the practice of relying upon imaginative experience as the primary means of arriving at basic and enduring truths. Since rational analysis is seen as inadequate to grasp the essential significance of the poet's various moods, he uses repeatedly a process of 'redefinition'. By this I mean that he does not dissect an event to reveal its meaning, but restates it in other terms, approaches it from another angle to see how it looks from there. The experience is redefined so that the totality of its significance can be gathered from the different accounts of it.

There are two distinct forms of this redefinition process. The first is its local use, where its function is to make clear the nature of a current emotional state. This is apparent in the tendency to follow a section describing an experience with another trying to place it in the poet's continuing development or evoking a related situation to which it can be compared. Section vii, for instance, describes how the poet goes to Hallam's door but finds no one there. In section viii this event is considered from the point of view of an imaginary happy lover who discovers that his fiancée is not at home when he calls; he is analogous to the poet in section vii and provides another way of looking at the same situation. The differences are also important, however: the lady will presumably be at home tomorrow, but Hallam can never return. This mode of operating is invaluable to a writer like Tennyson who is concerned to express the nature of an elusive emotion—Shelley's 'To a Skylark' is a splendid example of its extended use. The experience is redefined in other terms so that its essential qualities can be distilled.

The second form taken by this process is vital to the large-scale structure of *In Memoriam*. The poet repeatedly alludes after a period of time to an earlier event so that the intervening change of attitude can be immediately seen. The development of his experience is charted primarily by these reminders of earlier scenes which bring out the difference in the poet's outlook. This is most evident in the sections which refer back explicitly across the poem—Christmas, spring, the anniversaries of Hallam's death and the visits to the yew tree all show the poet's attitude measured against recurring external events. In section ii, for example, the yew tree is seen as a figure of deathly constancy, but when he returns in the spring he finds that the yew does experience 'the golden hour / When flower is feeling after' (xxxix). There can be such a thing as love and happiness in the face of death, he now realizes, but sorrow still controls his mind: 'Thy gloom is kindled at the tips, / And passes into gloom again'. His state of mind is progressively redefined in terms of his altered attitudes to the same object.

The importance of this same process in the work and thought of Wordsworth and Coleridge has been expounded by Stephen Prickett.[35] He stresses that to them growth was only possible through the realization of the inadequacy of previously adopted patterns of perception, through the reaction of new experiences on what had gone before. This theory of mental development which is explicit in 'Tintern Abbey' or 'Frost at Midnight' is the implicit structural basis of *In Memoriam*. The earlier poets show how thinking over former attitudes brings them to a new formulation; in *In Memoriam* the reader must perceive for himself how the poet's emotional response is progressively redefined, but the signs are all there in the writing. This process, like the other aspects of the poem discussed in this chapter, will appear again and again in the detailed discussion of language which is to follow.

I have suggested that Tennyson's way of finding values by which to live is related to Romantic modes of thought and that it affects various aspects of the structure of *In Memoriam*. The section-sequence is a superb form for embodying moment by moment the poet's changing moods and ideas without forcing them into a rigid frame; the redefinition process is necessary to capture the poet's states of mind and to chart his attitude as it evolves. These facets of the poem have perplexed and alienated critics, but the full story is even more complicated. There are aspects of the poem—of meaning and language—which do not allow us simply to say, it is a Romantic poem and we must treat it as such. It is also objective, impersonal and general; in other words, it exhibits characteristics usually associated with the Enlightenment.

Of course, this dichotomy between Romantic and neo-classical attributes is relative and is not meant to imply that one group of qualities is completely absent in a writer normally connected with the other. The distinctive factor in Tennyson's approach is the strong presence of both extremes. Consider these remarks he made:

[35] *Coleridge and Wordsworth: The Poetry of Growth* (London, 1970).

This is a poem, *not* an actual autobiography . . . 'I' is not always the author speaking of himself, but the voice of the human race speaking thro' him.

It is rather the cry of the whole human race than mine. In the poem altogether private grief swells out into thought of, and hope for, the whole world . . . It is a very impersonal poem as well as personal.[36]

These comments are the antithesis of the Romantic reliance upon subjective experience, but they too indicate one side of *In Memoriam*. Here we see Tennyson not simply singing like the linnet, but writing to the end of expressing the voice of the human race; he has almost adopted the Enlightenment stance of universal intelligibility, acceptability and familiarity. The poem is conceived of as stating a common human position which will be recognized as true and relevant by the whole of mankind. Though I have asserted that the rearrangement of the sections during the poem's composition does not affect its appearance as a diary, it does show the dichotomy in Tennyson's approach. *In Memoriam* is a record of his experience, but at the same time it is designed to be the voice of the human race. Wordsworth, we know, quite often modified his experience when he used it in his poems, but his alterations were of a completely different kind. He is characteristically to be found concealing the fact that another person was present who also found the event important; he emphasizes the uniqueness of the experience to him. Tennyson, on the other hand, typically generalizes his feelings in *In Memoriam*, stressing that they are common to many people. He insists at the same time on both individuality and generality.

The poem was accepted by its Victorian readers as being of relevance to them, and it is most significant that *The Prelude*, published in the same year, achieved nowhere near the success at the time despite Wordsworth's reputation and the uncertain reviews of Tennyson's earlier work. The repeated references to other people in related situations (often, it may seem to us, rather Victorian situations) contributes powerfully to this generalizing effect. The poet is like young men and girls who have lost their lovers, mothers and fathers who have lost their sons, widows and widowers. He may well say in section xcix that the myriads who have memories of births, bridals and deaths 'count as kindred souls; / They know me not, but mourn with me'. The poet's expression of his own loss comes to stand for the feelings of all bereaved people; to his

[36] *Memoir*, I, 304–5; Knowles, 'Aspects of Tennyson', p. 182.

readers *In Memoriam* represented in part at least what oft was thought.

Certain Romantic poets would perhaps have claimed that what they wrote was in some sense the cry of the whole human race, but Tennyson is distinctive in the deliberate way he sets about generalizing his experience and making it relevant to public issues. The whole process is very carefully managed. At the beginning of the poem the poet has lost the values he had lived by, his whole view of life has been shaken. For the most part, however, he is too absorbed in his immediate grief to think of that. Nevertheless, the question of Hallam's immortality leads back to larger issues, and the problems of life after death, contact between the dead and the living, the future of mankind and God's attitude to His creation feature strongly in sections xxxiv–lvii. Before, the world looked good to the poet and he assumed it was good; now it looks bad, and to prove it good is not easy. He finds himself completely unable to resolve the difficulties he has raised. So after section lvii he drops these problems, leaves them on one side, and turns instead, in a series of less intense sections, to consider the relative positions of Hallam and himself. He thus acts out the reliance upon experience which I have described as basic to *In Memoriam*. Unable to resolve his doubts by dogma or reasoning, he falls back on the personal. It is only as a result of the private vision of section xcv that he can return to public issues: reassurance in his personal life gives him the authority to speak with confidence on the general subjects he had been forced to abandon. He has not proved the world good, but he has had a personal experience which makes him believe that it is, and Hallam becomes an advance guard in the onward march of mankind.

The poet's confidence in speaking of public subjects at the end of the poem is, therefore, completely justified dramatically: the standards which were lost when Hallam died have been found again, and now have a far more secure basis. The poet has discovered his values in his own experience in Romantic fashion, but the resulting affirmation goes beyond the problematic rationalisations which the Romantic might achieve. It is very general in its scope and very specific in its details. At the end of *In Memoriam* the poet takes up a position on 'the feud of rich and poor', 'ancient forms of party strife', 'false pride in place and blood, / The civic slander and the spite' (cvi). All this is quite different from the linnet compelled to sing, from the black-blooded melancholic. In the Romantic period, according to Graham Hough, 'The emphasis shifts from social man to the individual man, when he is alone with his own heart or alone with nature'. We find both these emphases in *In Memoriam*.

The prime factor in the poem which encourages us to view it in the Enlightenment way as a carefully wrought artifact is the high degree of stylization which we usually find in the details of the language. Some element of stylization is perhaps always present in poetry, but such writing as,

> Sweet after showers, ambrosial air,
>   That rollest from the gorgeous gloom
>   Of evening over brake and bloom
> And meadow,   (lxxxvi)

is as self-consciously ordered as the sequence of sections is (apparently at least) casual. In the details of Tennyson's language we find all the artificiality and the concentration upon making an object to be admired for its beauty which is usually associated with the eighteenth century. There is no shortage of examples—

> Fair ship, that from the Italian shore
>   Sailest the placid ocean-plains
>   With my lost Arthur's loved remains,
> Spread thy full wings, and waft him o'er.   (ix)

> One whispers, 'Here thy boyhood sung
>   Long since its matin song, and heard
>   The low love-language of the bird
> In native hazels tassel-hung'.   (cii)

We feel that every word is picked individually and polished before use. At no time does Tennyson seem to want us to feel that he is using the language of men, that he is writing things down as they come to him. As we read *In Memoriam* we are always fully conscious that it is a work of art; it is not just the linnet singing because he must express his unruly emotions, but also toil cöoperant to a carefully designed end.

This is not to say, however, that the language of the poem is the same throughout. Indeed, it has been accused by Baum of having 'too much variety, both of style and of content'.[37] Here we see the

Tennysonian paradox in its full glory. The variety of content is the result of the need to show the poet's experience: Tennyson's Romantic approach to the problems of human existence demands that he include the fulness of life, for general reflections can result only from the felt reality of experience. The variety of style, on the other hand, results from a determined matching of language to content whereby ornate diction and syntax are used for lofty subject matter and a more prosaic mode for the commonplace; in other words, we have here the Enlightenment notion of *decorum*. When Baum compares sections lix and cxxii he is taking a considered declaration of intent—

> My centred passion cannot move,
>   Nor will it lessen from to-day—

and placing it beside an ecstatic celebration of the possibility of communion with the dead—

> The wizard lightnings deeply glow,
>   And every thought breaks out a rose.

The language is appropriate to the thought of each section.

This eighteenth-century principle of decorum, which was based ultimately on the belief that everything was put in its proper place by God and that the artist's task was respectfully to display this order, is fundamental to Tennyson's language—despite the subjectivity and irrationality of his outlook. Bernard Groom brings out this tendency by remarking how Tennyson admired Swinburne's *Atalanta in Calydon*, but 'asked whether it was *"fair"* to use the language of the Bible in poems so antagonistic to the spirit of Christianity. For Tennyson, it was a matter of poetic decorum and intellectual integrity to respect the historical associations of words and their religious implications'.[38] The rise and fall of emotion which is the basis of *In Memoriam* is matched with a variation in the degree of elaboration in language, but the two nevertheless stem from what have traditionally been opposed views of the nature of poetry.

The language of *In Memoriam* is adjusted according to the demands of decorum whilst maintaining a continual artificiality which defies the Romantic canon of spontaneity. Tennyson's avoidance of

[38] Bernard Groom, *The Diction of Poetry from Spenser to Bridges* (Toronto, 1955), pp. 252–3.

startling effects and his cultivation of the nuance produces an air of
delicate restraint which contributes further to the neo-classical tone
of the poem. He rarely jerks us violently by strange juxtapositions of
words or jarring rhythms; thus we see the preponderance of images
drawn from nature and the lack, for instance, of twin compasses
(though Tennyson admired Donne's poem for its 'wonderful
ingenuity'[39]). This delicate shading of detail will be seen in all
aspects of Tennyson's language. The reader must attend closely if,
for example, he is to appreciate solely from the repetition of the
words 'true and tried' that the Epilogue is written to the same man
as section lxxxv and thus completes a smooth movement from
isolation in grief to involvement with other people; or if he is to
notice how the attribution of the story of the raising of Lazarus
to *'that* Evangelist' (xxxi) reminds the reader that the incident is
reported in only the one Gospel and is thereby the more uncertain.
Rather than dislocating language to force it into his meaning,
Tennyson is to be found gently modifying it to suit his requirements.

Over against the record of a man who broods upon his loss until
a personal vision brings reassurance, then, is the delicate and
elaborate stylization of language in *In Memoriam*. Even section lix,
which has been mentioned as an example of relatively straightforward language, employs rhetorical exclamation and inversion,
personification and archaism—'O Sorrow, wilt thou rule my blood'.
There is a Romantic and a classical impulse in Tennyson's poem.
Study of the manuscripts makes it clear that both these tendencies
were present throughout its composition; it is not true, as critics
have guessed, that the earliest written sections were spontaneous
overflows of feeling in simple language whilst the later ones reveal
the falsity of their emotional stimulus by their artificial manner.
Section ix ('Fair ship, that from the Italian shore / Sailest the placid
ocean-plains'), for instance, was one of the first, whereas section vii
('Dark house, by which once more I stand / Here in the long
unlovely street') is not in the Trial Edition of 1850, though Nicolson surmised that it was 'obviously an actual experience'.[40]

The result of this consistent stylization is an affirmation through
language of an order and design of which Tennyson was personally
only precariously assured. His language habits are in many ways
those of the Enlightenment: they often irradiate the sense of a

[39] *Memoir*, II, 503.
[40] Nicolson, *Tennyson*, p. 297; and see Baum, *Tennyson Sixty Years After*, p. 116.

harmonious system which we find in Pope. Several critics have noted the likeness of the two writers, and Tennyson remarked how the perfection of some lines by Pope brought tears to his eyes.[41] In both cases the self-conscious creation of a beautifully made object implies a desire to aver an ultimate order in the universe.

However, in so far as Tennyson has this confidence in the human condition, it comes from very different sources. For Pope in the *Essay on Man*, Heaven

> sees with equal eye, as God of all,
> A hero perish, or a sparrow fall,
> Atoms or systems into ruin hurled,
> And now a bubble burst, and now a world.

Cosmic disaster is also faced towards the end of *In Memoriam*:

> The fortress crashes from on high,
> The brute earth lightens to the sky,
> And the great Æon sinks in blood,
>
> And compass'd by the fires of Hell;
>   While thou, dear spirit, happy star,
>   O'erlookst the tumult from afar,
> And smilest, knowing all is well.   (cxxvii)

Tennyson's warrant for equanimity through all is his personal belief that Hallam is still watching, whereas Pope had always known that 'The general Order, since the whole began, / Is kept in Nature, and is kept in Man': anyone could see that 'to reason right is to submit'. The language of these two quotations is similar, but Tennyson has not Pope's jaunty neatness. He does not divide his shorter lines into balanced clauses; the classical proportion is there in the successive matchings of clauses and line lengths, but the whole impression is heavier and not entirely free from an overtone of gloom. The affirmation which is implied in Tennyson's language was wrung from his nineteenth century world, whereas Pope could cheerfully celebrate a system which had secure foundations in the corporate beliefs of his society.

In *In Memoriam* the reliance upon intense personal experience

---

[41] Quoted by Sir Charles Tennyson, *Alfred Tennyson* (London, 1949), p. 452; see also Wilson, *Axel's Castle*, p. 14, and William Paton Ker, *Collected Essays* (London, 1925), I, 268.

as a way to truth suggests the Romantic linnet who has to express his unruly feelings. Yet, at the same time, the stylized language, like the attempt to represent the feelings of all mankind, implies a desire to regain Enlightenment values of order and design through toil cöoperant to an end. Of course, neither pole was ever more than a matter of emphasis. Romantic poets in fact fashioned their poems into works of art, they could make general declarations about the nature of human existence, and they sometimes wrote in ornate language (one thinks especially of Keats). Nevertheless, in *In Memoriam* we find a strong movement out towards *both* poles. Tennyson's mode of finding value in life is exceptionally subjective and the shaping of his poem shows it in many ways, but at the same time he makes a large claim for the general applicability of his experience and preserves decorum in diction within a consistently high degree of stylization. Abrams sums up the change the Romantics introduced:

> The first test any poem must pass is no longer, 'Is it true to nature?' or 'Is it appropriate to the requirements either of the best judges or the generality of mankind?' but a criterion looking in a different direction; namely, 'Is it sincere? Is it genuine? Does it match the intention, the feeling, and the actual state of mind of the poet while composing?'[42]

None of these questions by itself will serve for *In Memoriam*. A far more complex response is demanded.

We may speculate briefly on the reasons for this duality in Tennyson's writing. They may lie, as Auden suggested, in his character, and the 'tidiness' may be 'a *defence*, as if he hoped that through his control of the means of expressing his emotions, the emotions themselves, which he cannot master directly, might be brought to order'.[43] Other writers, however, have seen a general trend back towards classical qualities in the mid-nineteenth century. Edmund Wilson finds a reaction, specially prominent in France, against the looseness and sentimentality to which Romanticism was open, and Walter E. Houghton produces a lot of evidence of English disenchantment with introspective poetry.[44] In the Victorian period thought turned inexorably towards the problem of faith, but people were tired of being depressed by morbid personal

[42] Abrams, *The Mirror and the Lamp*, p. 23.
[43] W. H. Auden, *Tennyson: An Introduction and Selection* (London, 1946), p. xviii.
[44] Wilson, *Axel's Castle*, pp. 12–14; Houghton, *The Victorian Frame of Mind*, pp. 334–336.

doubts. Hence the liking for the heroic leader and narrative verse where one could see people coping with life, rather than the laments of the individual who could not see his way through the intellectual mist left by the loss of confidence in religious faith.

Obviously a return to the effortless security of the Enlightenment was impossible, and hence *In Memoriam* shows values being derived from personal experience in the Romantic manner. Nevertheless, the poet could exert himself to relate his work to the feelings of ordinary people, and this Tennyson does, as well as stating through the stylization of his language his ultimate orientation towards stable values. His determination to make in his poems something as perfect and highly wrought as possible is less a sign of a confident belief in an existing order than of a need to create a small piece of sanity and design within a general chaos. Several of his remarks about poetry in *In Memoriam* are concerned with the question 'What hope is here for modern rhyme' (lxxvii), and his desire for perfection may be seen as an attempt to raise a monument in the shifting sands of modern life. The vision described in section xcv gave hope for the eventual triumph of good, but only through his art could Tennyson recapture immediately the harmony and beauty which the Enlightenment had observed in the functioning of the whole universe.

In the last analysis there may be no contradiction at all. D. G. James notices just the same dichotomy in Arnold, but argues that the impulse towards the classical is in fact another kind of Romantic yearning:

> the classical becomes only a symbol for the inviolable thing, the other, the unattainable, the transcendent; and it is erected into such a symbol only by a certain play of self-deception, and by a refusal to face historic realities. Because this is so, the hunger for the classical in the modern spirit is a useless form of escape from its own nature and destiny; and this is what is in Arnold's [1853] Preface.[45]

James is severe, but it is doubtful whether this form of Romantic aspiration is more suspect than any other, or than the Enlightenment certainty (in the face of all the facts, it must seem to us) that all is well. The more difficult it is to account for the vicissitudes of human life, the more desperate will be any positive assertion, until the point when it is recognized that no assertion at all is possible. Tennyson did not reach this point but it was only through a very personal

[45] James, *Matthew Arnold*, pp. 59, 65.

mystical experience that he was able to arrive at a secure position. His eagerness to move from his vision to general issues shows the same desire for a system in the universe that we find in his language. The structure and language of *In Memoriam*, then, are the product of a desperate need for order in the absence of any clear and agreed means of establishing it. In these conditions it is perhaps not suprising that Tennyson's poetry contains elements which seem to be contradictory when viewed in the light of what was possible in the eighteenth and early nineteenth centuries.

I have been using the traditional pigeon-holes in my division of *In Memoriam* into two groups of attributes, but they have no sanction other than tradition and the fact that they seem to be helpful in considering two groups of artists and thinkers. As far as I can see, there is no reason why they should not co-exist in the extreme form they take in Tennyson's work. The need to recognize an order in existence will frequently occur alongside a consciousness of the recalcitrance of the evidence, and the dichotomy is liable to be manifested in the themes and language of art. Tennyson was evidently aware of the difficulties created in an uncertain world by the will to believe; he sets the tone for *In Memoriam* in the opening Prologue:

> We have but faith: we cannot know;
>   For knowledge is of things we see;
>   And yet we trust it comes from thee,
> A beam in darkness: let it grow.

If we keep these statements and desires in mind, we should be able to read the poem in the spirit appropriate to its historical origins. The tendencies I have been discussing in this chapter could be re-classified in terms of 'the beam and the darkness', for they reflect the hopes and doubts which are at the basis of Tennyson's stance in *In Memoriam*. There is no complete reconciliation—how could there be?—but the several elements derive an ultimate unity from their single source in the fully self-conscious intellectual and emotional position which Tennyson displays in the poem.

The modern reader is compelled by this unusual bundle of characteristics to approach Tennyson in a complex way. Critics have their own predilections, and the duality I have described is liable to mean that Tennyson will please neither those who require reality of emotional impulse, those who want every rift loaded with ore, nor those who like their poetry hard and sane. He is not so easily categorized. These general considerations will reappear in my last chapter, but their implications for the study of the language of *In Memoriam* will be evident throughout. With their aid I hope to demonstrate Tennyson's 'practice', as he puts it in section lxxv, 'In fitting aptest words to things'.

III

DICTION:
SIMPLE WORDS AND COMPLEX MEANINGS

DICTION is concerned with the words selected by the poet. As Mrs. Nowottny has pointed out, there is some confusion in the use of the term, resulting from indecision about whether it refers to words in isolation or as they interact with each other.[1] Sometimes when we talk of diction in literature we say that it is 'ornate' or 'drawn from everyday language' or 'influenced by the terminology of psychoanalysis', and here we seem to be referring in a general and absolute way to the writer's preferences. But when we speak of 'appropriate' diction, of 'every word in place', of 'fruitful ambiguity' or of characters in a novel each having 'a distinctive mode of utterance', we are at least implicitly considering words in relation to their context. Only very limited statements can be made about the diction of a poem without taking into account the context of each word under examination. An alternative way of phrasing this point would be to say that the important issue is the contribution of a word to the density of structure which I described in my first chapter as characteristic of poetic language. Sometimes it will prove possible to generalize about the use of certain types of diction in the poem as a whole, but for the most part I will be concerned with the intricate interrelations between words.

The diction of *In Memoriam* has aroused considerable hostility in unsympathetic critics, and I therefore propose to build this discussion round a refutation of Harold Nicolson's all-embracing judgment that 'of all poets, Tennyson should be read very carelessly or not at all'.[2] Studies of Tennyson have often been marked by a crisis of confidence which makes the critic assume that if more than one meaning is possible at any point then Tennyson was probably confused or, if the complexity seems to fit in, successful despite himself. This is the attitude of Cleanth Brooks, who thinks it 'substantially true' that Tennyson did not build his doubts 'into

---

[1] *The Language Poets Use*, pp. 26ff.; and I. A. Richards, *The Philosophy of Rhetoric* (New York, 1936), pp. 51–7.
[2] *Tennyson*, p. 233.

D

the structure of the poetry itself as enriching ambiguities'.[3] There is no evidence that, as Brooks claims, Tennyson sought to avoid ambiguity and other kinds of complexity; his quoted remarks suggest the opposite—'Then he spoke of Milton's Latinisms, and delicate play with words, and Shakespeare's play upon words'.[4] I wish to show that the diction of *In Memoriam* is often woven into subtle and complex structures of language and that careless reading is likely to provide the least satisfactory approach.

The assumptions underlying this crisis of critical confidence can be illustrated from one of its more extreme exponents, Paull F. Baum in his study, *Tennyson Sixty Years After*. Section i is analysed there at some length,[5] and Baum observes that 'dead selves' is ambiguous:

> I held it truth, with him who sings
> To one clear harp in divers tones,
> That men may rise on stepping-stones
> Of their dead selves to higher things.

Baum says that 'dead selves' might mean one's past experience during this life or one's improvement from incarnation to incarnation, but though he finds the ambiguity 'suggestive' he thinks there must be one 'right' interpretation after all. I would say, on the contrary, that there are three meanings here, three ways in which men may rise. The phrase is about a man's development in his life on earth (the sort of development we see in the poet during *In Memoriam*); about the individual's progress after death (the poet's desire to believe that Hallam still exists somewhere becomes an important theme); and about the perfectibility of mankind as a whole (the possibility, which the poet eventually affirms, that man may be 'The herald of a higher race'). Hallam's death has opened up three principal areas of deep anxiety, and they are all comprised in this one phrase; the poet's optimism has been destroyed in one blow. The lines express in embryo the main themes of the whole poem.

Baum is even less happy about the rest of the section, for he persists in finding confusion where I see complexity. The poet wants to cling to his grief for fear that love should vanish with it:

---

[3] Cleanth Brooks, 'The Motivation of Tennyson's Weeper', in John Killham, *Critical Essays on the Poetry of Tennyson* (London, 1960), p. 177.
[4] Hallam Tennyson, *Memoir*, I, 277—Mrs. Rundle Charles writing of 1848.
[5] Pp. 303–6. On section i see also L. Metzer, 'The Eternal Process: Some Parallels between Goethe's *Faust* and Tennyson's *In Memoriam*', *Victorian Poetry*, I (1963), 189–96.

'Let Love clasp Grief lest both be drown'd, / Let darkness keep her raven gloss'. Baum objects to the latter line because Milton's parallel usage in *Comus* (line 251) is in a very different context. Comus is speaking of the enchanting power of the Lady's song: 'At every fall smoothing the Raven downe / Of darkness till it smil'd'. There is no contradiction here. The effect of the virtuous Lady's song is so great that it even smooths the raven down of darkness— that is, it softens the deathly evil of Comus. Tennyson's poet, however, is more extreme, and would not have his darkness of grief and death charmed away even for a moment. The allusion boldly links the poet with Comus, and his determination to resist consolation with opposition to Christian virtue. The poet's desire to preserve his love whatever the cost is most forcibly expressed.

The parallel with *Comus* runs right through the section. The first lines we considered ('men may rise on stepping-stones') reflect the opening lines of Milton's poem:

> Yet som there be that by due steps aspire
> To lay their just hands on that Golden Key
> That opes the Palace of Eternity.[6]

Like those to whom the Attendant Spirit refers here, the poet used to think that men could aspire to eternal life, but he now ranges himself with Comus and darkness and rejects the optimistic Christian creed. The insistence on keeping the raven gloss of darkness develops the loss of faith described in the first lines of the section, for the poet goes further than Comus by refusing to be charmed even temporarily by the virtuous Lady.

The section continues, 'Ah, sweeter to be drunk with loss, / To dance with death, to beat the ground'. Here Baum questions, 'Does "to beat the ground" mean to hurl oneself in despair upon the ground, to beat one's head on the ground; or is it a Latinism merely repeating "To dance"?—a difficult choice'. Once again, we do not have to make a choice. The line partly means 'to despair', with to me the further suggestion of beating on the actual ground where the dead person is buried in a macabre effort to get in. It is also a Latinism, and is in fact the literal meaning of *tripudiare*, 'to dance a religious dance'. The poet's dance is religious, but in a deliberately pagan form. 'To beat the ground' does, at this level, repeat 'To

---

[6] The opening of *Comus* seems relevant also to sections lxiv and xciii, as editors have noted. The epigraph to the early poem 'The Hesperides' is drawn from *Comus*.

dance with death': all the three phrases in these two lines are ultimately repetitious (they are syntactically similar as well) and may be
thought of as simulating the movement of a dance. There is, moreover, a further allusion to *Comus*: 'Come, knit hands, and beat the
ground / In a light fantastic round' (143). These lines end Comus'
speech inciting his 'crew' to wantonly abandon themselves to
emotion, and the allusion again fits section i exactly. As we have
seen, the poet rejects Christian consolation and identifies himself
with the pagan Comus, refusing to have darkness smoothed away.
Like Comus, he will abandon himself in a ritual dance of emotional
indulgence.

This parallel with Milton's poem provides a consistent scheme
against which to measure the poet's attitude; the extremity of his
position is indicated by the fact that in *Comus* the issue is between
good and evil. His resolution to cling to grief is presented as deliberately opposed to an optimistic faith. By means of a delicately
sustained allusion Tennyson succeeds in packing his lines with deep
religious, moral and mythological implications. There is much more
useful complexity here than Baum—or those who think that
Tennyson is best read carelessly—will allow. Baum puts his finger
on several subtleties of expression, but he begins in each case by
assuming mere confusion, so blinding himself to the virtues of the
section—which no one would claim as among the most powerful in
In Memoriam.

The crisis of confidence in Tennyson's diction seems to break
down into two paradoxically related notions. On the one hand it is
accepted that the language is simply straightforward and that
Tennyson's aim was just to make plain what he meant—this is
behind the way Baum takes it for granted that there must be one
meaning to 'dead selves'. On the other hand, it is assumed that
Tennyson sought, by disguising his meaning in vague or ornate
diction, to give his writing a merely artificial elevation which results
only in the spuriously 'poetical'. This second idea underlies Baum's
criticism of 'Let darkness keep her raven gloss' and 'to beat the
ground' and his conclusion that 'Tennyson has chosen to be deliberately cryptic and "poetic" at all costs' (p. 305). The second
notion is the subject of the next chapter, the first (that Tennyson is
straightforward) I propose to deal with by showing how the juxtaposition of quite unexceptional words produces complex effects if
we look closely.

.   .   .

One cause of the impression that the diction of *In Memoriam* is straightforward is probably the fact that the words themselves are almost always easy to understand—we do not think of Tennyson as torturing the language into his meaning. The revision of line 9 of section xxxvi suggests that this surface simplicity was Tennyson's aim, for the mention in the Harvard loosepaper and the Trinity manuscript of 'the Logos' is replaced in the published version by 'the Word'. This comprehensible diction certainly seems to have been appreciated by contemporary readers; one wrote, 'A spirit of wonderfully subtle sympathy is displayed in that poem, or series of poems, and in his deepest and tenderest sorrow he is in language most simple'.[7] The concern of the Victorian poet to gain a public for his writing has been much discussed in recent criticism,[8] and the superficial simplicity of the language of *In Memoriam* may have been caused by the desire for a wide public; at any rate, it was no doubt a major factor in the poem's contemporary popularity.

Nevertheless, Tennyson's diction is not always drawn from language in everyday use, or even from the poetic tradition, for he is able to devise new words when he feels the necessity. He is apparently the first user of 'intervital' ('between lives'—xliii), 'orb' as a verb (xxiv) and 'plumelets' ('minute plumes'—xci). Compounding is Tennyson's favourite way of forming new expressions to suit his need, though almost nothing remains in *In Memoriam* of the excessively delicate usages he is supposed to have spent ten years removing from his first volumes of poetry. The compound is particularly valuable in suggesting the identity or simultaneity of two notions which would otherwise be separated by language as we normally use it. In section xlviii the poet says that Sorrow

> rather loosens from the lip
> Short swallow-flights of song, that dip
> Their wings in tears, and skim away.

'Swallow-flights' catches exactly the idea of a swallow on the wing. The compound has the advantage of making neither element in it seem subordinate. It is not a swallow which is flying, or an act of flying which happens to involve a swallow; it is both at once, a

---

[7] Archibald C. McMichael, *Reflections By The Way* (Ayr, n.d.—but *Maud* is recently published), p. 114.

[8] E.g. E. D. H. Johnson, *The Alien Vision of Victorian Poetry* (Princeton, 1952).

swallow-flight. One thinks also of 'hourly-mellowing' (xci) and 'ever-breaking' (cxxiv). Here is another example:

> O mother, praying God will save
>   Thy sailor,—while thy head is bow'd,
>   His heavy-shotted hammock-shroud
> Drops in his vast and wandering grave.   (vi)

Is it a shroud or a hammock?—a hammock like a shroud or a shroud like a hammock? It is both at once, rather like a metaphor in which tenor and vehicle are completely intertwined. This example links the security of the hammock with the horror of the shroud, whilst playing upon the notion that the dead only sleep. It also looks forward to the process by which the dream, and finally and more satisfyingly the vision, becomes the means of contact with the dead.

The compound is extremely useful for expressing the mystery and paradox of other-worldly experience, as in the 'silent-speaking words' of Hallam's letters in section xcv, or the 'Cloud-towers by ghostly masons wrought' which appear to the poet in the ominous phantasmagoria of section lxx. They are not towers or clouds, but an irreducible amalgam of the two. The rationale of the method is explicit in section cxxi: 'Sweet Hesper-Phosphor, double name / For what is one'. At best, Tennyson's compounds are highly creative. Whereas the device suggests sensuous self-abandonment in the early volumes, in *In Memoriam* it shows a rigorous concern with choosing the right expression for the idea. It can pin down a thought precisely and economically and is particularly useful for preserving intact a notion which ordinary language would falsify by breaking it down into separable elements.

By and large, however, it is true that Tennyson uses simple, straightforward diction. But simple words can achieve complex effects, depending on the context they are placed in. Our use of language is very much involved with the fact that in a given situation there are some expressions which we expect and others which we do not. In the context, say, of a group of people sitting at a meal, we would expect the words 'Please pass the . . .' to be followed by a word from a rather small range to do with things to eat or drink or which contain food or drink—say 'fruit cake' or 'broccoli'. If, on the other hand, we were behind the counter in a baker's shop, we might still expect 'fruit cake', but 'paper bags' would also be a possibility, whereas this would be as surprising at the dining table as

'broccoli' would be at the baker's. Words which we might expect in
a given situation are said to collocate with each other—'by collocation is meant the habitual association of a word in a language with
other particular words in sentences'.[9]

The poet, who exploits all the resources of language to the full,
can gain great effect from the use of this fact—as Empson puts it,
'a word in a speech which falls outside the expected vocabulary will
cause an uneasy stir in all but the soundest sleepers'.[10] In section
lxxii the day is commanded to 'sow the sky with flying boughs'.
'Day', the grammatical subject, is so far from 'sow' that we have
almost forgotten it, and we assume that the wind is meant. On a
literal level, so it is, but in the poet's mind the 'reason' for the storm
is that this is the anniversary of Hallam's death, and thus it is right
that the day itself should be seen as the originator of the effects in
nature. We are thinking of weather and landscape, and therefore
sowing, blowing boughs and the sky are not out of place; they are
all simple words, but their conjunction is highly meaningful and
paradoxical in this section. Sowing the sky is a reversal of the usual
practice, and it negates the life-giving natural cycle: it means death.
The boughs are torn from their proper, fruitful positions on the
trees and flung at random into the air, where they have no place and
no useful function—even, perhaps, as Hallam has been frighteningly
wrenched from the earth where his potentialities might have been
fulfilled, and transplanted to an alien element. Tennyson does not
supply a scene of simply arbitrary destruction: it is the active reversal
of what is usually a constructive principle which gives the line its
strength.

This example shows quite clearly how simple words can be juxtaposed so as to yield complex meanings. It also illustrates the other
main reason why the power of Tennyson's diction has been over-
looked. The line is one of the most striking in the poem, but it
nevertheless relies upon very subtle nuances for its effect; the
collocational gap between the words is at first glance slight and we
have to look carefully to see how remarkable the description is.
This is almost invariably true of the diction of *In Memoriam*, which
is in this respect completely in line with the generalization about

[9] Robert H. Robins, *General Linguistics, An Introductory Survey* (London, 1964), p. 67.
See also J. R. Firth, 'Modes of Meaning', *Essays and Studies*, new series, IV (1951), 118–
49, and Spencer and Gregory, *Linguistics and Style*, p. 73.
[10] William Empson, *Seven Types of Ambiguity*, 3rd edn. (paperback, London, 1961),
p. 4.

Tennyson's language which I made in the previous chapter. He characteristically works in language which is superficially unremarkable: we must expect, not violent shocks, but delicate shades of meaning which gently modify our response. The surface maintains a classical calm, although monsters may be raging in the depths. Tennyson seems to have been very sensitive to slight nuances of language:

> Then he spoke of the great richness of the English language due to its double origin, the Norman and Saxon words. How hard it would be for a foreigner to feel the difference in the line
>
> > An *infant* crying for the light,
>
> had the word *baby* been substituted, which would at once have made it ridiculous.[11]

My argument, then, is that beneath the apparently simple and unremarkable diction of *In Memoriam* are effects of great complexity resulting from the juxtaposing of quite ordinary words. The careless reader may easily miss the point, for Tennyson does not deal in obviously extraordinary collocations. The need is now for further examples to support my claim.

> What hope is here for modern rhyme
> > To him, who turns a musing eye
> > On songs, and deeds, and lives, that lie
> Foreshorten'd in the tract of time?

Section lxxvii is the last of a group concerned with the transience of poetry, and it devalues deeds and lives as well by representing all as deprived of even their actual proportions by the diminishing effect of perspective. The vast, unbounded 'tract of time' is an emotionally charged image, but it is placed alongside a reductive reference to poetry as 'modern rhyme'. We see a similar juxtaposition of great and small in 'a musing eye', where a lurking reminder of the Muses is subordinated to the notion of a casually thoughtful observer. This confrontation of grand and trivial diction continues in the next lines:

> These mortal lullabies of pain
> > May bind a book, may line a box,
> > May serve to curl a maiden's locks,
> Or when a thousand moons shall wane

[11] From a conversation of 1892, quoted by Hallam, Lord Tennyson, *Tennyson and His Friends* (London, 1911), p. 218.

> A man upon a stall may find,
>   And, passing, turn the page that tells
>   A grief, then changed to something else,
> Sung by a long-forgotten mind.

'Lullabies' further degrades the poet's art, suggesting that its function is only to soothe the writer; but to link it with 'mortal' is to violate with thoughts of death all its usual connotations of peaceful domesticity providing security and rest for the fretful child. In this packed line 'mortal' has two references—to the poetry itself (it will not live) and to its subject matter (it is about Hallam's death). These are lullabies 'of pain' because they both describe and mitigate the poet's suffering. Such economy is not usually associated with Tennyson. Up to this point the tone of the section has been fairly elevated, but the two central lines of this stanza descend heavily to the mundane with thoughts of binding books, lining boxes and curling hair. We can see Tennyson building up the effect of a random list of trivia in the Trinity manuscript, where the second line of this stanza at first read, 'May be the lining of a box'. The last line requires yet a further shift in our reaction: 'when a thousand moons shall wane' is diction of a quite different kind, and it restores suddenly the wide sweep of time and space which opened the section. The moon also carries connotations of romantic love, but in this context the pair of lovers in the moonlight is overwhelmed by a succession of thousands more such couples. The line therefore suggests not only length of time, but the instability of human aspirations; the moon is also an image of change.

In the third stanza the diction drops again to the mundane man by the bookstall, but he is further juxtaposed with the 'long-forgotten mind', another phrase redolent of dreamy, romantic feelings. The diction puts the fate of modern rhyme before the reader by joining in one sentence the elevated and the inconsequential. The imagination-stretching evocations of the passing of the years correspond to all that is noble in the poet's activity; the trivial events juxtaposed with them figure the insignificance of poetry—or any human action—in the total scheme of things. There is no resolving this disparity; the poet instead decides to disregard it:

> But what of that? My darken'd ways
>   Shall ring with music all the same;
>   To breathe my loss is more than fame,
> To utter love more sweet than praise.

The 'tract of time' of the first stanza is narrowed down to 'my darken'd ways'; though the poet's individual path is gloomy, it forms a more manageable unit than the vast stretch of time with which he began. The strength of the last two lines comes from the fact that their content is almost identical, the great difference being that between the meanings of 'loss' and 'love'. In ordinary language we would not regard these two words as habitually associated, but in *In Memoriam* they have been linked several times already so that by this section they are established as a set collocation—we expect to see them together as we do 'bread and butter'. The affirmation to which they contribute is reinforced by our awareness of their previous occurrences. They carry all the triumph of the poet's victory over time by reminding us of his resolution in the first section of the poem to hold by his love. Their appearance here is therefore at least some kind of answer to the poet's disquiet at the power of time to diminish human achievement, for he has maintained his devotion to his friend. The very fact that he is still pursuing his theme of love and loss asserts human values in the desert of the tract of time. Section lxxvii shows Tennyson precisely controlling his diction so that we must read carefully if we are to appreciate the full connotations of his words and their delicate contributions to the structure.

Section xxi also affords interesting study from this point of view. It is in the pastoral mode with the poet making pipes from the grasses of the grave, but Tennyson's diction does not remain at the conventional level. Travellers pass by and comment unfavourably on his activity; though this happens occasionally in the pastoral tradition, it nevertheless tends to interrupt the mood. But it is quite definitely broken in the fourth and fifth stanzas:

> A third is wroth: 'Is this an hour
>   For private sorrow's barren song,
>   When more and more the people throng
> The chairs and thrones of civil power?
>
> 'A time to sicken and to swoon,
>   When Science reaches forth her arms
>   To feel from world to world, and charms
> Her secret from the latest moon?'

'The chairs and thrones of civil power', and still more 'Science', seem quite out of place in the pastoral world (related considerations appear in 'Lycidas', but even there it is noticeable that Milton is careful to pull the poem together by employing traditional diction whenever he can). The effect is to make the reader conscious, through dramatic presentation, of the differences between the values of the Golden Age and of the modern era. In pastoral poems to sit and pipe love songs is the ideal, but now one is expected to give prime attention to public issues.

If we look more closely at the second stanza quoted, we find that the way in which science is introduced is more subtle yet. The poet has been rebuked for singing of love, but the language used by the traveller is in fact that of sexual attraction: science 'reaches forth her arms / To feel' and 'charms / Her secret from the latest moon'. The first collocational surprise was the introduction of science into the pastoral, but then follows a second, for the language of love is used to describe science so that we come full circle. In the context the moon must also remind us of love, but '*latest* moon' emphasizes the irrelevance of such factors to the worldly traveller. He is interested in novelty and in being up to date, not in the abiding worth of love. The difference in values between the poet's devotion to his friend and his critic's pressing of public issues is doubly insisted upon. The public world breaks in on the pastoral but even as it does so the pastoral value of love is reasserted through the diction.

My last example is section lxxxii:

> I wage not any feud with Death
>   For changes wrought on form and face;
>   No lower life that earth's embrace
> May breed with him, can fright my faith.
>
> Eternal process moving on,
>   From state to state the spirit walks;
>   And these are but the shatter'd stalks,
> Or ruin'd chrysalis of one.
>
> Nor blame I Death, because he bare
>   The use of virtue out of earth:
>   I know transplanted human worth
> Will bloom to profit, otherwhere.

> For this alone on Death I wreak
> The wrath that garners in my heart;
> He put our lives so far apart
> We cannot hear each other speak.

Here again we find a highly ironic use of the language of love in the third and fourth lines. It is the earth which may 'embrace' and 'breed with' Hallam, whereas the poet is cut off from physical contact. This gruesome notion is supported by the use of such expressions as 'I wage not any feud' and 'I wreak the wrath', which have distinctly Gothic connotations. In such a context the macabre emphasis on the physical corruption of death seems appropriate.

The references to organic growth continue through the next stanzas. If we compare them, as we are encouraged to do by the repetition, we find a development from the life stimulated by the corpse, through the suggestion in the second stanza that human life is a plant which is cut down at death, to the full flowering of the spirit in an existence after death: 'I know transplanted human worth / Will bloom to profit, otherwhere'. This plant diction does not really constitute an extended metaphor—it is largely dead metaphor which might almost occur in conversation—but rather just a recurrence of words from the same area of meaning. We find it at each stage of the thought, taking appropriate connotations from its context but at the same time providing a stable image against which we can measure the development of the argument. We notice also that, despite the poet's claim that he is not disconsolate, the growth in the first two stanzas is linked absolutely to destruction, so that the most obvious and appealing aspect of organic life is denied immediately it is evoked. The third stanza describes a full flowering, but again we find the poet's discontent breaking through in the great prominence given to 'otherwhere'. Tennyson uses simple words throughout, but their interactions are complex, for there is a denial underlying the apparent affirmation.

The last stanza gives the cause of the poet's complaint: 'He put our lives so far apart / We cannot hear each other speak' ('far apart' is in clear contrast to 'earth's embrace'). After all the exalted talk of the 'eternal process' the poet's need is revealed as pathetically humble and mundane. The desire for renewed contact with Hallam confirms our suspicion that 'the spirit walks' (line 6) alludes to the possibility of his return as a ghost. Line 6 is primarily about the sublime notion of the soul's progress through its afterlife, but there is an underlying suggestion that a more functional appearance of his friend as a ghost would please the poet much better, for then they might speak. Once again we find that Tennyson's diction is cunningly chosen so as to undermine the apparent equanimity of the early part of the argument. The last stanza also contains the conclusion of the series of words denoting growth. The poet has described various kinds of life, but they provide him with no harvest which could satisfy and fulfil him: he has only 'The wrath that *garners* in my heart'. This is the final, resentful answer to the first three stanzas. Hallam may be blooming somewhere else, but the fruits are hardly available to the poet; he 'garners' only wrath born of frustration. It is that one word which really makes it plain that the section is *not* saying 'I am perfectly happy about all these aspects of death, it is just that one that worries me', but protesting bitterly at the whole process which has deprived the poet of his friend. The structure of the section is more complex and economical than it may appear at first sight, for although Tennyson may seem to employ unremarkable collocations, closer examination shows the words finely interweaving throughout the sixteen lines.

All the examples I have given bring out slightly different aspects of Tennyson's diction and if I gave more this would continue to happen. They have in common the appearance of classical simplicity and unruffled balance which is characteristic of the language of *In Memoriam*, but they also have an underlying complexity. There is no reason to suppose that Tennyson aimed merely to state a plain meaning unambiguously. Only the surface is straightforward and careful reading is essential if we we are to probe the subtle interactions of the words in the poetic structure.

IV

DICTION:
THE VAGUE AND THE POETICAL

'TENNYSON has chosen to be deliberately cryptic and "poetic" at all costs', says Baum.[1] I attempted to answer this charge in relation to section i in the previous chapter, but the notion has some currency, and I now propose to deal with it in more detail. F. R. Leavis writes of Rosetti's 'shamelessly cheap evocation of a romantic and bogus Platonism—an evocation in which "significance" is vagueness'. Dr. Leavis considers this to be characteristic of the poetry of Tennyson and his contemporaries, and sees it as exemplifying that separation of feeling from thinking 'which the Victorian tradition, in its "poetical" use of language, carries with it'.[2] This opinion has the sanction of the Pelican Guide: 'Far from opening up new possibilities, Tennyson helped to narrow and restrict, to establish a conventionally held notion of the "poetic" '.[3]

Yet the sections I discussed in the previous chapter surely demonstrate that the choice of words in *In Memoriam* is often sensitive and exact. The point may be made once more from section xlv, where manuscript variants show Tennyson tightening up his language. The poet is talking about the development of individuality in a baby:

> So rounds he to a separate mind
>> From whence *clear* memory may begin,
>> As thro' the frame that binds him in
> His isolation *grows* defined.

The Huntington manuscript reads for 'clear', 'his', and for 'grows', 'is'. In both cases Tennyson replaces a fairly neutral word with one which adds significantly to the meaning. In the first revision he alters the crude statement which implies that all memory begins with consciousness (he puts forward the opposite opinion in the previous section) and allows for the possibility of pre-conscious memories;

---

[1] *Tennyson Sixty Years After*, p. 305.
[2] F. R. Leavis, *The Common Pursuit* (London, 1962), pp. 47–8; see also F. N. W. Bateson, *English Poetry and the English Language*, 2nd edn. (New York, 1961), pp. 98–9.
[3] Robin Mayhead, 'The Poetry of Tennyson', in *The Pelican Guide to English Literature, VI: From Dickens to Hardy*, ed. Boris Ford (London, 1958), p. 243.

in the last line he abandons the simple copula, with its implications of a swift and easy change, and instead calls up the delicate idea of a gradual growth. The description becomes more appealing (indeed, *evocative*) as it becomes more accurate. These lines display a most discriminating choice of diction: their significance has nothing to do with vagueness.

Certainly there are places where the diction of *In Memoriam* is unjustifiably vague and uninspired; in a poem of this length it would be surprising if there were not. There is a tendency, for instance, to over-use a few adjectives which are so common and ill-defined as to have little meaning. 'Fair' occurs 18 times, 'happy' 16 times and 'sweet' 21 times. They all mean something in the region of 'nice, good, pleasant, beautiful' and they can have little success in making the reader aware of any specific properties in the objects they purport to describe. This weakness is liable to occur when the poet is trying to explain Hallam's qualities:

> Heart-affluence in discursive talk
> From household fountains never dry;
> The critic clearness of an eye,
> That saw thro' all the Muses' walk;
>
> Seraphic intellect and force
> To seize and throw the doubts of man;
> Impassion'd logic, which outran
> The hearer in its fiery course.   (cix)

Unfortunately Tennyson is more impassioned than logical here. One wonders just what 'heart-affluence' is, whether 'discursive' means 'conversational' or 'reasoning'—it would be repetitive in either sense, for we already have 'talk' and 'logic'—and whether 'fiery' really adds anything when we already have 'impassion'd'. The metaphors are mixed and unilluminating; 'household fountains' appears absurd if we visualize it, and a 'walk' seems a strange thing to 'see through'. This is Tennyson at his worst. Even so, we do not find here the spurious 'poeticality' of which he has been accused; one senses rather a failure to achieve an adequate form of expression.

But to criticize verse like this is easy and only to pick at the subject. A broader approach is required if we are to penetrate the essential nature of Tennyson's diction. If he can write poetry as subtle and meaningful as some of my examples have shown, how is it that he can also arouse charges of cultivating the vague and 'poetical'? The short reply (as far as *In Memoriam* is concerned) is that Tennyson should plead guilty but challenge the validity of the law under which he is indicted. I believe that this dissatisfaction with the language of *In Memoriam* springs from a failure to take account of the strange way in which, as I have claimed, Tennyson combines Romantic and Enlightenment attitudes. These factors are crucial to an understanding of Tennyson; they do not detract from the quality of his poetic achievement, but they very much affect the nature of it.

I propose to discuss the 'poetical' first, leaving vagueness till later. I pointed out in Chapter II that a major element in the classical impulse behind *In Memoriam* is the air of conscious artifice which Tennyson's verse habitually displays. He does not disguise the fact that it is a poem we are reading, a carefully fashioned work of art which he has been at pains to perfect. His writing is always deliberately stylized and his adherence to the principle of decorum ensures that the most elevated diction is employed for the loftiest and most deeply felt subjects. I well remember that as a student I had 'read' the following passage several times before I realized that it refers to the conception and birth of a child:

> And, star and system rolling past,
> A soul shall draw from out the vast
> And strike his being into bounds,
>
> And, moved thro' life of lower phase,
> Result in man, be born and think,
> And act and love . . .

Tennyson may seem to go a long way round here, but who would wish it otherwise? The elaborate delicacy is perhaps Victorian, but it has an appropriate dignity—decorum, in fact—as Tennyson approaches the end of *In Memoriam*. I wish to make two points. The first is that the ornate and stylized mode of writing is itself as valid as any other (in music or the visual arts this would not be questioned). One may dislike this kind of verse, but to condemn it just for being itself is simply to close one's mind to the convention in which it is working; it would be as well to complain of the improbability of the impenetrable disguises in Elizabethan plays (an early critic of Tennyson's ornateness was Bagehot—who found the same fault in Shakespeare[4]).

The second point is that Tennyson's language, however 'poetical' it may appear, is in fact working very hard. In the lines quoted from the Epilogue the reference to the stars is the last of a whole series in which Venus, the star of love, has figured, often explicitly, in connection with Hallam, and its presence here makes us think of the dead friend benevolently blessing this new union. Both the 'system rolling past' and the soul striking 'his being into bounds' conclude Tennyson's use of circle imagery (which I shall later discuss in full). On the one hand we have the vast system of the universe, including Hallam's star, which revolves in its infinite courses, and on the other the earthly limits of the body which the soul of the expected child is about to enter, but here at the end of the poem the two are connected in one great movement which embraces both the eternal and the temporal. The mention of the foetus passing in its development through stages corresponding to lower orders of animate life is also highly relevant, for it stands for the way in which the human race must 'move upward, working out the beast, / And let the ape and tiger die' (cxviii). Even as the unborn child is 'moved thro' life of lower phase' until it becomes fully human, so the whole of mankind must pass beyond the baser passions until 'the crowning race' becomes an actuality. We may say that Tennyson goes a long way round here if we assume that his purpose is merely to find a 'poetical' way of talking of conception, but if my reading of these lines is accepted then it must be agreed that Tennyson could hardly have been more economical. We must not conclude that we have exhausted any poem by Tennyson when we have decided that it seems nice and poetical—any more (as I urged in the previous chapter) than we must allow ourselves to be deceived by the superficial simplicity of the language.

In section x the poet says he would prefer that Hallam's remains, rather than being lost at sea, should be buried in a churchyard: 'sweeter seems / To rest'

> . . . where the kneeling hamlet drains
> The chalice of the grapes of God;

[4] 'W. Bagehot on *Enoch Arden* [*1864*]', in John D. Jump (ed.), *Tennyson, The Critical Heritage* (London, 1967), pp. 282–93.

E

> Than if with thee the roaring wells
> Should gulf him fathom-deep in brine;
> And hands so often clasp'd in mine,
> Should toss with tangle and with shells.

Observe how appropriate the periphrasis about the churchyard is to its context—it stands in complete opposition to the horrific alternative possibility. Its idyllic elegance is at the furthest remove from the violent picture of hands drifting about in the sea, but it also brings in several relevant associations. It presents the most homely and appealing aspects of the Christian life, the gathering together in peace of a whole community with one simple purpose, and at the same time insists on the central Christian mystery whereby the physical grapes become the means to spiritual blessedness in eternity. This notion interacts most strangely with the disaster of Hallam's death and the poet's obsession with the fate of his body, for spiritual survival seems irrelevant both in terms of the dead friend whose actual presence is so strongly desired, and in terms of the poet who is on the edge of despair. Indeed, these lines even raise in our minds a doubt as to the benevolence of a God who can allow Hallam to be so threatened with a watery grave—the chalice is drained. By elaborating his diction beyond a simple statement that it would be better if Hallam were buried in a churchyard, Tennyson manages to introduce several deeply relevant implications.

Yet these lines have been explicitly criticized. Harold Nicolson quotes them and declares that 'the simplicity essential to his meaning is marred by the elaboration of the language in which that meaning is conveyed'.[5] Why is simplicity essential? It is no more so than natural-sounding dialogue in grand opera. Nicolson is refusing to accept the convention within which Tennyson is operating— namely the eighteenth-century tradition of decorum whereby elevated diction is essential for an exalted theme. It would be as helpful to criticize Pope for making Eloisa speak in rhyming couplets. If we fail to take account of this classical strain in Tennyson's art we are liable to miss the very real relevance of such lines as these. The point is what he does within his chosen manner of writing. The periphrasis of section x is significant not because of its prettiness but because it contributes in several ways to the structure of the section.

---

[5] *Tennyson*, pp. 290–1.

Of special interest in this connection is Tennyson's use of poetic diction—words and phrases which had with the course of time come to be particularly connected with verse, rarely appearing in other contexts. This kind of diction is particularly associated with the period of the Enlightenment, and Wordsworth began his career by attacking it in the preface to *Lyrical Ballads*:

> Poets and Men ambitious of the fame of Poets, perceiving the influence of such language, and desirous of producing the same effect without being animated by the same passion, set themselves to a mechanical adoption of these figures of speech, and made use of them, sometimes with propriety, but much more frequently applied to feelings and thoughts with which they had no natural connection whatsoever.

Wordsworth's diagnosis is clearly related to the charge of spurious 'poeticality' which I am endeavouring to answer.

Tennyson's use of poetic diction is by no means as extreme in *In Memoriam* as in his earlier volumes. J. F. A. Pyre has a representative list of such words which he finds and dislikes in the volumes mainly up to 1842,[6] and it is interesting to see how few of them occur here. None of the following appears: amber, amorous, azure, bloomed, cedarn, chrystal, chrystalline, enchanted, flavorous, fringed, impearled, odorous, sheeny. 'Divine' is used, but not in the 'melancholy eyes divine' sense ('Mariana'); 'honied' occurs in lxxxix, but in context with 'buzzings'; 'orient' is in lxxxvi, but is used of the evening star; 'crisp' is found in xlix, but the *N.E.D.* does not mark it as poetical; and, to complete Pyre's list, 'ambrosial' occurs in sections lxxxvi and lxxxix. Pyre also has a list of 22 'verbal oddities' (pp. 231f.), but only four of them are used in *In Memoriam* and one of those is 'wold'—the natural word, of course, for a Lincolnshire man to use, and neat evidence of the dangers of attempting to interpret language from a distance in time or space. The total proportion of words in the poem which might be called poetic diction is in fact a little more than one a section.

Quite often 'poetic' words are merely synonyms for ordinary diction, apparently chosen because they happen to fit better into the verse. They can function in more subtle ways, however, and our general awareness of traditional diction in the poem encourages us to perceive ambiguities involving the operation of archaic meanings. In section lxxii the poet speaks of the day's 'quick tears',

[6] J. F. A. Pyre, *The Formation of Tennyson's Style* (Madison, 1921), pp. 226–8.

and whilst one sense is that the rain is falling fast, we may also think of the more 'poetic' meaning, 'living'. Rain is often thought of as life-giving, but to the poet at this time it is an agent of destruction and 'quick' is highly ironic. As in the case of the wind sowing the sky with flying boughs, a creative principle is reversed.

There are two similar examples in section lxi:

> And if thou cast thine eyes below,
>   How dimly *character'd* and slight,
>   How dwarf'd a growth of cold and night,
> How blanch'd with darkness must I grow!

> Yet turn thee to that *doubtful* shore,
>   Where thy first form was made a man . . .

One suspects in 'character'd' the older meaning, 'portrayed' (it is hard to distinguish detail from Hallam's height), but we must also in this context think of the word as referring to the poet's qualities and as partaking of the prevailing mood of humility. 'Doubtful' suggests on the one hand the poetic diction usage 'giving cause for apprehension' (the earth is a place of trouble for mankind) and on the other the sense 'undecided, ambiguous' (again the idea of Hallam being unable to see clearly). The dual meanings of both are functional in the section. Both tell us that it is difficult for Hallam to see what is happening on earth, implying the improbability of the friends renewing contact during the poet's life. At the same time, 'character'd' also suggests the poet's personal inadequacy and 'doubtful' invokes the unsatisfactory nature of earthly life compared to 'thy second state sublime'. Poetic diction need not constitute a false mode of creation: it can supply helpful ambiguity.

In Memoriam is pervaded by a sense of conscious artifice which to me seems so far from being substitute for feeling as to be a great cause of it. In such a context diction slightly removed from the ordinary may be the most appropriate. The poet is talking about how his home will appear after he has left it:

> Till from the garden and the wild
>   A fresh association blow,
>   And year by year the landscape grow
> Familiar to the stranger's child;

> As year by year the labourer tills
> His wonted glebe, or lops the glades;
> And year by year our memory fades
> From all the circle of the hills.   (ci)

The syntax of these lines is clearly stylized and they must appear very artificial—principally because of the repetition of 'year by year' at the beginning of the line. Yet this repetition is essential, for it makes us realize that each of the three statements so beginning has a certain amount in common: in each case time is passing—inevitably, we feel. But in the first statement the landscape is *growing* familiar to the stranger's child, whilst in the third the memory of the poet's family is *fading*. These two contrasting processes set up a strong movement beneath the superficially similar accounts of the passing of time. In the middle is the second statement about the labourer, and his two activities parallel the growing and the fading: he tills the glebe (growing) and lops the glades (fading). Both processes come together in the labourer because he goes on with his tasks year by year in the same place: the natural cycle of the countryside continues.

Such poetry is obviously impressive, but what of the poetic diction word 'glebe'? Does it matter that it is not the name we would give to a field and is therefore likely to evoke a less powerful impression of a real man working on a real farm? A real field would divert us from the sense of process which we abstract from the passage: it would withdraw our attention from the essential feature of the structure. In highly stylized lines like these a 'poetic' word can be better since it will match the artificial syntax. Tennyson thereby avoids the incongruity into which Wordsworth sometimes falls—as Raleigh said, 'Wordworth's flattest lines come from "prose choice of words" without keeping to "prose order" '.

The usefulness of stylized diction in creating true poetic significance is even better illustrated by section lxxxvi. Since they are relatively infrequent, we are bound to notice a section containing several 'poetic' words and a number which are nearly so—sweet, ambrosial, gorgeous, gloom, brake, bloom, rapt, dewy-tassell'd, horned flood (which is in *Paradise Lost*), fancy, crimson, odour, orient, ill, brethren. This is an extraordinary proportion, yet these lines are among the most admired; poetic diction cannot always be vicious (indeed, Wordsworth did not say that it was). The stylization here exhibits a movement, based upon the visual idea of the air rolling towards the poet and then on away from him.

> Sweet after showers, ambrosial air,
>   That rollest from the gorgeous gloom
>   Of evening over brake and bloom
> And meadow, slowly breathing bare
>
> The round of space, and rapt below
>   Thro' all the dewy-tassell'd wood,
>   And shadowing down the horned flood
> In ripples, fan my brows and blow
>
> The fever from my cheek, and sigh
>   The full new life that feeds thy breath
>   Throughout my frame, till Doubt and Death,
> Ill brethren, let the fancy fly
>
> From belt to belt of crimson seas
>   On leagues of odour streaming far,
>   To where in yonder orient star
> A hundred spirits whisper 'Peace'.

At the same time as the air flows onto and away from the poet it is described in an increasingly expansive way: it begins as 'air', 'slowly breathing', and then 'fans' the poet, and is at last 'leagues of odour streaming far'. We see the same enlargment of scope in the water images, from 'showers' to 'the horned flood' to 'belt on belt of crimson seas', and in the light-dark images, which brighten from 'gloom' through 'shadowing' to 'crimson' and finally the 'orient star'. As the denotations of the images swell and brighten, so do their connotations. As the poet's state of exalted calm becomes apparent 'crimson seas' comes to suggest the crimson of love which suffuses the landscape of eternity at the ends of sections xlvi and ciii, and we recognize the 'orient star' as Hesper, the star of love where spirits whisper 'Peace'. The poet's perspective expands during the section to include vast distances, and so his unhappy feelings are swept aside by the prospect of an ultimate reunion in love. The whole is expressed in one long sentence, a complicated piece of syntax which slowly unravels itself in one broad movement till we at last come to rest (whispering perhaps, from shortage of breath) at 'Peace'.

In section lxxxvi the poetic diction is perfectly compatible with
the high degree of patterning; the stylization pervades all elements
of the language so that we appreciate the onward flowing and
swelling movement which figures the poet's acceptance of life. The
diction also confers a distinct air of *ceremonial* on the whole section;
it is as if the poet were taking part in a ritual, not strolling out in the
country. We sense a formal celebration of the peace of mind which
the poet has at last attained (and which is a necessary precondition
of the vision of section xcv). The tone of ceremonial which the
ornate language produces encourages us to see great significance
in the breeze, but it is no mere imitation of the 'poetic', for the
section is densely structured. The movement of the breeze figures
the coming of peace to the poet—and, indeed, it seems distinctly
Pentecostal (a similar rising wind is associated with the mystical in
xcv and cxxii). The rolling air symbolizes the sweeping away of
doubt and death, and our sense that something more than a blowy
day is in question is fortified by the ceremonial tone which the
diction largely creates.

The ornate language, which to some has seemed merely 'poetical',
is essential to the effect of section lxxxvi. It would be foolish to
suggest that Tennyson's elaborate diction always results in such
complex and subtle poetic structures, for that would be to ask more
than any poet writing in any mode gives us. My point is that Tennyson's language is as good a base for great poetic achievement as any
other. I conclude this part of my case with a discussion of the use of
the pastoral convention in *In Memoriam*, for this form of expression,
confined as it is largely to poetry, may well be thought of as contributing to a sense of bogus 'significance'.

Tennyson wrote in 'To E.L. on his Travels in Greece':

> And trust me while I turn'd the page,
>   And track'd you still on classic ground,
>   I grew in gladness till I found
> My spirits in the golden age.

There is no doubt of the meaningfulness to him of the pastoral
tradition which reaches back through *Adonais*, Milton and Virgil
to Theocritus and the poems attributed to him.[7] The strongest

[7] For Tennyson's admiration of Theocritus, see Hallam Tennyson, *Memoir*, I, 383;
I, 341; I, 222; and II, 495. For other discussions of the pastoral in *In Memoriam*, see J. H.
Buckley, *Tennyson, The Growth of a Poet* (Cambridge, Mass., 1960), pp. 115-18 and Joseph
Sendry, '*In Memoriam* and *Lycidas*', *PMLA*, LXXXII (1967), 437-43.

reflections of the pastoral are in sections xxi, xxii and xxiii—the poet sings, he is by the grave, he takes the grasses and makes pipes, he talks of Pan, Argive Heights and flutes of Arcady. The whole description calls up the idyllic pastoral way of life. With these clues we soon notice other references to the convention. All the mentions of the morning and evening stars, for instance, relate to the closing of Virgil's Tenth Eclogue; 'Lycidas' also ends with Hesperus and the Platonic motto to *Adonais* was translated by Shelley himself as,

> Thou wert the morning star among the living,
>   Ere thy fair light had fled;—
> Now, having died, thou art as Hesperus, giving
>   New spendour to the dead.

The pastoral convention is important in *In Memoriam* because it places it in relation to the elegiac tradition. This contributes to the classical tone of Tennyson's language and provides a genre to give the reader some familiar starting point in such an individual poem. The literary convention also helps Tennyson to generalize the poet's grief, to make it seem to represent the sorrow of mankind. Part of the classical side of *In Memoriam* is an impersonality in its tone which makes it more than the story of one man. As the domestic analogies extend the contemporary range of the poet's loss, so the pastoral allusion deepens its field of reference in time. We think of the poet's grief as like that of the ancient Greek writers and this both ennobles and generalizes the whole poem.

The major function of the pastoral in *In Memoriam* is as an image for an idyllic pre-lapsarian state. Modern commentators agree that a prime feature of the convention was its evocation of a purer way of life than that of the urban poets. Kermode points out that a distinction between simple and complex conditions is fundamental to the pastoral—the shepherd was chosen for this supposedly natural, idle, contemplative and creative mode of existence.[8] The pastoral is a manifestation of man's perennial longing for a paradise; this basis is clear in Virgil's Fourth Eclogue, which deals with the Golden Age. Then faith and truth dominated, all were safe and free, it was always spring, warm breezes blew on smiling flowers which always bloomed, men were fed without slaughter or effort.

---

[8] Frank Kermode (ed.), *English Pastoral Poetry from the Beginnings to Marvell* (London, 1952); see also Sir Walter Wilson Greg, *Pastoral Poetry and Pastoral Drama* (London, 1906).

The pastoral allusion introduces all this weight of traditional meaning into *In Memoriam*—

> And all we met was fair and good,
>   And all was good that Time could bring,
>   And all the secret of the Spring
> Moved in the chambers of the blood;
>
> And many an old philosophy
>   On Argive heights divinely sang,
>   And round us all the thicket rang
> To many a flute of Arcady.   (xxiii)

Tennyson consistently associates the idyllic pastoral state with life before Hallam's death: it is in those 'four sweet years' that the poet locates the Golden Age. In section xxiv he says plainly,

> If all was good and fair we met,
>   This earth had been the Paradise
>   It never look'd to human eyes
> Since our first Sun arose and set.

The life together of Hallam and the poet had all the beauty, freshness and innocence of the Garden of Eden—and as with Eden and the Arcadian Golden Age, it was the entry of death into the poet's pre-lapsarian world which marked its end. Tennyson wrote in a letter of 1863, 'Cauterez, which I had visited with my friend before I was twenty, had always lived in my recollection as a sort of Paradise'.[9]

Language which evokes the pastoral genre is, then, used by Tennyson with consistent awareness of its deeper implications, not as a means of giving an illusion of the 'poetical'. But it does not only correspond to the period before Hallam's death; the most vital point about the Golden Age in *In Memoriam* is that after the reassuring vision of section xcv it is expected to come again in another form. The poet's hope for the future of mankind is expressed in language which refers us again to the Arcadian paradise, but now it is not the innocent condition which was ended by Hallam's death, but a world of peace and wisdom to be achieved when man has developed himself to 'a higher race'. Section cv takes up the pastoral image and, as several commentators have observed, alludes to Virgil's Fourth Eclogue:

[9] Hallam Tennyson, *Memoir*, I, 491–2.

> No dance, no motion, save alone
> What lightens in the lucid east
>
> Of rising worlds by yonder wood.
>   Long sleeps the summer in the seed;
>   Run out your measured arcs, and lead
> The closing cycle rich in good.

Virgil wrote:

> Ours is the crowning era foretold in prophecy:
> Born of Time, a great new cycle of centuries
> Begins. Justice returns to earth, the Golden Age
> Returns, and its first-born comes down from heaven above.
> Look kindly, chaste Lucina, upon this infant's birth,
> For with him shall hearts of iron cease, and hearts of gold
> Inherit the whole earth—yes, Apollo reigns now,
> And it's while you are consul—you, Pollio—that this glorious
> Age shall dawn, the march of its great months begin.[10]

Even as it was death which brought the end of the former Golden Age with Hallam, so it is the victory over death represented in sections xcv and ciii which makes it possible for another paradise to follow. The Fourth Eclogue, moreover, has traditionally been regarded as an anticipation of the birth of Christ, and Tennyson uses the same figure when he ends section cvi, 'Ring in the Christ that is to be'. The spiritual iron age which followed Hallam's death can be succeeded, as the poet knows from section xcv, by a glorious new era of peace if mankind will abandon gods of gold and follow the example of Hallam—'a noble type / Appearing ere the times were ripe' (Epilogue).

Tennyson has seized upon exactly the most fertile aspects of the pastoral and emphasized them, so as to bring out the relationship between the Golden Age which was lost at the beginning of the poem and that which is hoped for at the end. The promise for the future is presented in the same terms in the Epilogue, where the bride enters 'glowing like the moon / Of Eden on its bridal bower' and her eyes 'brighten like the star that shook / Betwixt the palms of Paradise'. Tennyson is consistent in his use of pastoral diction right to the conclusion of *In Memoriam*. This kind of literary artificiality is much more than a substitute for true poetic creation,

---

[10] C. D. Lewis (trans.), *The Eclogues of Virgil* (London, 1963).

for it has important functions in the total structure. The pastoral convention helps to generalize and impersonalize the poem's themes by linking them to an established tradition, whilst also providing a resonant image which embodies the poet's confidence in the future and its organic connection with the past. It fits perfectly into the stylization of language which Tennyson habitually employs—indeed, it could hardly operate without it. Such stylization is by no means a way of achieving spurious 'significance': it is of the very essence of Tennyson's poetic creativity.

We must turn now to the question of vagueness. On this count too I believe that as a rule Tennyson is the best judge of the appropriate diction. Those who remark his vagueness seem to conflate two kinds of imprecision: vagueness of statement—not working out the subject properly but attempting to obscure the lack of thought in inclusive and ill-defined generalizations; and vagueness of visual detail—using evocative and hazy description to create an aura of the mysterious, again disguising a lack of real substance. These two kinds of vagueness seem to be regarded as having a common effect, bestowing upon the language a sense of some great underlying significance which proves, upon closer examination, to be bogus. The implication is that Tennyson and his contemporaries thought that this was how 'poetic' language should be or, at any rate, that it was the best they could manage.

Vagueness may, however, be appropriate; as Wittgenstein pointed out, the instruction 'stand roughly here' may be perfect where 'more exact' advice would lead to confusion. In *In Memoriam* we find vague statements which we may call dramatic—that is, they express an idea which the poet does not, and cannot, comprehend or explain in a more precise way. An example will make clear what I mean:

> For all we thought and loved and did,
> And hoped, and suffer'd, is but seed
> Of what in them is flower and fruit.

In these lines from the Epilogue we have some idea of what is meant by 'seed'—human life as we know it—but we can understand little of the nature of the flower or fruit. Clearly things are expected to get better in time, but in just what way is neither stated nor implied: we are simply told that it will stand in the same relation to what we have now as the flower and fruit do to the seed. The reason why these lines are vague about the 'one far-off divine event' is that the poet *does not know* what the event will be like, and there is even a lingering doubt as to whether it will occur at all.

Vagueness of diction in such circumstances is surely not culpable. It is justified dramatically, for it describes something of which the poet, in his situation, has only a hazy notion. It has often been remarked that the Prologue too expresses no more than a strong hope for the future:

> We have but faith: we cannot know;
>   For knowledge is of things we see;
>   And yet we trust it comes from thee,
> A beam in darkness: let it grow.

Dr. Leavis' comment on Hopkins is interesting in this context, for he seems to have a contrast with Tennyson in mind. He says that the Roman Catholic poet had

> a habit of seeing things as charged with significance; 'significance' here being, not a romantic vagueness, but a matter of explicit and ordered conceptions regarding the relations between God, man and nature.[11]

It seems as if Tennyson is being blamed for being uncertain about his commitment to Christianity, but it is reasonable that if he was unsure about the existence or nature of God, then he should say so. The poet hopes that all will turn out for the best and that is as far as he can go. This kind of vagueness is just what we would expect in *In Memoriam* for, as I pointed out in Chapter II, Tennyson believed that 'nothing worthy proving can be proven'. It is an essential corollary of the intuitive way of acquiring wisdom; Hopkins' situation was utterly different, for he was able to support his theology with the authority and traditions of the Church.

Once again we see that true understanding of *In Memoriam*, and of the demands it makes on Tennyson's skill with language, depends upon an appreciation of his basic attitudes. This time it is the Romantic slant in the poem which is relevant. *In Memoriam* is based upon the premise that statements about the truths which most vitally concern mankind cannot be definite: the poet can make only such assertions as are warranted by his experience. This Romantic attitude co-exists with the stylization of diction which I have dis-

[11] *The Common Pursuit*, pp. 51–2.

cussed earlier in the chapter, and that is perhaps why critics have been led astray. Tennyson is not as confident in the order of things as his language might at first imply. The insecurity of his faith is completely explicit and in such a context vagueness of statement is fully appropriate.

It should not be supposed, however, that Tennyson is claiming licence for loose and indecisive writing, as we can see by comparing the last stanza of section cxxxi with his first thoughts. The two readings are about equally imprecise, but in his revisions Tennyson makes his vague statements much more subtle and relevant. The poet will 'trust',

> With faith that comes of self-control,
> The truths that never can be proved
> Until we close with all we loved,
> And all we flow from, soul in soul.

The following version appears in the Harvard manuscript:

> With ever more of strength and grace
> The truths that never can be proved
> And come to look on those we loved
> And That which made us, face to face.

Notice that the early draft is not conspicuously bad as poetry; even so, Tennyson was not prepared to rest there. The revised first line shows a clear improvement, for it gives some idea of how 'strength and grace' or 'faith' are to be attained: through the exercise of 'self-control'. Thus Tennyson finally reiterates his belief that man's advancement depends on man himself. In the third line 'close with' is far more expressive than 'come to look on' for, as K. W. Grandsen points out,

> it suggests both 'the closing cycle' when God in man will be fully revealed, and also the closing or coming together of two people in love: thus beautifully bringing into unison the two principal themes of the poem.[12]

'Close with' is much more intense than the draft for it makes us realize that, instead of merely looking at his friend, the poet will be completely reunited with him. The change from 'face to face' to 'soul in soul' again emphasizes, in the alteration from 'to' to 'in', the

---

[12] K. W. Grandsen, *Tennyson: In Memoriam* (London, 1964), p. 19.

fulness of the poet's expected involvement with Hallam, whilst also bringing out the spiritual nature of the ultimate meeting.

The final important difference between the two versions is in the reference to God: 'That which made us' becomes 'all we flow from'. 'Flow' links the stanza to the water imagery that often suggests eternity in the poem (section ciii, for instance), and also to the 'spiritual rock' of the first stanza. There the 'living will' is asked to 'flow thro' our deeds and make them pure'; in the last line it is 'we' who flow and the implication is, therefore, that we ourselves are, in our spiritual essence, part of the living will. A static notion of the Maker is replaced by a dynamic one which represents mankind as involved with the Godhead in a developing creation. Instead of the conventional phrase of the first draft Tennyson gives us an image which adds significantly to the section's account of the relationship between God and man. As a statement of a faith to live by, section cxxxi remains conspicuously vague in comparison with Hopkins' Roman Catholicism—'all we flow from' is, if anything, less precise than 'That which made us'. Tennyson's revisions improve these lines so that they contribute more powerfully to the poetic structure by giving a fuller and more refined account of his vague beliefs.

Vagueness of pictorial detail is often related to the same basic trends in Tennyson's thinking—his reliance upon subjective experience and ultimately the vision for his most deeply felt beliefs. The trance which enables the poet to transcend the limits of time and space and make contact with his dead friend is of the greatest significance in *In Memoriam*. To express honestly and credibly the essence of such other-worldly experience must be an extremely difficult task, and vagueness can be very helpful. The apparently precise may falsify, giving a mere illusion of exactitude in an area where no one can hope to achieve full comprehension. In the Lincoln manuscript we can see that in section cxxiv Tennyson first wrote 'And *doubt* began "believe no more" ', but changed it to 'I heard *a voice* "believe no more" '. The draft was more specific in that it claimed to tell us who or what spoke to the poet, but the line is better with this detail left vague. We may think of the voice as 'doubt' if we wish but it could also represent several other things. The revision implies what I take to be the fact: we do not really understand who or what it is that 'speaks' in this way. The line is mysterious, not in order to be 'poetical', but because the event was to the poet mysterious.

Tennyson was evidently aware of the problem of describing the supernatural in language. At the visionary climax of the poem, section xcv, he declares:

> Vague words! but ah, how hard to frame
> In matter-moulded forms of speech,
> Or ev'n for intellect to reach
> Thro' memory that which I became.

That which is essentially beyond our comprehension must be explained—more than that, made actual—to the reader through 'matter-moulded forms of speech'. Language, which is best suited for expressing our everyday needs, must be adapted to experiences which are beyond time and space. In section xcv itself at the climax of the vision, Tennyson altered the line '*His* living soul was flash'd on mine' to read '*The* living soul'. His son noted, 'He preferred, however, for fear of giving a wrong impression, the vaguer and more abstract later reading'.[13] Tennyson was right to perceive the need for a certain vagueness when attempting to express 'that which is', the innermost essence of spiritual awareness. He was always anxious that his poetry should be accurate, and in this case accuracy could be best achieved through diction which is in itself less precise. We should also notice that the preferred reading is very appropriate to the poem, for in section xci the poet envisages two kinds of supernatural manifestation. Hallam may appear in the shape in which he was known in time or, more wonderfully, 'beauteous in thine after form, / And like a finer light in light'. 'The living soul' suggests the second kind of experience.

Much more could be said about section xcv from this point of view, but I have discussed it elsewhere[14]—and there are many other examples in *In Memoriam* of Tennyson's skilful use of pictorial vagueness to make the mystical real to us. In section ciii the poet dreams that he is summoned to the sea (presumably) of eternity where Hallam is waiting in a great ship:

> And while the wind began to sweep
> A music out of sheet and shroud,
> We steer'd her toward a crimson cloud
> That landlike slept along the deep.

[13] *Works, The Eversley Edition*, ed. Hallam Tennyson.
[14] *The Major Victorian Poets: Reconsiderations*, ed. Isobel Armstrong, pp. 58–67.

The description is visually imprecise. 'A crimson cloud' goes as far as we could expect towards expressing the nature of eternity, but Tennyson blurs the account still further with the epithet 'land-like'. The cloud is their destination but a ship usually sails to the land; this is both cloud and land. To represent heaven more specifically would be dishonest and less impressive; it may well be true that, as Tennyson himself said, 'Milton's vague hell is much more awful than Dante's hell marked off into divisions'.[15] The idea that there are things which we cannot know objectively and precisely is basic to the very intuitive and experiential nature of *In Memoriam*. Dramatic vagueness, so far from being a weakness, is one of the ways in which this aspect of Tennyson's thought is presented to us.

We may conclude with section lxx, where the poet is trying to imagine Hallam's face, but finds his view blocked by a sequence of nightmare images:

> Cloud-towers by ghostly masons wrought,
>   A gulf that ever shuts and gapes,
>   A hand that points, and palled shapes
> In shadowy thoroughfares of thought;
>
> And crowds that stream from yawning doors,
>   And shoals of pucker'd faces drive;
>   Dark bulks that tumble half alive,
> And lazy lengths on boundless shores.

This excellent evocation of a horrible dream sets off perfectly the conclusion of the section when, 'beyond the will', Hallam's face does appear to calm the poet's soul. There are two earlier versions of this section in the Lincoln manuscript and they show how helpful vagueness is to Tennyson here. The first line quoted read '*A fort* by ghostly masons wrought'; with the vaguer replacement we are left wondering whether the poet saw clouds or towers. We must conclude that the apparition was neither the one nor the other but something unlike anything we have ever seen on earth. We see also that Tennyson added 'shadowy' to the fourth line quoted; again, the point is not to summon up a bogus illusion of poetry but to express the reality of a deeply mysterious vision. A predecessor of the fifth

---

[15] Hallam Tennyson, *Memoir*, II, 518.

line runs, 'And lamps that wink at yawning graves'. 'Graves' is more specific than 'doors' but Tennyson's improvement leaves us to imagine where the doors might lead; we may think of the graves yielding up their dead but the air of uncertainty is appropriate to the nightmare atmosphere.

We are similarly left in doubt about the form of the 'palled shapes', 'dark bulks' and 'lazy lengths', for although there is the appearance of a list of details, they are given little distinctive individuality. Perhaps even more important, no attempt is made to explain the significance of any of these strange manifestations. This peculiar combination whereby the poet enumerates in apparent detail without giving any explanation or precise visual impression is peculiarly effective in expressing the numinous; it is beyond our comprehension and vague diction ensures that we sense its enigmatic nature.

My claim for Tennyson's vagueness, then, is that very often it *does* give the impression that something significant is in question, but this is no mere substitute for meaningful poetic structure. We must recognize the distinction between an experience whose essence can be only vaguely intuited and which is therefore best described in diction which suggests its imprecision, and a failure to discover a true form for a subject. To be sure, Tennyson sometimes slides into the latter shortcoming, but critics who accuse him of cultivating a false significance in order to imitate the 'poetical' are probably objecting to his subject matter rather than his language. *In Memoriam* cannot be properly understood without an appreciation of the strong anti-materialist reliance upon intuition. The Romantic belief that ultimate truth is unknowable and that we can only grope our way subjectively towards it forms a basic element in Tennyson's thought, and its extreme manifestation is the vision which transcends ordinary reality. In this context the examples I have considered exhibit through the vagueness of their diction experiences which are truly significant in the poem.

Difficulties in appreciating Tennyson's poetic power seem to me to dissolve when we take proper account of his classical qualities— which involve elaborate diction—and his Romantic outlook— which appears at its fullest in his reliance upon the mystical. When we read with confidence we find that these two aspects of his language are very far from being a means of evoking the spuriously 'poetical'. They are often at the very foundations of the closely woven poetic structure of *In Memoriam*.

F

V

SYNTAX:
RELATIONSHIPS AND EMPHASIS

> Of all the elements necessary to make an utterance meaningful, the
> most powerful is syntax, controlling as it does the order in which
> impressions are received and conveying the mental relations 'behind'
> sequences of words.[1]

THE term *syntax*, as I propose to use it, refers to the grammatical
function of words and their relations with each other in the structure
of the sentence.[2] We will be concerned with those elements in the
language—tense, mood and voice in verbs, pronouns and articles,
word order—whose function is to make connected sense out of
what would otherwise be just a string of words. Our task is rather
different from the study of diction, for in syntax the number of
possible forms is limited. Tennyson remarked that he could have
written 'baby' in the line, 'An infant crying in the night', but he
could in fact have substituted a vast range of other words—mother,
dog, lexicographer, lonely person, mock turtle; in diction the field is
almost boundless. But for the first word in the line there were only a
few possibilities—a(n), the, the absence of article, some, any. The fact
that the area of choice is narrower does not, however, make syntax
less important; it means that a great deal can hang upon an element
which is both small and familiar (we use 'an' all the time without
noticing it, unlike 'mock turtle'). Unless we read carefully we may
fail to notice the significance of syntax in the poetic structure.

The general characteristics of the syntax of *In Memoriam* are
exactly those we might expect from the two preceding chapters.
Firstly, Tennyson's syntax is unobtrusive. He does not, as a rule,
violate the norms of language; he prefers to exploit the capacities
of ordinary forms. He repeats the same structure, varies word order
within the accepted limits and capitalizes on the potential ambiguities and contrasts in articles and pronouns. We do not find him
turning the whole system upside down and remaking it according

---

[1] Nowottny, *The Language Poets Use*, p. 9.
[2] See Robins, *General Linguistics*, pp. 180 and 190; C. L. Wrenn, *The English Language*
(London, 1949), pp. 106–7 and 130–2; and Ullmann, *Language and Style*, p. 111.

to his own requirements. Violent dislocations of language are likely, particularly in a long poem, to produce diminishing returns, whilst subtle modulations of the norm can be as startling in their own way. In this respect Tennyson's syntax is of a piece with his diction, as I described it in Chapter III: on the surface at least, it is simple, unobtrusive, unremarkable.

Such strange syntax as we find in *In Memoriam* comes mainly from compression of one kind, namely the omission of auxiliary verbs:

> O not for thee the glow, the bloom,
>   Who changest not in any gale,
>   Nor branding summer suns avail
> To touch thy thousand years of gloom.   (ii)

We have to understand 'is' in the first lines and 'do' in the third. At times Tennyson carries this feature about as far as is possible, presumably in the interests of condensation. It is the key to the disputed stanza of section xv, where commentators have found a mixture of tenses:

> The forest crack'd, the waters curl'd,
>   The cattle huddled on the lea;
>   And wildly dash'd on tower and tree
> The sunbeam strikes along the world.

These verbs are all in the present tense after the pattern of the preceding line, 'The rooks are blown about the skies'. The omission of auxiliary verbs adds to the general effect of the storm by creating uncertainty and disorder, and is more specifically relevant because in the first line the confusion is between active and passive forms of the verb. When we find that the waters have not curled themselves, but are *being* curled, we appreciate more forcibly the extent to which the storm has deprived these natural forms of their own powers of motion: they move only at the whim of the unruly elements. This is in accord with the way the rooks are 'blown about' the skies instead of flying through them, and with the effect of the storm on the poet, who is similarly incapacitated and impelled to 'dote and pore on yonder cloud'. The wild unrest makes the poet, like the forest and the waters, unexpectedly passive. The temporary ambiguity in the syntax makes us more fully aware of the implications of the reading we must finally adopt.

But as a rule Tennyson's syntax stays close to accepted forms.

One is pleased to find this view confirmed by the mathematics of others. Mats Redin[3] counted the departures from regular word order in eleven poets from Pope to Sassoon, and shows that Tennyson has almost the lowest proportion of irregular constructions—4·8 per cent (6 per cent in rhymed verse) compared with Wordsworth's 11·2 and Pope's 21·8. Over half Tennyson's 'deviant' forms are displacements of the Adverbial, and in this respect English allows considerable licence anyway. William E. Baker[4] shows Tennyson using easily the highest proportion of 'regular' sentences out of thirty poets writing between 1870 and 1930. Baker in particular has defined his terms according to his own purposes, but these figures do strongly confirm the claim that Tennyson's syntax is usually unobtrusive.

The second general point about the syntax of *In Memoriam* concerns its habitual stylization, and this too is what we would expect after studying the diction of the poem. Tennyson's syntax reminds us that the poem is a work of art which he has perfected—'toil coöperant to an end' in the Enlightenment manner. The co-existence of these two attributes may seem paradoxical, but consider this stanza:

> Now fades the last long streak of snow,
>   Now burgeons every maze of quick
>   About the flowering squares, and thick
> By ashen roots the violets blow.   (cxv)

The inversions of subject and verb in the first two lines (though familar enough in poetry) are the only real deviations from normal English usage. Otherwise we have very little that could not readily be found outside a poem, but Tennyson persistently departs from the simplest constructions so that the syntax seems always just to one side of ordinary language. The use of the simple present tense ('fades' rather than 'is fading') is rather strange; the promotion of the adverbs and adverbial phrase ('Now', 'thick', 'By ashen roots') to the start of their clauses is quite acceptable as a means of gaining emphasis, though boldly used in the last clause; and, over all, there is the repetition of the same construction ('Now fades ... Now burgeons'), giving a rhetorical air to the stanza. In fact, it is faintly reminiscent of the 'Elegy Written in a Country Churchyard', though

---

3 *Word-Order in English Verse from Pope to Sassoon* (Uppsala, 1925), pp. 180ff.
4 *Syntax in English Poetry 1870–1930* (Berkeley and Los Angeles, 1967), p. 170.

Gray's images are distinctly more precious and his rhythms less varied:

> Now fades the glimmering Landscape on the Sight,
> And all the Air a solemn Stillness holds;
> Save where the Beetle wheels his droning Flight,
> And drowsy Tinklings lull the distant Folds.

The characteristic syntax of *In Memoriam* does not move very far from ordinarily permitted forms, but it contributes to the general tones of classical stylization which we find in other aspects of Tennyson's language.

This mode of writing is often completely justified. In the stanza quoted the initial stressing of 'Now' brings out the poet's new-found joy in the present and the distinction between how he feels at this point in the poem and how he has felt for so long. For the first time the spring seems to bring him a new birth of life and hope, and he can exult in the present instead of mourning for the past. The other inversions throw the emphasis in each case onto the verb, so that the *activity* which is going on all around becomes the most important aspect of the scene. This too suits the poet's new mood: the verbs evoke movement, growth, fluxation, and bring to the fore his joyful acceptance of change in everything that lives. He has come a long way since his determination in section i to cling to grief and his wish in section ii to identify with the unchanging yew tree. The repetition of the same clause structure reflects the simultaneity of all these signs of spring and the unity of the poet's response to them: correspondent events are given similar syntax. The formalization is integral to the structure of the section, for it leads us to the most important aspects of the meaning.

I have been trying to suggest that in general the syntax of *In Memoriam* is both unobtrusive and stylized. In the process I may have begun to demonstrate how significant syntax can be in the poetic structure. The two examples I have discussed represent the lines the argument will now take: in section xv we saw how small grammatical items are important because they indicate the nature of the relationships between the various elements in the sentence; in section cxv word order was shown as determining the emphasis which we are obliged to give to the several aspects in the description. These two functions, which are performed uniquely well by syntax, are the subject of this chapter.

Articles, demonstratives and pronouns are all ways of showing the speaker's relationship to the person or thing in question. In a simple expression like 'this boy' the choice of demonstrative indicates either that the boy is nearby or that he has been spoken of recently; 'my boy' suggests that he is specially connected to the speaker; 'you' is appropriate when he is actually present. The point could hardly be simpler, but the implications of the choice in terms of personal relationships could be immense.

I argued in Chapter II that *In Memoriam* is essentially structured on the poet's developing experience. This is often presented in terms of the poet's external surroundings, and if we are to accept his experience it is vital that we believe in his descriptions.

> Unwatch'd, the garden bough shall sway,
>   The tender blossom flutter down,
>   Unloved, that beech will gather brown,
> This maple burn itself away.   (ci)

In these lines the items in the scene are all referred to as if they were actually visible to the poet. This is most obvious with 'this' and 'that', with their 'over there' pointing effect, but the definite articles in the first two lines constitute a similar claim of recognition.[5] This use of the definite article occurs most frequently in speech when the object of attention is there for all parties to see, and its employment here is a way of insisting on the actuality of the beech and so on: the poet can see them there in front of him. The device is very common in *In Memoriam*:

>   ice
> Makes daggers at the sharpen'd eaves,
>
> And bristles all the brakes and thorns
>   To yon hard crescent, as she hangs
>   Above the wood . . .   (cvii)

'Yon' is an overt route to the same goal. We take it that the poet is actually looking at the moon and the woods because he uses the syntactic forms which are reserved for such occasions, and our belief in the reality of his experience is strengthened by seeing him in relation to external phenomena.

[5] For the functions of the definite article see M. A. K. Halliday's chapter in *English Studies Today*, 3rd series, ed. George I. Duthie (Edinburgh, 1964), pp. 25–36; and for a generally suggestive discussion see Sir George Rostrevor Hamilton, *The Tell-Tale Article* (London, 1950).

A variation on this effect is illustrated in the following lines:

> So find I every pleasant spot
> In which we two were wont to meet,
> *The* field, *the* chamber and *the* street,
> For all is dark where thou art not.   (viii)

Here the definite article refers neither to something the poet sees, nor to a place which is generally known or which has been previously introduced, but to something the poet recognizes in his own mind. He is thinking of particular places with which *he* is familiar, and because he speaks of them in this direct way we are drawn inside his mind. He is inconsiderately, as it were, assuming information which we do not have; we catch him off-guard, revealing his own knowledge and attitude. We are made aware that the poet has intimate preconceptions which we cannot share: the fact that the article's claim for recognition functions directly for the poet but not for us is the major point of the line.

We find the poet particularly immersed in his own view of things at the start of the poem when he becomes emotionally involved with the ship which is bringing back Hallam's remains. In section xii he describes how his mind leaves his body and goes out over the sea. He names no objective, but we read, 'I . . . reach the glow of southern skies, / And see *the* sails at distance rise'. What sails?—the sails which have obsessed him to the point where he is unconscious of any need to specify in greater detail. He can speak of them without it occurring to him that they may not be as familiar to others because he is absorbed in his very special relationship with them. This example is particularly interesting because of the close proximity of '*the* glow of southern skies', where 'the' means 'the kind of glow which we all know exists in such regions'. This we can recognize without any difficulty, but it is immediately followed by 'the sails' which are so personal to the poet: we become keenly aware of the point at which his mind diverges from the everyday concerns common to us all, and thus of his existence as a sorrowing individual. It is the definite article which conveys this information to us.

I have talked of the importance of mystical experience in *In Memoriam* and of the appropriateness of a certain vagueness of diction as a means of expressing it. Tennyson has only 'matter-moulded forms of speech' with which to make the reader comprehend and believe in the transcendental. The article can be of use in this situation, for whilst 'the' demands recognition and acceptance, 'a' can represent the strange and unknown. Sorrow is speaking:

> 'The stars,' she whispers, 'blindly run;
> A web is wov'n across the sky;
> From out waste places comes a cry,
> And murmurs from the dying sun'.   (iii)

The contrast between the two articles here consistently sets off the known from the mysterious. The poet can cope with the stars, the sky and the sun, for they are visible and familiar, but 'a web' and 'a cry' are of a different order of experience. The web is both the purposeless courses of the stars and a veil which conceals light and meaning from us, and the cry is both a proclamation and a lament. The poet can barely comprehend these manifestations, and their alien nature is signalled by the prominent contrast between 'a' and 'the'.

We can see again how small grammatical elements illuminate relationships in section lxx, which I discussed apropos of vague diction. At the beginning of the section the definite article shows that the poet understands the gloom and the hues which he can see, and the face which he recalls:

> I cannot see the features right,
> When on the gloom I strive to paint
> The face I know; the hues are faint
> And mix with hollow masks of night.

The last line quoted begins the series of horrific images which block the poet's vision, and 'hollow masks' has no article; indeed, there is no definite article at all throughout the two succeeding stanzas which present the ominous phantasmagoria. 'The' would imply familiarity and recognition, but the nightmare is strange and ghastly. In the last stanza the sequence is broken:

> Till all at once beyond the will
> I hear a wizard music roll,
> And thro' a lattice on the soul
> Looks thy fair face and makes it still.

The wizard music is still mysterious, but in the last line the poet finally gains some kind of communion with the dead. In the first stanza he sought '*The* face I know', but now he speaks to his friend instead of about him: '*thy* fair face'. The more direct and intimate second person pronoun shows us that Hallam is, in the end, actually present to the poet. This shift from 'the' to 'thy' delineates exactly the change in Hallam's relationship to the poet during the course of the section. We might notice also the verbs 'see' and 'look': in the first line the poet is actively trying to *see*, but in the last stanza he is passive as the face *looks* on him (the earlier draft in the Lincoln manuscript reads 'I cannot *get* the features right' in the first line, and the correspondence is absent). When the vision comes the poet does not have to do anything, just to wait while it looks on him. The verbs work with the changes in the article (and the vague diction) to make the reader believe in the actuality of mystical experience.

So far I have been concerned largely with the way in which Tennyson uses articles to bring out the nature of the poet's relationships to persons or things, but the last example has taken us on to pronouns. Francis Berry points out that the personal pronoun is 'the one Part of Speech which presupposes human relations and human situations',[6] and we would expect it to be important in *In Memoriam*. The poem is fundamentally an account of the poet's developing attitude, and the way in which he sees the connection between Hallam and himself is a major part of it. Tennyson can select either 'thou' or 'he' to stand for Hallam, and he has used this power consistently and meaningfully.

At the start of the poem Hallam is usually 'he', for the poet is dominated by the fact of the friend's absence and has no warrant for believing that a direct address could reach a listener. The pathos of this situation is explicit in section vii, where the poet attempts 'thou', but is frustrated by Hallam's inability to respond. 'Behold me', he says, but no one is listening and he is compelled to recognize the awful fact of death in the flat statement, '*He* is not here'. He attempts to assume a continuing 'thou' relationship but feels obliged to acknowledge its impossibility. 'Thou' occurs in section viii, but in a context which stresses only the separateness of the two men: 'For all is dark where thou art not.' Hallam's existence is denied immediately it is suggested, and the paradoxical-sounding line leaves us with an impression of futility.

After this the second person pronoun is not used of Hallam for thirty sections, but we do find it used of the ship bearing the body

---

[6] *Poet's Grammar* (London, 1958), p. 3. Cf. Hasan, 'Linguistics and the Study of Literary Texts'.

back to England, and often so that at first we think it refers to the
dead man. Section xiv begins 'If one should bring me this report, /
That thou hadst touch'd the land to-day', but we find that the ship,
not Hallam is meant by 'thou'. The same thing happens at the
start of section xvii: 'Thou comest, much wept for: such a breeze /
Compell'd thy canvas'. In both cases the reader is made initially
to confuse the ship and Hallam, and this shows how involved the
poet is with the voyage. He is using the ship as a surrogate for his
friend's return and pouring all the emotion which belongs to the
fact of his death into a desire for the arrival of the vessel which bears
his body. The use of the intimate personal pronoun expresses this
projection. The transference is in fact reciprocal, for as the ship is
seen as a person, so the dead friend has become little more than an
object—in section x the poet alludes to him as 'thy dark freight,
a vanish'd life'. This adaptation of 'thou' to the ship is deeply
poignant: we think that the pronoun should refer to Hallam, but he
is only a corpse and no more responsive to direct address than the
boat in which he forms a part of the cargo. The word which should
affirm a warm, close relationship is used to deny one.

The pronoun 'we' is perhaps the strongest for suggesting harmony
and intimacy, but instances of it in the first third of *In Memoriam*
are backward-looking, set firmly in the past—for example, 'The path
by which we twain did go' (xxii). Here 'we' is connected to the
pastoral idealization, and sadly contrasts former pleasures with
present sorrows. The most hopeful line in the first third of the poem
occurs in section xlvii, where the poet concludes that souls must
retain their integrity beyond death, and therefore 'I shall know him
when we meet'. The tremendous certainty in this line proceeds
from 'shall', with its sense of determination, from 'when', which
flatly assumes that the event will occur (cf. 'if'), and from the
movement through the pronouns by which 'I' and 'him' are first
placed in a positive relationship and then superseded by 'we',
implying that the reunion has been accomplished. In this section 'we'
is used with great confidence for the future, but the optimism does
not last. From section xl 'thou', 'he' and occasionally 'we' all occur
in reference to Hallam, according to the poet's mood. He is determined to construct a credible present relationship between himself
and Hallam, but his attempts must ultimately fail because they have
no basis other than common sense or wishful thinking. Only the
vision of section xcv can provide a secure belief. In section ciii,

which completes the poet's hopes for the future by showing in a dream his final reunion with Hallam, the dead man is 'he' until the last stanza when the two are joined together in eternity: '*We* steer'd her toward a crimson cloud / That landlike slept along the deep'.

As a result of the authority imparted by these visions a twin movement begins with Hallam as its subject. He is both the source of the poet's individual assurance and an exemplar for the future progress of mankind. In this latter role Hallam is sometimes 'he', but 'thou' is always used when the poet is thinking of him in personal relationship to himself. I mentioned that his desire to use 'thou' was frustrated in section vii; here, in its partner, cxix, he seems to employ the form as many times as he can:

> And bless thee, for thy lips are bland,
> And bright the friendship of thine eye;
> And in my thoughts with scarce a sigh
> I take the pressure of thine hand.

The purposefulness of this contrast with section vii is shown by the Lincoln manuscript draft of cxix, which reads, '*The* face is bright, *the* lips are bland / *He* smiles upon me eye to eye ... I take the pressure of *his* hand'. The change in pronouns, as I have tried to show, brings out the change in attitude. The 'he' of the first part of *In Memoriam* has been replaced by 'thou', for the poet at last feels sure that Hallam is there to hear him. Finally, in the last stanza of section cxxx, the personal pronouns circle and balance each other, suggesting the kind of reciprocal relationship which had before been only a 'backward fancy' from the past:

> Far off thou art, but ever nigh;
> I have thee still, and I rejoice;
> I prosper, circled with thy voice;
> I shall not lose thee tho' I die.

Tennyson's subtle use of articles and pronouns to bring out the nature of his relationships with persons and things shows him well able to exploit the potentialities of syntax—though, as with diction, we must pay careful attention, for the classical impulse in his writing ensures that we will not find him obtrusively dislocating the structure of ordinary language.

Word order is also concerned with relationships—grammatical

relationships between words in sentences: we recognize the subject, for example, by the fact that it precedes the verb. However, it is the optional variations within a given clause structure which tend to be significant for poetic language. The uses of word order we shall be considering here do not, as a rule, involve alternative kinds of grammatical connections, but a choice between different sequences of presentation—or, between giving emphasis to different elements in the sentence (parallel syntax, which is exceptionally frequent, is reserved for separate discussion). Tennyson writes,

> The hills are shadows, and they flow
>   From form to form, and nothing stands;
>   They melt like mist, the solid lands,
> Like clouds they shape themselves and go.   (cxxiii)

If we were to reduce the last two lines to a more straightforward form, say 'The solid lands melt like mist and shape themselves and go like clouds', we would not alter the grammatical function of any of the words or phrases, but the order in which we encounter them. The subject, verbs and complements act in the same way, but Tennyson has put them into a more expressive arrangement. 'The solid lands', instead of coming first, are sandwiched between the mist and the clouds so that they seem completely engulfed by images of insubstantiality; and 'go' is made starkly to end the sentence and the stanza so that the solid lands seem to slide suddenly away into a an indefinite void. Tennyson's deployment of word order for emphasis makes the account far more dramatic and alarming.

Although he sometimes uses inversions which we accept only in poetry (e.g. subject and verb), Tennyson often gains his effects, as in the foregoing example, from within the resources of ordinary language. We may observe further how he uses word order to place emphasis on the most important elements by comparing the first stanzas of three parallel Christmas sections:

> With trembling fingers did we weave
>   The holly round the Christmas hearth;
>   A rainy cloud possess'd the earth,
> And sadly fell our Christmas-eve.   (xxx)

Again at Christmas did we weave
 The holly round the Christmas hearth;
 The silent snow possess'd the earth,
And calmly fell our Christmas-eve.   (lxxviii)

To-night ungather'd let us leave
 This laurel, let this holly stand:
 We live within the stranger's land,
And strangely falls our Christmas-eve.   (cv)

The classical tone of conscious formality is present in all three, even though the word order is almost that of ordinary language. The prime function of these sections is to provide a series of chronological fixing points against which the poet's changing attitude can be measured, and word order is used to throw into relief the most significant aspects of his response on each occasion.

The first thing we notice is the trio, 'With trembling fingers', 'Again at Christmas' and 'To-night ungather'd', all of which stand out because the prepositional phrase is normally placed last in the clause. The first phrase insists on the overt sorrow of the family, whereas in the second, 'Again at Christmas', there is an element of dull repetition, of carrying on as usual. A year has passed bringing some calmness, but no real solution. In the third section the opening inversion brings out the sense that something special is about to happen, for the emphasis is on tonight as opposed to other nights: a habit is to be broken. The family has left the old home with its associations with Hallam, and the visions of sections xcv and ciii have made the traditional consolation less meaningful. Christmas has become 'an ancient form / Thro'' which the spirit breathes no more', and the section ends with hopes for the advent of 'The closing cycle rich in good'. It is also fitting that the most obvious manifestation of this breach with tradition (the fact that the laurel is ungathered) should take a prominent place. The effectiveness of this opening can be compared with Tennyson's initial version, printed until 1863, in which the section began, 'This holly by the cottage-eave, / To-night, ungather'd, shall it stand'. These lines are less good for several reasons, and they notably fail to take us straight to the point in the manner of the opening we now have.

A further inversion in the last line of each of the stanzas throws the adverb into prime position, again stressing what is individual about the poet's attitude on each occasion. In section xxx it is sadness, in lxxviii calmness; in cv 'strangely' is particularly important, for it refers not only to the absence of familiar faces but also to the strange behaviour which the poet is now adopting. The prominence of these adverbs results from the inversion of subject and verb in the three last lines, and this should help us to notice the difference in tense between sections xxx and lxxviii, where the poet speaks in the past, and cv, where we find the present tense and injunctions for the immediate future. This contrast is a major cause of the excitement which pervades section cv: it adds a sense of immediacy and urgency which reflects the poet's new confident outlook. The other two sections saw the poet dominated by memories of the past and Tennyson chose his tense accordingly; now the poet rejects the old forms and looks forward to the future, and the tense is again appropriate. Tennyson make his syntax push the verbs forward to our attention so that we notice the part they are playing.

Emphatic word order can operate over the length of a whole section, as we can see in lxvii, where the poet, who is in bed, imagines Hallam's burial place:

> When on my bed the moonlight falls,
>   I know that in thy place of rest
>   By that broad water of the west,
> There comes a glory on the walls:
>
>   .   .   .
>
>   The mystic glory swims away;
>   From off my bed the moonlight dies.

In the first stanza the prepositional phrases 'on my bed' and 'in thy place of rest' stand out because they occur initially in their clauses. This forces us to notice their similarity (a bed is a place of rest)— and then their dissimilarity. Despite the euphemism, Hallam's condition is very different from the poet's, yet the equivalence in syntax points up the way in which they are nevertheless joined together by the strange trance. In the last line quoted (line 10) the end of the experience is marked by another displacement, 'From off my bed': the moonlight goes even as it came. The prominent prepositional phrases keep the movement of the poet's thought clear and, by stressing the *place*, emphasize the spatial leaps which his imagination makes. Both the distance and the connection are brought to our notice. The section concludes with another inversion:

> And then I know the mist is drawn
> A lucid veil from coast to coast,
> And *in the dark church* like a ghost
> Thy tablet glimmers to the dawn.

This must surely be deliberate. Section lxvii first has the poet in bed, then he thinks about the burial place, then comes back in his mind to the bed, and finally goes out once more to the dark church. Each of these movements is signalled by an inversion which pushes the phrase naming the place to the front of its clause. The syntax insists on the dream's mysterious power to transcend physical separation.

We may conclude with a discussion of one of the occasional very long sentences which Tennyson controls so well (section lxxxvi, which was instanced in the previous chapter, is rather similar). In section xiv the poet begins, 'If one should bring me this report', and goes on to talk about the ship arriving and how it would appear and then, more fantastically, imagines that Hallam might come walking off it and the things they would do and say. He ends (still in the subjunctive mood):

> And I perceived no touch of change,
> No hint of death in all his frame,
> But found him all in all the same,
> I should not feel it to be strange.

The main clause does not come until the twentieth and last line of the section. Suzanne Langer has said that 'the tension which music achieves through dissonance, and the reorientation in each new resolution to harmony, find their equivalents in the suspensions and periodic decisions of propositional sense in poetry'.[7] The syntax here, which builds up a massive sum of *If*s in order to resolve them all in a one-line *Then*, produces just the effect which Mrs. Langer describes. The section is very startling because the series of *If*s becomes more wildly improbable as it continues, and yet the main clause for which we have been waiting proclaims that the whole thing would *not* be strange. As we read the list of possibilities

---

[7] Quoted by Donald Davie, *Articulate Energy* (London, 1955), p. 18.

we become progressively more convinced that they must be rejected, but to the poet they are all quite credible. This, of course, is
the main point of the section, and it demonstrates how far the poet
is the victim of his 'fancies' (as in sections xiii and xv) at this stage
of the poem. By ordering his sentence so that the reader is led in
suspense from the unremarkable to the impossible, and then having
the poet affirm that to him they all seem likely, Tennyson gives the
strongest emphasis to our impression of the poet's state of mind.

Section xiv shows Tennyson using syntax for emphasis on the
scale of clauses rather than the phrases of the earlier examples. At
this point it will be best to break off, for further discussion of word
order at this level must involve parallel syntax, which merits a
separate chapter. I hope I have said sufficient to indicate the general
character of Tennyson's syntax in *In Memoriam* and the variety of
effects he can gain from it.

VI

SYNTAX: A PATTERN OF THOUGHT

There rolls the deep where grew the tree.
O earth, what changes hast thou seen!
There where the long street roars, hath been
The stillness of the central sea.

I QUOTE this stanza from section cxxiii as one of very many which demonstrate Tennyson's predilection for successive uses of the same clause or phrase structure, that is, for parallel syntax. The air of formal perfection which we often find in the language of *In Memoriam* is very much a product of this kind of syntax. In this stanza the clauses balance each other completely: every form is related to another and the whole group drawn in tightly together as a self-sufficient unit.

There are five clauses, pivoting on the third, 'O earth, what changes hast thou seen!' This summarizes the stanza and also qualifies its equilibrium by introducing an emotional note through the exclamation. Each of the remaining clauses is related to the other three, so that every possible combination is included. I will list the correspondences in an attempt at clarity:

1. The clauses within each of the two sentences belong together. 'There rolls the deep' and 'where grew the tree' are similarly structured, and the there-where form exerts a strong internal pull. And the same is true in the last two lines.

2. We pair the clauses according to their functions in their sentences, linking the two 'there's and the two 'where's: 'There rolls the deep' goes with 'There hath been the stillness', and 'where grew the tree' goes with 'where the long street roars'.

3. We relate the clauses in respect of the tenses of the verbs, and this produces a further different set of pairs. 'There rolls the deep' corresponds to 'where the long street roars', for both depict present conditions, whereas the remaining two clauses are in the past—'grew' and 'hath been'.

Each clause is parallel, in various ways, to all the others. This incredibly detailed and complicated three-way structure takes us as

G

close to the essence of Tennyson's stylized language as any feature we have yet considered (though this is not the place to discuss the alliteration and assonance of this stanza, which are also formidable). The balance is complete, precise, immaculate; nothing is left out, nothing overbalances the pose and perfect equivalence. The image which comes to mind is the movement of a watch, but that is the eighteenth-century figure for the functioning of the universe. Here is the full paradox of the linnet and the artifact: the frightening account of the instability of external nature is conveyed in syntax which is formally perfect. But the poet's equanimity here is founded not on satisfaction with the processes of erosion in themselves, but on a Romantic determination to disregard them and live by the truth of the imagination: 'But in my spirit will I dwell, / And dream my dream, and hold it true'.

Parallel constructions occur in *In Memoriam* at the rate of about five per hundred words (a proportion somewhat higher than Wimsatt gives for the prose of Johnson, Addison and Hazlitt[1] and about the same as I find for Pope—though his figures, unlike Tennyson's, include many antitheses. There is in fact a book on parallelism in Tennyson;[2] it contains some useful remarks but consists mainly of lists of examples). The air of stylized patterning which parallel syntax brings to the language is pervasive, and greatly furthers the cohesion and regularity of the verse. The stanza from section cxxiii is closely unified within itself; the balanced syntax makes its form appear deliberate—almost tidy (it is saved by the exclamation in the second line). The trend is towards similarities rather than differences, familiarity rather than novelty. We are conscious of coherence and clarity of outline before all else. The whole tendency of Tennyson's language could be described in the words which Gerard Manley Hopkins used to explain the effect of metre:

> Now the force of this recurrence is to beget a recurrence or parallel-
> ism answering to it in the words or thought and, speaking roughly
> and rather for the tendency than the invariable result, the more
> marked parallelism in structure whether of elaboration or emphasis
> begets more marked parallelism in the words and sense. And more-
> over parallelism in expression tends to beget or passes into parallelism
> in thought.[3]

---

[1] *The Prose Style of Samuel Johnson*, p. 26.
[2] Émile Lauvrière, *Repetition and Parallelism in Tennyson* (London, 1910).
[3] *The Journals and Papers of Gerard Manley Hopkins*, ed. Humphrey House and Graham Storey (London, 1959), pp. 84–5.

In the language of *In Memoriam* we see a mutual reinforcing of pattern which answers exactly to Hopkins' account. Tennyson's rhythms are not marked by spectacular variations any more than his diction, he builds up a long poem by repeating a stanza form (which is itself notable for the repetitions of rhyme), and parallelism is the most striking feature of his syntax. All aspects of his language work towards an effect of homogeneity, integration and order.

Parallel syntax frequently occurs in alliance with line-length so as to suggest a smooth and meditative outlook in which disagreeables are brooded upon rather than clashed together. The iterative structure accumulates thoughts rather than twisting and turning in an involuted chain of logic, and this makes it highly appropriate for the elegiac subject matter of *In Memoriam*. In fact, the syntax is distinctly reminiscent of the Bible, for Hebraic verse was based on the principle of parallel constructions (as Hopkins remarked in the letter just quoted). G. W. Allen observes,

> The structure of Hebraic poetry, even in English translation, is almost entirely lacking in subordination. The original language of the Old Testament was extremely deficient in connectives, as the numerous 'ands' of the King James version bear witness. It was a language for direct assertion and the expression of emotion rather than abstract thought or intellectual subtleties.[4]

Perhaps I can demonstrate this point by writing out two passages of equal length in a way which will bring out the extent of the parallelism. The first example is from section ciii, the second from *Deuteronomy* 1:28. Equivalent constructions are placed immediately underneath each other whereas different forms follow on to the right.

In Memoriam
And still as vaster grew the shore
      And roll'd the floods in grander space,
          The maidens gather'd strength
             and grace
             And presence, lordlier than before;
And I myself,
     who sat apart
       And watch'd them,
             wax'd in every limb;
           I felt the thews of Anakim,
             The pulses of a Titan's heart.

[4] *Discussions of Poetry: Form and Structure*, ed. Francis Murphy (Boston, 1964), p. 62.

Deuteronomy 1:28
Whither shall we go up?
our brethren have discouraged our heart,
            saying,
                    The people is greater
                            and taller than we;
                    the cities are great
                            and walled up to heaven;
                    and moreover we have seen the sons of the Anakims there.

Then I said unto you,
                    Dread not,
                    Neither be afraid of them.

I hope it will be apparent that these passages are very similar in design. Almost every phrase and clause in each is followed by another of analogous form, and both use 'and' in preference to other conjunctions. A quotation from another writer on perhaps the same subject but with different preoccupations may clinch the argument:

> The change took place, as I showed, through the unconscious development of a transpersonal control point; a virtual goal, as it were, that expressed itself symbolically in a form which can only be described as a vision of God. The dreams swelled the human person of the doctor to superhuman proportions, making him a gigantic primordial father who is at the same time the wind, and in whose protecting arms the dreamer rests like an infant.

I have not put this passage by Jung[5] in the diagram because although it is considerably longer than the others it contains almost no repetitions of structure and would run across several pages; 'and' occurs only once. I have selected these examples solely because of correspondences in their content and I believe they are typical.

Tennyson also uses 'climactic parallelism', a form which students of Biblical verse have found important: 'Here the first line is itself incomplete, and the second line takes up words from it and completes them':[6]

                    Peace and goodwill, goodwill and peace,
                    Peace and goodwill, to all mankind.   (xxviii)

---

[5] Quoted by Howard W. Fulweiler, 'Tennyson and the Summons from the Sea', *Victorian Poetry*, III (1965), 39.
[6] S. Driver, quoted by G. W. Allen in *Form and Structure*, ed. Murphy, p. 65.

SYNTAX: A PATTERN OF THOUGHT

> The lightest wave of thought shall lisp,
>   The fancy's tenderest eddy wreathe,
>   The slightest air of song shall breathe
> To make the sullen surface crisp. (xlix)

> How dimly character'd and slight,
> How dwarf'd a growth of cold and night,
> How blanch'd with darkness must I grow! (lxi)

As the Eversley editor says, 'That my father was a student of the Bible those who have read *In Memoriam* know' (p. 207). The poem is full of allusions to the Bible, the sections describing domestic situations analogous to the poet's are like parables, and the resemblance in language is at times really explicit—in section ciii Hallam speaks: ' "Enter likewise ye / And go with us:" they enter'd in'.

The undercurrent of ritual language in *In Memoriam* seems very appropriate to the elegiac theme. T. S. Eliot decided that it could 'justly be called a religious poem',[7] and this is broadly true. *In Memoriam* is about God, death and the renewal of life, the rhythms of the seasons, man's relationship with the physical universe, the prospect of life beyond the grave and the possibility of communication with the dead. All this is the stuff of religion as well as elegy, and the authoritative and sometimes incantatory tone deriving from the reminiscence of Biblical syntax fits the poem very well. When the poet is talking of 'Our little systems', 'the little lives of men', 'The man I held as held as half-divine', 'The daily burden for the back' or 'The very source and fount of Day' (I am just skimming through the first twenty-five sections), overtones of religious language add a proper sense of ritual and thoughtful dignity. It is again a matter of decorum. Parallel syntax often suggests that the poet is considering fully the significance of any statement, that he is lingering upon its implications and expounding all its consequences, rather than flashing out in random directions as the whim takes him. It may also cause us to read with an incantatory inflection, as, for instance, when the poet is celebrating the mystery of Hallam's continuing presence:

> Thy voice is on the rolling air;
>   I hear thee where the waters run;
>   Thou standest in the rising sun,
> And in the setting thou art fair. (cxxx)

[7] *Selected Prose*, p. 172.

The poet's song is of 'comfort clasp'd in truth reveal'd', and the meditative, religious tone associated with the Hebraic writings helps Tennyson to achieve a fit mode of expression. We should not be surprised that Queen Victoria told him, 'Next to the Bible *In Memoriam* is my comfort'.[8]

Parallel syntax is not always, of course, a good thing. It is dangerous because it can continue indefinitely; it offers a ready mould into which a whole succession of thoughts can be poured without the writer feeling any impulsion to shape them in any individual way or press them to a strong conclusion.

> To draw, to sheathe a useless sword,
>   To fool the crowd with glorious lies,
>   To cleave a creed in sects and cries,
> To change the bearing of a word,
>
> To shift an arbitrary power,
>   To cramp the student at his desk,
>   To make old bareness picturesque
> And tuft with grass a feudal tower.   (cxxviii)

It is as if the clause structure gained its own momentum and Tennyson was unable to stop making them. Parallelism makes the syntax very plain, and if the substance is weak—a string of irritable generalizations, as here—then the effect is one of great triteness. Clause follows clause, but we seem to get nowhere.

Tennyson's parallelism is often, however, appropriate to his subject matter.[9] The similarity in syntactical structure makes us focus on correspondences in the sense of the clauses whilst at the same time being aware of the sequence of which they are a part. Both the succession in events and the equivalence between them is conveyed. By section cxvii the poet has overcome his worries about the effects of time so far as to expect 'Delight a hundredfold'

> For every grain of sand that runs,
>   And every span of shade that steals,
>   And every kiss of toothed wheels,
> And all the courses of the suns.

The parallel syntax here gives a strong sense of *process*, for we are

[8] Hallam Tennyson, *Memoir*, I, 485.
[9] On the relation of syntax to meaning see Davie, *Articulate Energy*, chapter VII.

conscious simultaneously of the persistence of the pattern and the onward movement of the sentence. The repetition in form gathers an impetus which is transferred to the subject matter so that the whole account imparts a feeling that the process is inevitable. The passage of time can be gauged in four ways—the hour glass, the sundial, the clock and the orbits of terrestial bodies—but whatever we use as a measure, time passes just the same. It is inexorable.

Parallelism is splendidly suited to the expression of process, and Tennyson has much occasion to use it in this way in *In Memoriam*. The poem is about time, the seasons, erosion, evolution, the movements of the planets, the inevitability of death, the cycles of the future. In section xxii the poet says that Death

> broke our fair companionship,
> And spread his mantle dark and cold,
> And wrapt thee formless in the fold,
> And dull'd the murmur on thy lip,
>
> And bore thee where I could not see ...

The momentum in the syntax is transferred to the implacable action of Death. We can see the method applied to the movement of the seasons in section lxxxv:

> But Summer on the steaming floods,
> And Spring that swells the narrow brooks,
> And Autumn, with a noise of rooks,
> That gather in the waning woods,
>
> And every pulse of wind and wave ...

The pulsation in the elements and the rhythmic revolutions of the natural cycle are represented by the iteration in the sentence structure.

Parallel syntax need not affirm an inexorable process however. The similarity in clause structure may be used to set off the differences between successive statements, as we can see later on in section lxxxv:

> So hold I commerce with the dead;
> Or so methinks the dead would say;
> Or so shall grief with symbols play
> And pining life be fancy-fed.

Here the repeated form presents qualifications of the first attitude, reducing it from its optimistic assertion to the bluntly realistic. We come down through the syntax in regular and well-defined stages—like gears in a car—until we reach a level where the poet can cope with the load of his grief without distortion. The parallel clauses make clear this gradual descent to the realistic so that we appreciate the poet's determination not to indulge his fantasies. Section xviii provides a similar but more extended example. The ship bearing Hallam's body has at last arrived, and the poet must somehow deal with the excessive emotional power with which he had invested it. His return to a degree of stability is again shown in a tendency to make large claims and then withdraw them; and parallel syntax again marks out the differences. He begins, ' 'Tis well, 'tis something; we may stand / Where he in English earth is laid', but the next stanza opens, ' 'Tis little . . .' The ship has returned and, of course, it does not help the poet much, as he slowly recognizes here. The rest of the section continues to use parallel clauses to express his determination to be realistic, as he speaks of 'the head / That sleeps or wears the mask of sleep', and of 'The life that almost dies in me; / That dies not, but endures with pain'. In each case the extravagant way of looking at things is discarded for a more balanced view. The repetition in structure is in accord with the attempt to reassess the situation but at the same time points up the differences in attitude.

The challenge to perceive connections which parallel syntax presents is found in quite an obvious way in section l, where each stanza begins, 'Be near me when . . .' We are liable to conclude that the stanzas are of equivalent status rather than following successively in an argument. The subtlety lies in the fact that this is only partially true: the stanzas do not follow logically, but they do exhibit a significant sequence. The first stanza is the most personal, dealing with the poet's physical response when 'the blood creeps, and the nerves prick / And tingle'. The second is more abstract and shows the poet in more speculative mood, seeing Time and Life as purposeless and malevolent. The third is the most general, broadening out to a view of men as 'the flies of latter spring', maintaining their petty lives for a brief hour and then passing, we infer, into oblivion. But the last stanza moves in a new direction:

> Be near me when I fade away,
>   To point the term of human strife,
>   And on the low dark verge of life
> The twilight of eternal day.

The poet naturally turns from the vicissitudes of life to envisage his own death, but this is not merely a change in time perspective, for the final stanza also shows a development in his thinking. At last the poet has some dim hopes of an eternal day in which his friend might really be near him. The section is not ultimately despairing. The identical openings of the stanzas set off the adjustments in the poet's thought and make us juxtapose the changing attitudes. They encourage us, for instance, to compare the last lines with 'Be near me when my light is low', the first—the contrast in the magnitude of the two lights (a candle burning low and, potentially at least, the sun) expresses the expansion in the breadth and hopefulness of the poet's conception.

As well as illustrating the ways in which parallel syntax can relate to the argument, section 1 (which has fifteen parallels altogether) shows how this clause structure can build up emotional pressure. The repetition of the same form seems to imply the poet's involvement in his subject:

> Be near me when my light is low,
>> When the blood creeps, and the nerves prick
>> And tingle; and the heart is sick,
>> And all the wheels of Being slow.

Lauvrière says, 'there is, especially in emotional moods, a natural tendency to cast successive thoughts in the same mould until the very matter of words or the power of emotion be exhausted'.[10] The blood creeps *and* the nerves prick, *and* tingle (the line break emphasizes the persistence of the parallel), *and* the heart is sick . . . the poet seems compelled to continue in the one form until the intensity of his depression is consumed. The reader is held in the same structure of thought while the poet forces through it all the pressure of his emotion. The point is again very clear in the third stanza:

> Be near me when my faith is dry,
>> And men the flies of latter spring,
>> That lay their eggs, and sting and sing
>> And weave their petty cells and die.

Parallel syntax often has this effect of conveying the intensity of the poet's emotions. We see it when he is talking of the idyllic time before Hallam's death:

[10] *Repetition and Parallelism in Tennyson*, p. viii.

> And all we met was fair and good,
>> And all was good that Time could bring,
>> And all the secret of the Spring
> Moved in the chambers of the blood.   (xxiii)

The repetition shows the poet's deep feeling that absolutely everything ('all . . . all . . . all') was in harmony. He thinks of their journey
through France:

> as of old we walk'd

> Beside the river's wooded reach,
>> The fortress, and the mountain ridge,
>> The cataract flashing from the bridge,
> The breaker breaking on the beach.   (lxxi)

The same concord was experienced in all these places, and the poet's
reluctance to leave the list manifests his involvement in the memory.
One more example finds the poet imagining the ship which is
bringing Hallam's body:

> I hear the noise about thy keel;
>> I hear the bell struck in the night:
>> I see the cabin-window bright;
> I see the sailor at the wheel.   (x)

The parallel syntax shows the poet gripped by his impulsion to
follow the form through until his emotional need is expressed, but
we should notice also that the scene is arranged so that each clause
takes us nearer to the ship—one would first be aware of the noise,
then more specifically of the bell, then one would see the windows,
and finally the sailor. The similarities between the clauses show the
poet's involvement, whilst the differences indicate more precisely,
through a kind of emotional montage, his desire to move in as close
as he can to the ship. We observe his mind constructing the picture
and pursuing his imaginings to the ultimate detail, the living human
figure—though it is not, sadly, Hallam.

Parallel syntax, as well as imparting a characteristically meditative
Biblical tone to *In Memoriam*, can give a strong sense of process in a
series of events, point up movements in the poet's thought and
convey the intensity of his emotion. Yet the prevalence of the form
is so great that we might expect it to show some further relationship

to the characteristic cast of Tennyson's mind and the themes of the poem. Syntax governs the kinds of connections we make between expressions, perhaps even between ideas, and the dominance of one kind of construction should signify the existence of a habitual pattern of thinking.[11]

The issue becomes even more conspicuous when we realize that parallelism is an aspect of an even more common feature, namely Tennyson's tendency to use successively clauses which have the same general function in the sentence. In other words, I am including not only those clauses which are internally of similar construction (parallel clauses) but also those which are alike in that they stand in the same relationship to the structure of the sentence in which they occur. A stanza from section lxvi should demonstrate:

> The shade by which my life was crost,
> Which makes a desert in the mind,
> Has made me kindly with my kind,
> And like to him whose sight is lost.

In the first two lines are two clauses which tell us more about 'The shade'. They are both in the same general syntactic relationship to it, but each has its own shape and we could not call them parallel. They are introduced by different forms of the relative pronoun, have different subjects, and are in different tenses and voices; yet they both act in the same way as qualifiers of 'The shade'. In the last lines too we would not say that 'kindly with my kind' is very similar to 'like to him whose sight is lost', but both expressions have the same function of telling us what the shade 'Has made me'.

Each of these pairs of clauses adds material which builds up our impression of the poet's state of mind. The first recalls, unexplicitly, the image of the path of life (cf. section xxii), and then develops that mental landscape into a spiritual desert; the second gives a literal answer to the query about his sociability and then introduces the simile of the blind man which runs through the next two stanzas. The point is made, but through the accumulation of clauses with the same function, rather than by a deepening logical penetration involving a chain of clauses successively modifying one another. And, moreover, if we look at the whole section we find that out of a total of eighteen clauses, eight are main clauses in four pairs, and six of

---

[11] For a full discussion of the evidence on the relationship between language and thinking, see Denis Lawton, *Social Class, Language and Education* (London, 1968).

the subordinate clauses fall into groups of two and four, amassing detail about the main clauses. Compare 'Loves Growth' by Donne:

> If, as in water stir'd more circles bee
> Produc'd by one, love such additions take,
> Those like so many spheares, but one heaven make,
> For, they are all concentrique unto thee.

Here no two clauses stand in the same relationship to each other. We start with a condition in which a comparison is nested, then follows the consequence ('Those like so many spheares, but one heaven make'), and finally a causal clause of explanation. Like Tennyson in section lxvi, Donne is dealing with one fairly simple notion, but each clause develops the subject in a different kind of way. Two distinct thought processes are involved. A diagram would show Tennyson's clauses ranged in a series, but Donne's dotted around with connecting lines going in all directions and indicating varying types of relationship (a string of elephants, trunk to tail, as opposed to a wagonload of monkeys). Donne's structure is in complete contrast with that which Tennyson uses to expound his image of the blind man:

> He plays with threads, he beats his chair
> For pastime, dreaming of the sky;
> His inner day can never die,
> His night of loss is always there.

Tennyson's tendency in *In Memoriam* to repeat clauses of the same general function rather than continually strike out new and diverse connections amounts to a recognizable pattern of thought. His syntax lingers over a given idea, adding descriptive particulars or restating it in another form: I propose to call it *analogical* as opposed to *analytic*. A notion is not explored in depth and explained, but approached from various angles on the same plane, turned round and reformulated until the meaning emerges from the total account. Subordinate clauses do not often tax us with whys and wherefores, conditions and results, causes and effects—and when they do, each structure is repeated before the argument moves on; they give us a stronger impression of the essential nature of the object, feeling or event by presenting it in different words or images or by adding descriptive details. We receive a further notion of what the experience is *like* so that we can more nearly grasp its exact quality, not an analysis of its composition or of how it came to be as it is. (This contrast is argued by more rigorous linguistic methods in Appendix A.)

Section cxxiv has been generally regarded as one which carries much of the thought of *In Memoriam*:

> I found Him not in world or sun,
>   Or eagle's wing, or insect's eye;
>   Nor thro' the questions men may try,
> The petty cobwebs we have spun.

The syntax I have been describing is evident in the list of the first two lines and in the redefining of 'the questions' as 'petty cobwebs'. Tennyson makes his point by giving a further derogatory account of philosophical speculations rather than by arguing against them. He is suspicious of reason:

> If e'er when faith had fall'n asleep,
>   I heard a voice 'believe no more'
>   And heard an ever-breaking shore
> That tumbled in the Godless deep;
>
> A warmth within the breast would melt
>   The freezing reason's colder part,
>   And like a man in wrath the heart
> Stood up and answer'd 'I have felt'.

The poet heard two things: 'a voice' and 'an ever-breaking shore'; his response was also dual: a warmth melted reason and 'the heart / Stood up and answer'd'. In the first pair he associates his doubts with the inexorable geological processes which have troubled him, in the second he includes both his opposition to reason and his positive alternative approach. Tennyson's syntax is perfectly adapted to this statement of his beliefs.

Section cxxiv makes plain Tennyson's reliance upon his personal experience. In Chapter II I linked this approach to his habit of establishing his emotional and intellectual position by returning to a situation or event to redefine his attitude to it. Subjective experience (however unsure) is the poet's only stay in an uncertain world, and in order to comprehend properly his mental state he repeatedly redefines it against familiar imagery and such occasions as Christmas, spring, and the anniversary of Hallam's death. The method is explicit in section cxxiv itself, for the poet declares that he was not like 'a man in wrath' after all, but 'a child in doubt and fear' (as in liv) who increased in wisdom until he became 'a child that cries, / But, crying, knows his father near'. The poet's developing attitude is continually measured against recurring external phenomena. The analogical mode of clause linkage I have been discussing is an aspect of this whole process of redefinition, for it shows the poet attempting to pin down in words the essence of an occurrence by reformulating it in other terms. Tennyson's syntax is completely in accord with his general approach to the problems of human existence and with his express convictions, as given, for instance, in section cxxiv, about the most promising way of seeking truth. It constitutes a pattern of his thought.

The principal antagonists of his subjectivism, as the poet sees it, are 'freezing reason' and scientific materialism—'Let Science prove we are' (cxx; we should remember that parallelism is also characteristic of the Bible). It is interesting to compare the syntax of *In Memoriam* with that of the book from which Tennyson drew much of his knowledge, Sir Charles Lyell's *Principles of Geology*. Lyell writes,

> If, then, it be conceded, that the combined action of the volcanic and the aqueous forces would give rise to a succession of distinct formations, and that these would sometimes be unconformable, let us next enquire in what manner these groups might become characterised by different assemblages of fossil remains.
>
> We endeavoured to show, in the last volume, that the hypothesis of the gradual extinction of certain animals and plants, and the successive introduction of new species, was quite consistent with all that is known of the existing economy of the animal world; and if it be found the only hypothesis which is reconcilable with geological phenomena, we shall have strong grounds for conceiving that such is the order of nature.[12]

As we might imagine, Tennyson's syntax is quite distinct from that appropriate to a scientific approach. A corresponding passage in *In Memoriam* is in simple sentences and entirely without subordination (except as it is occasioned by Nature being made the speaker):

> 'So careful of the type?' but no.
> From scarped cliff and quarried stone
> She cries, 'A thousand types are gone:
> I care for nothing, all shall go.

[12] Sir Charles Lyell, *Principles of Geology* (London, 1830–3), vol. III, pp. 30–1.

> 'Thou makest thine appeal to me:
> I bring to life, I bring to death:
> The spirit does but mean the breath:
> I know no more.'   (lvi)

Where Lyell asks us to concede and then to enquire, refers us back to his second volume, considers which hypothesis is reconcilable and finds strong grounds, the poet declares and redefines his experience until the full horror of it is apparent.

Walker Gibson has demonstrated the difference in point of view between Lyell and the poet—the way (specially in cxxiii) the latter speaks as if he were the immediate witness of the vast and extended changes which Lyell cautiously describes.[13] But Tennyson's analogical syntax is the strongest contrastive feature, even in the central part of section cxviii, where Gibson remarks 'a complexity of grammar that could equal the dependent clauses of any scientist'. Certainly the relationships between the parts of the nineteen-line sentence, in which the poet rehearses a scientific account of the development of the earth, are complex and varied, but the tendency to repeat a construction before moving on a step in the logic is still very evident. The world 'In tracts of fluent heat began, | *And* grew to seeming-random forms'; man

> throve *and* branch'd from clime to clime,
> The herald of a higher race,
> *And* of himself in higher place,
> If so he type this work of time
>
> Within himself, from more to more;
> *Or*, crown'd with attributes of woe
> Like glories, move his course, *and* show
> That life is not as idle ore,
>
> But iron dug from central gloom,
> *And* heated hot with burning fears,
> *And* dipt in baths of hissing tears,
> *And* batter'd with the shocks of doom
>
> To shape *and* use.

Almost every clause is followed by another of similar function.

·   ·   ·

[13] Walker Gibson, 'Behind the Veil: A Distinction between Poetic and Scientific Language in Tennyson, Lyell and Darwin', *Victorian Studies*, II (1958), 60–8.

Tennyson's syntax exemplifies a pattern of thought which I have termed analogical; it embodies a process of redefinition, thus according with his opposition to reason and scientific method and his reliance upon subjective experience. The syntax actually expresses his belief on these issues by making us perceive what kinds of connection he considers valuable. I would stress that Tennyson's analogical syntax, and its most obvious manifestation, parallelism, is not merely the negative response of a man frightened by science and logic. Donne's syntax has been admired as displaying 'a fidelity to thought and feeling':[14] the metaphysical poet is caught between traditional rhetoric and the new spirit of rational inquiry and it need not surprise us that his syntax is determinedly analytic (even, perhaps, to the point of exhibitionism). Tennyson's chosen pattern of thought is faithful to *his* way of thinking and feeling. He knew that science would not solve all problems and, moreover, that the attitude of mind which sometimes accompanied it could dangerously threaten the quality of human life—the poet declares with defiant (if somewhat heavy) irony,

> Let him, the wiser man who springs
>   Hereafter, up from childhood shape
>   His action like the greater ape,
> But I was *born* to other things.   (cxx)

The action of *In Memoriam* is concerned with the poet's mind and its relations with God and the universe. This emphasis on subjective and ultimately mystical experience means that considerations of time, space, condition and causality—all of which are played down in the analogical sentence structure—become relatively unimportant. In this respect *In Memoriam* seems a very modern poem. Things are experienced, they impinge on the poet, and he writes them down, tries to capture them as they affect him; it seems as if the sequence is given to us as it impressed the poet, uninfluenced by preconceived notions of a logical order in the universe. Section vii, for instance, begins with the poet apostrophizing the house; the dependent clauses add information about the associations which it has for him and the main verb, a sudden appeal to Hallam, is delayed till line 6:

---

[14] George Williamson, *The Donne Tradition* (Cambridge, Mass., 1930), p. 45.

> Dark house, by which once more I stand
> Here in the long unlovely street,
> Doors, where my heart was used to beat
> So quickly, waiting for a hand,
>
> A hand that can be clasp'd no more—
> Behold me, for I cannot sleep,
> And like a guilty thing I creep
> At earliest morning to the door.

Notice particularly how he moves from the reminiscence 'waiting for a hand' to the jarring present of 'A hand that can be clasp'd no more': here a whole chain of reasoned connecting links might be interpolated, but the poet just annexes his immediate feeling. 'Behold me' thrusts itself into the sentence in similar fashion as the poet's emotional need breaks through.

> He is not here; but far away
> The noise of life begins again,
> And ghastly thro' the drizzling rain
> On the bald street breaks the blank day.

There is no subordination here, just a series of main clauses strung together. This lack of formal links perhaps helps to cause the temporary ambiguity in the syntax of the first line, where we are liable initially to assume that 'but far away' refers to Hallam (despite the semi-colon). This temporary confusion is to the point, for the dismal daybreak is indeed related to Hallam's absence: it seems an external manifestation of the poet's despair. He records his sensations without comment, and the reader is forced to reconstruct the psychological mechanisms at work.

In other words, Tennyson's sentence structure is moving in the direction of *no* syntax.[15] Perhaps section vii is rather extreme—though the Prologue supplies similarly striking examples; like Hopkins, I speak rather for the tendency than the invariable result. Nevertheless, it is sometimes the case in *In Memoriam* that the more important connections are not made by the syntax at all; they lurk behind it for us to discover. The poet (apparently) relates the impressions in the order in which he feels them and we respond directly to the movement of his mind without the imposition of any intervening logical arrangement.

[15] Cf. H. M. McLuhan, 'Tennyson and Picturesque Poetry' in Killham, *Critical Essays*.

H

There is much to be said for this procedure. The way in which we divide up, categorize, restructure, and elucidate our sensations as we transpose them into language often has little to do with what we actually perceive. In his use of analogical syntax Tennyson seems to intuit that one might evade this misleading procedure. At the conclusion of section cxxii, where he is describing the trance condition, the clause structure simply juxtaposes the series of images:

> And all the breeze of Fancy blows,
> And every dew-drop paints a bow,
> The wizard lightnings deeply glow,
> And every thought breaks out a rose.

We almost read these lines *vertically*, as it were; the connections between the clauses are as self-effacing as possible and indicate nothing about the structure of the experience in question except, perhaps, that to attempt further analysis would be pointless. A sequence of images is as near as we can get. Confronting the reader with a series of immediate sensations in this way is faithful to the mode of thinking and feeling of a poet whose reliance is on subjective perceptions (it shows exactly the same mental processes as the building of a long poem out of a loose succession of sections). Tennyson is often working on the extreme edge of human experience; the basic structure of *In Memoriam* is emotional and analysis would be of little assistance in conveying its essence.

This tendency towards no syntax is naturally most marked in accounts of the mystical like the one just quoted—or section xcv:

> The living soul was flash'd on mine,
>
> *And* mine in this was wound, *and* whirl'd
> About empyreal heights of thought,
> *And* came on that which is, *and* caught
> The deep pulsations of the world,
>
> Æonian music measuring out
> The steps of Time—the shocks of Chance—
> The blows of Death.

I have italicized the 'and's to bring out the analogical structure, but in the last three lines even this unobtrusive form of linkage disappears and the phrases are just laid end to end. The totality of the vision can be conveyed in earthly language only by means of a series of images, and through his syntax Tennyson does his best to avoid imposing a meretricious order on the inexplicable and to preserve the simultaneity and equality of the impressions which compose it. The close of section cxxiv is comparable:

> And what I am beheld again
> What is, *and* no man understands;
> *And* out of darkness came the hands
> That reach thro' nature, moulding men.

The vision is described in two accounts here. The first is itself in dual form and states the absolute and enigmatic nature of the experience, echoing 'that which is' (xcv); the second takes up the images of darkness and the hand which have run all through the poem.

Tennyson's use of analogical (and parallel) syntax never quite cuts loose from conventional forms in its effort to recreate directly the quality of experience. Nevertheless, it is a bold innovation and certainly reflects his characteristic and explicitly preferred mode of thought. When we recall also the other effects of parallel syntax— both the local reinforcements of process, argument and emotional intensity and the all-pervading, meditative, Biblical tone—we must realize how much Tennyson is able to extract from the most neglected aspect of poetic structure.

VII

IMAGERY: PICTURES IN THE MIND

In literary studies the term 'imagery' is commonly used to cover two broad areas. On the one hand it is taken to refer to the sights and sounds of the physical world which the poet calls up in our imagination; on the other, it means more strictly figures of speech such as metaphor and simile.[1] When his family are leaving their old home, the poet says, 'Unloved, the sunflower, shining fair, [will] / Ray round with flames her disk of seed' (ci). The account of the sunflower forms a mental picture as we read, but only the flames, and perhaps 'Ray', are figurative; they represent the petals, whereas the rest of the description uses literal, botanical terminology. This chapter is about the pictures which Tennyson creates in our mind as we read *In Memoriam*. It would seem that to draw one's imagery from a wide range is often considered a virtue by modern critics, though it is not easy to see why this should be so—one would think that the relationship of an image to its context would be the most important factor. Tennyson's range is by no means remarkable; in fact, his imagery falls into four main groupings—religious, domestic, scientific and natural.

Obviously *In Memoriam* is much concerned with religious matters; the point was discussed in the previous chapter along with the Biblical tone which the syntax tends to create. The loss of Hallam shakes the poet's faith in a beneficent universe and throws into question the whole nature of life and death. The poet's crucial need is to believe that Hallam still exists and that they might eventually be reunited in some form—Lazarus came back from the dead, but he left no account of life beyond the grave (xxxi), and the poet can achieve no certainty. The geologists' demonstrations of the neutrality of nature arouse fears that it may be at strife with God (lv) and that man, 'Who trusted God was love indeed / And love Creation's final law', may be 'blown about the desert dust, / Or seal'd within the iron hills' (lvi). The problem is ultimately resolved only by the

---

[1] Cf. Rosemond Tuve, *Elizabethan and Metaphysical Imagery* (Paperback, Chicago, 1961), p. 3 and Ullmann, *Language and Style*, pp. 176–8.

visionary experience of section xcv, where the poet receives his own, individual revelation. In section cxxiv he recalls how

> what I am beheld again
> What is, and no man understands;
> And out of darkness came the hands
> That reach thro' nature, moulding men.

He regains his faith in an overall power for good in the universe, and in section cxxxi prays to the 'living will' to 'Flow thro'' our deeds and make them pure'.

The fundamental issue through all this is immortality and the survival of the love of the poet and his friend: in section cxx the poet declares, 'Like Paul with beasts, I fought with Death', and the allusion is to *1 Corinthians* XV where St. Paul asks, 'If after the manner of men I have fought with beasts at Ephesus, what advantageth it me, if the dead rise not?' And in *In Memoriam* 'the dead' means Hallam. Yet Tennyson seems to go beyond this position and make Hallam take on certain attributes of Christ. As early as section xiv the poet speaks of him as 'The man I held as half-divine', and in xxxvii he says, 'And dear to me as sacred wine / To dying lips is all he said'. The indications of this transference of divinity have been fully marshalled, though perhaps with some excess of ingenuity, by Ryals.[2] In section li Hallam or all the dead (it is unclear which) are said to

> watch, like God, the rolling hours
> With larger other eyes than ours
> To make allowance for us all;

in section lxxxvii the poet describes how before Hallam's death 'we saw / The God within him light his face'. The apotheosis is completed in section ciii, where Hallam appears 'thrice as large as man' to conduct the poet into eternity, and in cvii his birthday is honoured for the first time immediately after the family has declined to celebrate Christmas. The poet becomes like an apostle whose mission is to preach the example of Hallam—his faith, virtue, chastity even, his love of freedom and conservatism, his wisdom and his good manners. In section cxxix he is 'human, divine' and 'Dear heavenly friend': 'Behold, I dream a dream of good, / And mingle all the world with thee'.

[2] Clyde de L. Ryals, *Theme and Symbol in Tennyson's Poems to 1850* (Philadelphia, 1964), pp. 205–6, 223–4, 245–6, 255–9.

It is not altogether easy to know what to make of all this. For all the importance of Hallam in the poem, it seems almost incredible that Tennyson should have expected his readers to regard him as having affinities with Christ. The dissimilarity of the two figures makes their conjunction counter-productive, for we only become all the more aware that Hallam is *not* like Christ. We accept that he should be invested with qualities which we would do well to emulate, that he should be seen as surviving in some higher existence and that this should be a great comfort to the poet. But most of the more prominent aspects of the traditional Christian view of Jesus still do not fit. Hallam's birth, as far as we know, was unexceptional, his life was unfulfilled, and his death was arbitrary and unhelpful, and only in a loose sense followed by a resurrection. It seems that Tennyson wanted to stress three things: Hallam's elevation to some higher spiritual condition, his importance to the poet, and his exemplary qualities. But, taking these points in order, the divinity could surely be only such as all good souls might achieve; as an image for the poet's personal reassurance the identification seems presumptuous; and there are many more simple and credible ways of suggesting that someone is of a noble character.

There seems little gain in terms of the general scheme of *In Memoriam* if when Tennyson writes, 'Nor cared the serpent at thy side / To flicker with his double tongue' (cx) we think of Satan defeated by the Resurrection. And consider the extraordinary juxtaposition in cxi: Hallam had

> an eye,
> Where God and Nature met in light;
>
> And thus he bore without abuse
> The grand old name of gentleman.

In fact, Christian symbols hardly ever really come alive in this period of fragmentation and doubt; they appear to lack the weight of agreed implication they had, say, for Herbert. *In Memoriam* is itself an example of the tendency in modern times radically to rethink Christianity, and as soon as people start doing this its power as *the* great, universally accepted doctrine begins to fail. Sixteenth- and seventeenth-century controversies about whether God would prefer to be worshipped in Latin or English, or even about whether His Mercy extends to all or only a chosen few, do not affect the fundamentals of Christianity to the extent of questioning whether 'somehow good / Will be the final goal of ill' (liv).

When a creed loses its universality then its symbols must fragment as well. They become no longer dependable; they lack the sanction and resonance which grows with community belief. One has the same sense with Shelley in *Adonais* and 'Ode to the West Wind', and Hopkins has to work very hard as he wrestles with '(my God!) my God'. When Tennyson writes, 'They call'd me in the public squares / The fool that wears a crown of thorns' (lxix), the image seems flat and allegorical—it is a cipher which we could easily translate rather than a symbol enriched by its association with a complex and suggestive body of thought and feeling. If God and nature are at strife then what can be the significance of a crown of thorns? It can indicate little more than extreme suffering, for the total Christian message (which it would have called to mind in the seventeenth century) is in doubt. The first half of *In Memoriam* upturns the traditional Christian point of view with a classic instance of the modern fear that God may be dead, and it then becomes a little late to attempt to use the imagery as if its basis had never been questioned —and specially for the purpose of suggesting that Hallam is like Jesus.

Tennyson is on much surer ground when he alludes to Dante as a way of presenting visionary experience, for the medieval poet's cosmography seems far less tarnished with confusion, familiarity and casual usage. Bradley noticed similarities between Dante's Paradise and the stanza of section lxxxv which describes Hallam's reception in heaven:

> The great Intelligences fair
>   That range above our mortal state,
>   In circle round the blessed gate,
> Received and gave him welcome there.

The winding and whirling of the vision in section xcv, the references to the Empyrean, 'Æonian music' and 'boundless day' all recall such passages as

> straight the holy mill
> Began to wheel; nor yet had once revolved,
> Or e'er another, circling, compass'd it,
> Motion to motion, song to song, conjoining;

> Thus saw I move the glorious wheel; thus heard
> Voice answering voice, so musical and soft,
> It can be known but where day endless shines.[3]

Arthur Hallam was a translator of Dante, and Tennyson said that *In Memoriam* was a kind of Divine Comedy. The allusion to Dante's vision of heaven enables Tennyson to draw upon an established account of mystical insight in his efforts to make actual to the reader an experience which was essentially beyond human comprehension. Dante's quest for Beatrice was not unlike the poet's for Hallam, and his image of heaven adds both individuality and authority to the mysticism of *In Memoriam*.

When we turn to Tennyson's images of domestic situations we find ourselves very firmly grounded in the terrestial sphere. They present in microcosm the dual personal and general character of *In Memoriam*. The introduction of the poet's family and friends makes it more intimate and stresses the personal reality of the speaker so that we are more inclined to accept his account of his experience; the sections describing hypothetical family circumstances analogous to the poet's make it, as Valerie Pitt points out,[4] more general and impersonal, more the voice of the race, by suggesting that his plight is shared by many other people. We see the similarities between the poet and the bereaved parent, the widow or widower, the lower-class girl in love with a more respectable man, or the faithful wife of the preoccupied intellectual. This deliberate inclusion of the sorrow of other unfortunate people adds vitally to our sense that the poem aspires to the neo-classical qualities of universal intelligibility, acceptability and familiarity. The anniversary of Hallam's death wakens,

> To myriads in the genial earth,
> Memories of bridal, or of birth,
> And unto myriads more, of death.

> O wheresoever those may be,
> Betwixt the slumber of the poles,
> To-day they count as kindred souls;
> They know me not, but mourn with me.   (xcix)

And they did mourn with the poet, but their presence in *In*

---

[3] Paradise, beginning of Canto XII and end of Canto X, *The Divine Comedy*, trans. Henry Francis Cary (first pub. 1814), ed. Edmund Gardner (London, 1908), pp. 344, 339.
[4] *Tennyson Laureate* (London, 1962), p. 117.

Memoriam is a principal stumbling block for the modern reader. Houghton explains the Victorian cult of the home primarily in terms of the need for a shelter from the anxieties of modern life and a haven for the moral and spiritual values which were threatened by the commercial competition of working hours and the speculations of critical thinkers. At home one was safe.[5] One suspects that a reason why we feel so uneasy at (for instance) the vignette of the bride who will be able to return to her parents with her 'babe' (xl) is that this is the aspect of the Victorian scene which remains closest to our own attitude, from which we are least distanced. We may overlook Tennyson's folly on the Crimean War, for he had no notion of modern battle conditions as we experience them on our television screens, but his regard for domestic bliss, though surely not culpable, seems sentimental and irritating. Yet I have before me an engraving of 1870 which shows 'A morning drive in a goat cart for Princess Mary and her brother Adolphus, in the grounds of White Lodge, Richmond. Francis, the new baby born this year to the Duke and Duchess of Teck, is in his mother's arms'[6]—all amusingly reminiscent of press treatment of the current British Royal Family.

The domestic analogies—parables, we might call them—function also (as Miss Pitt again remarks) as a measure for the poet's grief. I have talked of Tennyson's need to define an emotional situation, to seize it in words, and comparison with a related figure can afford an extra dimension:

> Tears of the widower, when he sees
>   A late-lost form that sleep reveals,
>   And moves his doubtful arms, and feels
> Her place is empty, fall like these.   (xiii)

Here we have all the desire for Hallam's bodily presence and the notion of a specific place left empty, and at the same time the accepted context of marriage. We may be surprised at the physical intensity which these images of the family imply and the shift in gender which one of the friends undergoes, and uneasy at the poet's naïvety. Tennyson and his public were evidently completely unconscious of the sexual inferences which might be drawn from such imagery—or, indeed, from the whole poem. It would seem that Tennyson and Hallam conducted their friendship in the same

[5] *The Victorian Frame of Mind*, pp. 341–8.
[6] Alan Bott, *Our Fathers* (London, 1931), p. 14.

spirit, whatever its psychological basis may have been. Such it was to live in a pre-Freudian age!

Sometimes the redefining function of domestic imagery is obvious, for a lyric utterance by the poet is followed directly by a parallel situation. The experience at the 'Dark house' in section vii is paired with the 'happy lover' who 'learns her gone and far from home' (viii), and the comparison between the poet's grief and the tidal movement of the Wye in xix is succeeded by a distinction between the way in which bereavement is expressed by servants and children 'in a house / Where lies the master newly dead' (xx). An emotion is stated and then redefined (the same process that I described in the previous chapter) in an effort to grasp its essential qualities. The domestic analogies allow the poet and us a further perspective on his condition: we walk round it, inspecting it from various points of view so that we might comprehend it the better. Moreover, the general similarity between the several sections employing this imagery makes us compare them so that we are brought to realize the change in the poet's attitude. In sections vi, viii, xiii and xx he is simply like people who have lost loved ones; in lx, lxii and lxiv the separation between the two people need not remain complete—in fact the main theme is the circumstances in which they might be reunited; and section xcvii gives the closest relationship, with Hallam as the learned but distant husband and the poet as his wife who 'dwells on him with faithful eyes, / "I cannot understand: I love"'.

As I have suggested, the other form taken by domestic imagery, the references to the poet's family and friends, makes *In Memoriam* more personal, more like the poet's actual experience. The knowledge that Hallam is mourned by all the family makes him more real to us and helps prevent the poet's grief from appearing to exist in a vacuum. The whole family is conscious of the change from previous Christmases in section xxx, and in cv they all seem to agree that 'change of place, like growth of time, / Has broke the bond of dying use'. They are present at the opening of section xcv and give it a naturalistic starting point—though it is significant that the mystical climax of the poem could only take place 'when those others, one by one, / Withdrew themselves from me and night'. The whole structure of *In Memoriam* rests upon the authenticity of the poet's experience, and the presence of the family encourages us to accept him as a real person to whom such events could actually happen.

The sections in which the poet addresses his friends are addition-
ally important because they show his attitude to the outside world.
In section vi 'One writes, that "Other friends remain" ', but this is
no consolation to the poet, who declares: 'unto me no second
friend'. But by section lxxxv he feels able to offer his friendship
again; this new move out into society is stated more forcibly towards the end of the poem—'I will not shut me from my kind' (cviii).

Both strands of domestic imagery are important when we come
to the Epilogue. Critics have wondered whether it provides a
satisfactory conclusion to the poem, whether the marriage of his
sister is really any answer to the poet's problems. We must reply
that logically it is not, but poems work according to their own
principles. *In Memoriam* began with the loss of Hallam from the
family: that group is now to gain from the birth of a child who can
be seen in potential as a further step towards the 'higher race'. We
have had repeated comparisons of the poet to someone involved in a
marriage and pictures of him as one of a family group, and we can
therefore regard the marriage at the end as a symbolic representation
of his position. The Epilogue figures the poet's accordance with the
process of birth, marriage and death, and the expected birth of the
child corresponds to his own delivery into a fresher life: 'For I
myself . . . have grown / To something greater than before'. The
opening line indicates that the groom is the man who was addressed
in section lxxxv; the poet now finds joy in celebrating the marriage
of his new friend. Although Hallam is his mainstay and his ultimate
hope, he also needs companionship amongst the living, and the
Epilogue completes his movement outwards into normal social life.
Now that the basic loss of Hallam has been remedied ('I shall not
lose thee tho' I die') all else falls into place. The marriage in the
Epilogue demonstrates both the poet's acquiescence in everyday
life and his harmony with the universal pattern of birth, marriage and
death.

If domestic imagery has tended to repel twentieth-century commentators, Tennyson's interest in science has proved a major source
of scholarly excitement. It also bears upon the appropriateness of the
Epilogue, as John Killham has shown: a review, which Tennyson
probably read, of Robert Chambers' *Vestiges of the Natural History
of Creation* (1844)

> specially emphasized that the operation of the law of development
> depended entirely upon the 'generative system'. It is in consequence

of this, I suggest, that a marriage concludes *In Memoriam*; in marriage we come closest to participating in the cosmic purpose, though we must continuously seek to 'type' the qualities we desire to make permanent in man.[7]

The death of his friend left the poet ready to accept the gloomiest interpretation of the evidence of the geologists, which seriously threatened his faith in the status and independent volition of mankind (sections xxxv and liv-lvi). The time scheme of Genesis could not be true and man, so far from being the climactic creative act of a benevolent God, became merely a small item in a vast and apparently random process. He seemed at the mercy of natural laws which condemned each species to fight for its existence and allowed some to disappear; Lyell (and later, Darwin) displaced man from the centre of the earth, even as Copernicus and Galileo had made it difficult to regard him as the centre of the universe. But after the personal vision of section xcv the poet returns to general issues: he regains confidence in the onward development of mankind and decides that if the species are not established once and for all then progress is possible and man might be 'The herald of a higher race' (cxviii). The 'ordinary process of generation', as Chambers called it, must be the vital means to this advance, and therefore the poet celebrates it in the Epilogue; he is 'No longer caring to embalm / In dying songs a dead regret' because, as the marriage implies, he accepts as potentially advantageous the whole scheme of the universe— including the death of Hallam.

It would seem that things had changed since Wordsworth speculated in the Preface to *Lyrical Ballads* on whether 'the time should ever come when what is now called science, thus familiarized to men, shall be ready to put on, as it were, a form of flesh and blood'. But science had not become much more familiar, or 'ready to put on' anything: it forced itself upon Tennyson. He could not, like Wordsworth, stand back and wonder whether the scientists were yet behaving in a manner acceptable to poetry. As a thinking man he was obliged to realize that the scientist's view of the world affected him deeply, and this is an illuminating index of the extent to which the intellectual climate had beeome less secure during the intervening forty years.

Nevertheless, it is possible to overestimate the importance of

---

[7] John Killham, *Tennyson and The Princess* (London, 1958), p. 263; the whole of chapter XI is very helpful.

scientific imagery in *In Memoriam*. Tennyson is not a complete innovator in this respect—one may instance not only Shelley, but Thomson as well, for his *Autumn* also contains geological theories. He considers the possibility, argued by St. Jerome, that the sea may be sucked up through the earth to emerge as springs, but rejects it:

> Besides, the hard agglomerating salts,
> The spoil of ages, would impervious choke
> Their secret channels, or by slow degrees,
> High as the hills, protrude the swelling vales. (l. 766)

He prefers the notion of water being drawn up into the atmosphere by the sun and falling as rain, and this, moreover, exemplifies 'The full-adjusted harmony of things' (we notice at once the readiness with which Thomson accepts the theory which affirms an order in life—it displays an equanimity impossible to Tennyson). But observe also the bluntness of Thomson's scientific imagery, which is unequalled in *In Memoriam*. In the previous chapter I discussed some ways in which the poet defies the methods of rationalism and deals with scientific matters in his own forms of language, and this is his consistent practice. Sun-spots are 'wandering isles of night' (xxiv), the history of the earth is 'The giant labouring in his youth' (cxviii) and erosion is

> The moanings of the homeless sea,
> The sound of streams that swift or slow
> Draw down Æonian hills, and sow
> The dust of continents to be. (xxxv)

It is hardly true to claim, as one critic does, that Tennyson furnishes a whole new framework of terminology. Fossils are introduced by having Nature cry 'From scarped cliff and quarried stone' and the contending species are 'red in tooth and claw / With ravine' (lvi); the possibility that man and the lower animals might be more closely connected than one would wish appears as an admonition in very traditional imagery:

> Arise and fly
> The reeling Faun, the sensual feast;
> Move upward, working out the beast,
> And let the ape and tiger die. (cxviii)

Whilst Tennyson's scientific imagery is not really extreme—

neither new nor particularly bold in its terminology—one of the
interesting features of the unity of *In Memoriam* is his use of geological language to refer to social upheavals. In section xxi the
travellers who criticize the poet's singing cite not only science
reaching forth her arms, but also the fact that 'more and more the
people throng / The chairs and thrones of civil power'. It seems that
the two occurrences were about equally alarming to Tennyson, and
it is appropriate that towards the end of the poem they should be
brought together through his imagery. In section cxiii it is stated
that Hallam would have been

> A pillar steadfast in the storm,
>
> Should licensed boldness gather force,
>   Becoming, when the time has birth,
>   A lever to uplift the earth
> And roll it in another course.

The geological development of the earth is aligned with the moral,
social and political progress of humanity (as it seemed to Tennyson's
conservatism). The poet's fears of physical and social forces coalesce,
but Hallam is his reassurance on all fronts. In section cxxvii he links
'The red fool-fury of the Seine' to a catastrophe in which 'The
brute earth lightens to the sky, / And the great Æon sinks in blood',
but Hallam guarantees that all will be well. The use of such imagery
for social forces is by no means new, but in a poem where the
changing face of the earth has been an important theme the connection is unusually powerful, for it suggests that 'the whole creation moves' towards the 'one far-off divine event' (Epilogue).
Scientific imagery, as well as expounding the poet's anxieties about
the nature of the universe, impresses upon us the unity of Tennyson's thought.

   Natural imagery is, of course, closely interwoven with the poet's
attitudes to geology. I suppose most of us, when we think of nature
in poetry, think of Wordworth, but it is crucial to realize how different Tennyson's approach is—indeed, there is something to be
said for scrapping the term altogether in connection with Tennyson
and speaking instead of 'landscape' or 'the countryside'. Wordsworth
is concerned to examine the influence of nature on his mind and to
consider his position when he discovers that he no longer receives
the same inspiration from it. The question 'Are God and Nature

then at strife' (lv) is as far removed from his outlook as could be.
For Wordsworth nature is essentially stable—in the 1805 *Prelude*
he speaks of 'enduring things' (I, 436), of 'objects that endure'
(XII, 36); 'I had forms distinct / To steady me ... I still / At all
times had a real solid world / Of images about me' (VIII, 598f.).
And when he also recognizes the changing face of nature the point
is very different from Tennyson's 'I care for nothing, all shall go'
(lvi):

> By influence habitual to the mind
> The mountain's outline and its steady form
> Gives a pure grandeur, and its presence shapes
> The measure and the prospect of the soul
> To majesty; such virtue have the forms
> Perennial of the ancient hills; nor less
> The changeful language of their countenances
> Gives movement to the thoughts, and multitude,
> With order and relation.   (VII, 721f.)

Wordsworth sees the varying surface appearances of the hills and
finds that they add a pleasant diversity to his thought; Tennyson
hears the streams wearing down the mountains, sees cyclic storms
and a thousand types vanishing, and declares,

> The hills are shadows, and they flow
>   From form to form, and nothing stands;
>   They melt like mist, the solid lands,
> Like clouds they shape themselves and go.   (cxxiii)

His question is not of how one comes into the fullest relationship
with nature—it doesn't stay still long enough for that—but of the
very conditions of existence in the natural world.

For all this distrust of nature, it is nevertheless indispensable to
Tennyson as a poetical instrument. The break-down of the Enlightenment system was followed by the Romantic reliance upon
individual resources, and the poet was left in need of a value-bearing
language—the inadequacy of Tennyson's religious imagery emphasizes the point. The world of nature provided the obvious and
accepted solution to this demand for imagery with dependable
connotations. The immediate sight of 'Laburnums, dropping-wells of
fire' is perhaps little affected by a knowledge of the operation of
geological forces, and Tennyson could certainly rely on his readers'

settled assumptions about the value of beautiful natural objects. They are the major stable reference system in the poem, the main agency by which our excitement, pleasure, sorrow or pain are aroused.

Tennyson's exploitation of stock responses is by no means straightforward, however, for the poet's attitude to nature varies as he is initially alienated from and eventually reintegrated into the conditions of earthly existence. At the first spring the poet declares, 'No joy the blowing season gives, / The herald melodies of spring' (xxxviii); the second he looks forward to, asking 'Can trouble live with April days, / Or sadness in the summer moons?' (lxxxiii); and in the third he finds that

> the songs, the stirring air,
> The life re-orient out of dust,
> Cry thro' the sense to hearten trust
> In that which made the world so fair.   (cxvi)

This pattern of response is held completely consistently so that the uses made of natural imagery provide a running index to the poet's developing attitude. Our expectation that nature will appear as beneficent is not automatically satisfied; at first the poet is out of sympathy with the good things of nature, but gradually his outlook changes. I cannot at all understand why Ryals should say that 'Finding the rest of life harsh and repugnant, Tennyson turned, as did Wordsworth in disillusionment with the affairs of men, to nature, which was to serve in the initial stages of his grief as a consolation'.[8] If the poet turns to nature, it is to 'A hollow form with empty hands' (iii), to the yew tree (ii) which does not change like the rest of the natural world. It is the yew's 'thousand years of gloom' that appeal to him, for he sets his face against change and the movement of the seasons in his determination to preserve love. Like Wordsworth, he wants stability, but he has to go to the tree usually connected with death to find it, and the consolatory power of nature is denied. In section vii the 'blank day' fits the poet's mood, but all the feelings which we normally associate with dawn are violated. Break of day is established in our culture as a time for happiness, new beginnings, freshness, light and beauty, but Tennyson denies all these connotations. The poet's state of mind corresponds only to the deathly things in nature. Thus in section xv he could identify with the storm which is threatening the birds, trees and cattle, but in section xi

---

[8] *Theme and Symbol*, p. 198.

he is out of harmony with the peaceful morning which would 'suit
a calmer grief'.

Towards the beginning of *In Memoriam* the poet firmly denies
the pleasant connotations of nature; the happy scenes are couched
in the pastoral idiom and set in earlier times (as I pointed out in
Chapter IV). They are in complete contrast with the present. Now
the poet, deprived of personal support and alarmed by the geologists,
is conscious of 'The moanings of the homeless sea' which erodes the
land, and fears that love could only have 'bruised the herb and
crush'd the grape, / And bask'd and batten'd in the woods' (xxxv).
Before Hallam's death they walked

> Thro' lands where not a leaf was dumb;
> But all the lavish hills would hum
> The murmur of a happy Pan.   (xxiii)

Now the hills are drawn down by the streams and the woods are the
scene of orgies. Nature is merely man's grave, as he is 'blown about
the desert dust, / Or seal'd within the iron hills' (lvi). No wonder
the poet is alienated from the natural cycle and does not cheer up
when the first spring comes.

A lot of the power of the poem over its first readers must have
come from this frustration of conventional expectations. Tennyson
in 1850 was well in advance of most in his awareness of the significance of changing views of the earth's structure and in his readiness to consider a reversal of the Wordsworthian or eighteenth-
century attitude towards nature. K. W. Grandsen acutely points
out how in 'The Two Voices' one feels that Tennyson 'had genuinely
hoped for a more positive enlightenment [from nature] such as
Wordsworth had experienced, and is genuinely surprised at his
failure to get it'.[9] We may also recall how Wordsworth took several
stanzas to explain in 'Resolution and Independence' how it was that
he had sad thoughts despite the 'pleasant season'. When Tennyson's
poet revisits the yew tree in spring he finds that 'to thee too comes
the golden hour / When flower is feeling after flower', but his
Sorrow unhesitatingly denies that attractive image with the cynical
comment, 'Thy gloom is kindled at the tips, / And passes into gloom
again' (xxxix). There may be a period of happiness, but it can be
only a momentary glimmer in the dark night of our lives. Our
assumption about the goodness of nature is used to press home the

[9] *Tennyson: In Memoriam*, p. 26.

I

poet's despondency. His trust in nature has been betrayed (initially by Hallam's death and then, encouraged by that first shock, by anxieties over man's position in the world) and in the same way the reader is deceived in his expectation that natural objects with pleasant connotations will appear in contexts where his approval is required.

By the end of *In Memoriam* the poet has reached a position where he can refer to natural imagery with acceptance and pleasure, but this victory has been hard won and the recurrence of the same images reminds us of the trials and tribulations on the way. Towards the close of the poem he consistently rejoices in the processes of nature—with section vii we compare cxix ('I smell the meadow in the street')—and he finds it breathing or pulsing with life, unlike the dead thing he saw at the beginning:

> Thy voice is on the rolling air;
> I hear thee when the waters run;
> Thou standest in the rising sun,
> And in the setting thou art fair. (cxxx)

Hallam is absorbed into the oneness of the whole creation, and the poet's feeling of his continuing presence is his assurance of its ultimate goodness. Since the vision of section xcv he has regarded the universe as one great, harmonious system, for there he caught

> The deep pulsations of the world,
>
> Æonian music measuring out
> The steps of Time—the shocks of Chance—
> The blows of Death.

The life in nature is not its own, as it was for Wordsworth: it comes from the poet's awareness that Hallam and a higher spiritual reality can be glimpsed through it. And so *In Memoriam* ends with the marriage of the Epilogue, with the poet taking every opportunity to stress his contentment with the natural order. The young are placed in relation with the old, the dead with the living, and the unborn with those of future ages; and natural imagery is woven in with it all. The poet is now able to look forward to a people who will understand 'Nature like an open book'.

The Epilogue is a final expression of the poet's harmony with the conditions of men on earth, a harmony which was destroyed at the

beginning of the poem, but which he has regained after a long alienation. It takes two years—and the vision of section xcv—before he
can again acquiesce in the natural cycle. His grief does not simply
pass away with the spring in the traditional pastoral manner, for it is
too real and too bound up with anxieties about nature itself. The
three-year time scheme is in vivid juxtaposition with the poet's
changing response; the annual pattern of the seasons is at first
violated, but eventually accepted. Natural imagery is an index of
the poet's developing outlook, for we appreciate his position
by seeing him in relation to images which have agreed value
connotations.

In general, then, natural imagery is fully integrated into the
overall structure of *In Memoriam*. It also provides a credible background for the poet, but it is almost never true to say, as some critics
have, that it is merely for pictorial decoration. Very often scenic
description serves to arouse in the reader an emotional state equivalent to the poet's. We feel with his distress at the first anniversary of
Hallam's death because of our involvement with the natural imagery:

> Risest thou thus, dim dawn, again,
>   And howlest, issuing out of night,
>   With blasts that blow the poplar white,
> And lash with storm the streaming pane? (lxxii)

The second anniversary, on the other hand, is 'So loud with voices of
the birds, / So thick with lowings of the herds' (xcix). The account of
the landscape awakens in us a mood appropriate to the poet's
feelings, so that we intuit his emotional condition through concrete
images rather than by means of an abstract analysis. This is presumably why when Tennyson had first written 'The moon is out'
in section civ (Trinity manuscript) he changed it to 'The moon is
hid'—the obscuring of the light better suggests the poet's separation
from familiar comforts as he prepares to spend Christmas in a 'new
unhallow'd' environment. The method is obviously related to (and
supported by) the way in which the poet's outlook is indexed by
his attitude to nature, but it works at a more detailed and specific
level and through a more indirect—and sometimes more intense—
appeal to the reader's stock responses.
The poet dreams of the time when Hallam was alive:

> I walk as ere I walk'd forlorn,
>   When all our path was fresh with dew,
>   And all the bugle breezes blew
> Reveillée to the breaking morn.   (lxviii)

The description communicates the poet's happiness, the freshness
and exultation of that earlier time. Now he is 'forlorn', but his
previous condition is indicated solely by the tone in which the path
and morning are evoked. (We might notice also that, since the path
image has often been used for life, these lines imply not only one
specific occasion, but also the habitual mood of their time together.)
I take it that this use of natural description to convey the poet's
feelings is what Eliot meant in his familiar remark about an 'objective correlative'. The sensory experience communicated by the
description of external objects evokes in the reader an emotion
appropriate to the poet's feelings.[10] Hallam himself seems to be
making the same point in his review of Tennyson's 1830 volume.
One of the five things he specially admired was the 'vivid, picturesque delineation of objects, and the peculiar skill with which he
holds all of them *fused*, to borrow a metaphor from science, in a
medium of strong emotion'[11] ('Mariana' is the outstanding example
from 1830). The description arouses in us a state of mind correspondent to the mood of the speaker.

Sometimes Tennyson makes the connection between landscape
and feeling overt, as, for instance, in the two spring sections lxxxiii
and cxv. The first concludes:

> O thou, new-year, delaying long,
>   Delayest the sorrow in my blood,
>   That longs to burst a frozen bud
> And flood a fresher throat with song;

and at the end of the second the poet says:

>   and in my breast
> Spring wakens too; and my regret
> Becomes an April violet,
> And buds and blossoms like the rest.

---

[10] *Selected Prose*, p. 102.
[11] *The Writings of Arthur Hallam*, ed. T. H. Vail Motter (New York, 1943), p. 191;
cf. McLuhan, 'Tennyson and Picturesque Poetry', in Killham, *Critical Essays*.

In each case the equivalence of the spring and the poet's emotions
is made overt by a metaphor linking the two. But the correspondence does not only apply in these explicit lines—it is present throughout the concrete description of the season in the preceding stanzas:

> Where now the seamew pipes, or dives
> In yonder greening gleam, and fly
> The happy birds, that change their sky
> To build and brood; that live their lives
>
> From land to land.   (cxv)

We are well aware that this is more than background landscape.
I discussed the syntax of this section in Chapter V, remarking how
the emphasis is thrown onto the verbs and the poet's new delight
in movement and change. The tone of the verse is quite un-elegiac,
for the syntax never fits the line, and even runs over the end of the
stanza, as if the poet's excitement caused him to overflow the usual
bounds. The palpable delight in the sea birds is in contrast with the
suspicion of the ocean when it was bearing Hallam's body, for then
the poet thought of himself as a dove venturing out over an alien
element and moaning 'Is this the end?' (xii). His joy in the birds that
'change their sky / To build and brood' is even more significant,
for it was change which the poet feared so much at the beginning
of the poem, and movement in place which worried him as recently
as sections ci and cii. 'Brood' suggests his confidence in the whole
generative process of nature and contrasts with the image of the
widower in the early sections and looks forward to the marriage
in the Epilogue. The poet has overcome his doubts on all these
scores, and his mood could not be better given than by this natural
imagery.

The essential feature of this technique is the excessive emphasis
which is placed on the description—excessive, that is, for mere
description. We feel that the emotional pressure behind the writing
is so high that it must refer to something beyond itself. We look
naturally to the person of the speaker for a cause, and so the weight
of feeling is transferred to him. In section vii the poet goes to
Hallam's door, remembers how they used to meet, finds himself
alone and makes no direct comment. Instead he describes the
weather and the time of day:

> He is not here; but far away
> The noise of life begins again,
> And ghastly thro' the drizzling rain
> On the bald street breaks the blank day.

We receive a strong impression of the poet's despair. 'The noise of life' contrasts with Hallam's deadness and suggests that human existence is just a confused din; the dawn is not beautiful (as we expect dawns to be) but ghastly; the weather is horrible—at first Tennyson wrote 'dripping' (Harvard manuscript) but drizzle is far more depressing, partly because of its sound; and 'bald' and 'blank' are both dual-purpose adjectives which can apply as well to a despondent state of mind as to scenery. When I discussed this section in the previous chapter I pointed to the lack of explicit connections between clauses and the way in which we are thereby encouraged to reconstruct from his immediate sensations the poet's state of mind. In this last stanza the natural imagery is not overtly associated with his mood, but, because of its position in the section and the weight of emotional implication it seems to carry, we are forced to turn to the poet's mind for an explanation. The concrete description communicates the intensity of his feelings much more powerfully than any amount of straightforward analysis.

Fundamentally, all Tennyson is doing when he uses landscape to suggest emotion is playing upon a simple human tendency. People do commonly invest their surroundings (and their cats and dogs) with their own feelings—and, conversely, allow their environment to affect their mood. Tennyson seems to be completely aware of what he is doing. In section lxxii the poet says to the day, thou

> might'st have heaved a windless flame
> Up the deep East, or, whispering, play'd
> A chequer-work of beam and shade
> Along the hills, *yet look'd the same.*

Even had the weather been different, it would have seemed horrible to the poet—he is perfectly conscious of the attribution of emotion to landscape he is making, and conscious that the mind tends to find its own reflection in this way. He also realizes that nature exerts a reciprocal influence on our feelings:

> Yet oft *when sundown skirts the moor*
> An inner trouble I behold,
> A spectral doubt that makes me cold,
> That I shall be thy mate no more.   (xli)

The poet is fully aware that he is specially liable to these uneasy sensations under certain natural conditions, for as we see a reflection of our emotions in nature, so nature to some extent determines what those emotions are. 'Cold' in the third line is particularly appropriate, for as well as indicating the poet's shiver of fear it suggests the sudden chill which can come in the evening of a warm day.

The human tendency to effect an interchange—overt or implied—between emotions and environment is used with subtlety and discrimination in *In Memoriam*. Sometimes it involves the pathetic fallacy—for example, 'happy birds' in section cxv. Ruskin termed the attribution of human emotions to animals and things fallacious, but we are not, of course, supposed to believe in it literally—there is no reason why the figure should be inherently foolish. Tennyson uses the pathetic fallacy far less than his predecessors, as Josephine Miles has pointed out: in Gray, Collins, Keats and Shelley we find it every 40 or 50 lines, in Tennyson about every 90 lines.[12] Moreover, his practice is rarely conventional. The sea in section xi (which I considered in Chapter I) forms parts of a powerful structure of inter-relationships between the poet, the morning and his dead friend:

> Calm on the seas, and silver sleep,
>   And waves that sway themselves in rest,
>   And dead calm in that noble breast
> Which heaves but with the heaving deep.

The sea is given attributes which should be Hallam's were he alive, and the imagery doubles back on itself because 'sleep' and 'rest' are euphemisms for death. The repeated personification of the ship in the early sections, to take another example, expresses the poet's obsessional transference of his grief, and is not a random peculiarity but an indication of his psychological problem. There are many other instances—in section xcv the 'filmy shapes / That *haunt* the dusk' supply a hint of the vision which is about to occur, the trees '*Laid* their dark *arms* about the field' in a way which recalls the poet's desire for Hallam's touch, and the dusk is 'doubtful' because the light is uncertain and because it weakens his trust in the vision.

The yew tree, traditionally a simple emblem in graveyard laments, is in section ii a good example of the sublety and originality of Tennyson's involvement of natural objects with his own emotions.

---

[12] Josephine Miles, *The Vocabulary of Poetry* (Berkeley and Los Angeles, [1942]-46). For Tennyson's views, see *Memoir*, II, 73.

> Old Yew, which graspest at the stones
> That name the under-lying dead,
> Thy fibres net the dreamless head,
> Thy roots are wrapt about the bones.

In this first stanza the poet has done nothing but apostrophize the yew, but we know that it is its contact with the dead that attracts him. The last two lines quoted are strongly physical, and make us think of his desire at the beginning of the poem to regain the bodily presence of his friend. The tree is almost embracing the dead, as the poet would wish to do.

> The seasons bring the flower again,
> And bring the firstling to the flock;
> And in the dusk of thee, the clock
> Beats out the little lives of men.

Tennyson's technique of placing parallel clauses in succession and forcing us to make the connecting links operates to the full here. The implication is that man is set apart from the natural cycle described in the first two lines: he dies once and for all and is not renewed the following spring. Moreover, it seems as if the whole of man's life is lived out in the dusk of the yew: the fact of death is the ultimate controlling power in our entire existence. The third stanza discovers a further relevance in the tree, for it is to be distinguished from the rest of nature:

> O not for thee the glow, the bloom,
> Who changest not in any gale,
> Nor branding summer suns avail
> To touch thy thousand years of gloom.

The yew does not experience the glow and bloom of love, but remains in gloom despite the passing of time. The poet resolved in the previous section that love must clasp grief lest both be drowned, and he is able to identify with the tree because it does not change like the rest of nature but stays always fixed upon the dead. He too will resist the healing and changing power of time, for love must be preserved.

> And gazing on thee, sullen tree,
> Sick for thy stubborn hardihood,
> I seem to fail from out my blood
> And grow incorporate into thee.

The poet values the yew's constant devotion to the dead—and implies that he might himself prefer to die. Growing incorporate into the tree means abnegating his own personality in order to become one with an object, and 'incorporate', as well as 'united with', suggests 'incorporeal', that is, his soul leaving his body. By growing into the yew the poet would acquire the tree's contact with the dead; he would achieve the most complete involvement with Hallam by dying himself.

The tree grasps, nets and wraps, is gloomy, sullen and stubborn, but these manifestations give us an oblique and complex insight into the poet's emotions, not an easy and meretricious short cut. We should also remember that the whole procedure of relating feelings to nature (including the pathetic fallacy) stretches at least as far back in literary history as the earliest pastoral poetry—the Theocritan 'Lament for Bion' begins,

> Cry me waly upon him, you glades of the woods, and waly, sweet Dorian water; you rivers weep, I pray you, for the lovely and delightful Bion. Lament you now, good orchards; gentle groves, make you your breathing clusters, ye flowers, dishevelled for grief.[13]

Tennyson's employment of his ancient tradition of transferring emotion to landscape is in keeping with his use of the pastoral convention. The important thing is that it should be treated with freshness and with such precision of context that our responses are channelled into just those meanings which the author requires.

Tennyson's skill in this respect can be shown from section xci, where the poet asks to see a vision of Hallam. The four stanzas have a clear scheme to them:

st.1: When (description of spring)   st.2: Come, as you used to be
st.3: When (description of summer)   st.4: Come, as you are now.

The poet prefers the second kind of vision, we feel, and this becomes plain in the last stanza:

> Come: not in watches of the night,
>   But where the sunbeam broodeth warm,
>   Come, beauteous in thine after form,
> And like a finer light in light.

This second kind of vision of Hallam in his present heavenly form—a revelation of eternity, in fact—will be even beyond the power of

[13] *The Greek Bucolic Poets*, trans. J. M. Edmunds, Loeb Edn. (London, 1912).

light. The spirit of stanza two is unsatisfactory in comparison. It is associated with night, whereas day has more active and hopeful connotations; and it will not show Hallam at his best, for it will remind the poet of what Wilfred Owen called 'the undone years':

> Come, wear the form by which I know
> Thy spirit in time among thy peers;
> The hope of unaccomplish'd years
> Be large and lucid round thy brow.

The poet has already suggested (e.g. lxii) that what was left unfinished in Hallam's life is now more gloriously completed in eternity, and only the second kind of vision (stanza four) would represent this greater maturity.

The two stanzas of natural description which accompany the visions invest the whole idea of Hallam's return with a pleasant aura associated with the beauties of nature, but they also correspond closely to the kind of manifestation they each precede. Stanza one describes spring as opposed to the summer of stanza three, and is therefore generally appropriate to the lower degree of fulfilment, but the distinction is made precise by the detail of the language. Throughout the imagery of stanza one is a certain sparseness, a lack of abundance:

> When rosy plumelets tuft the larch,
> And rarely pipes the mounted thrush;
> Or underneath the barren bush
> Flits by the sea-blue bird of March.

This sense of scantness is most apparent in the 'barren' bush (it is presumably as yet leafless), but it is also there in the 'plumelets', which seem particularly diminutive and are only in 'tufts' anyway. Things have not yet come to fruition. The fact that the thrush 'rarely pipes' suggests both infrequency and thinness—the woods are not filled with a chorus of sound but very occasionally the thrush makes a meagre, almost nervous noise. And something of the same lack of fertility is felt in the last line too as the bird 'flits by': we have only a brief glimpse and it is gone.

All this conveys the poet's attitude to the possibility of Hallam appearing in his old form, and it contrasts with the second kind of vision, which is introduced by a description of summer:

When summer's hourly-mellowing change
    May breathe, with many roses sweet,
    Upon the thousand waves of wheat,
That ripple round the lonely grange.

This stanza is overflowing with abundance. As against the plumelets
and the rare piping of the thrush we have 'many roses sweet' and
'the thousand waves of wheat', figuring the increased maturity
which Hallam has achieved in eternity. The summer is also seen as a
state of 'hourly-mellowing' change, and this corresponds beatifully
to the continuing fulfilment of Hallam's potentialities in his present
existence. We see that the poet is no longer alarmed at his friend's
superior development, as he was in section xli ('No more partaker
of thy change'), for he attaches to it the pleasant sensations we
associate with the image of harvest. Moreover, the maturity and
fertility connected to a vision of Hallam in his 'after form' does not
only represent the perfection which Hallam is achieving; it also
suggests the likely effect on the poet of such a revelation. It will
create confidence in a deeper spiritual principle underlying everything, not just the personal consolation of a 'normal ghost'. This is
exactly what happens in section xcv, where the poet does not
simply experience the return of Hallam as he knew him on earth,
but 'The deep pulsations of the world'.

The natural imagery corresponds in minute detail to the two kinds
of vision. There is no explicit invitation to see the landscapes as
indicative of the quality of the apparitions, just the suggestion
that one might occur at one time and one at another; the shape of
the section and the intensity of the writing make us construct the
link for ourselves. Tennyson carefully controls the connotations of
his images so that our sympathetic response to natural objects is
precisely directed. He knows he can rely on our habit of associating
landscape and emotion and he uses our experience of these value-
bearing images to make us feel immediately the individual significance of the two visions.

By way of conclusion one may point out the extent to which the
four principal groups of images in *In Memoriam*—religious, domestic
scientific and natural—are inter-related. The poem is very much
concerned with the poet's attitude to God, death and change, and
the cycles of the seasons are used to indicate the development of
his accord with the processes discovered by geologists and with

existence in general. His return to normal social life is shown through appearances of his family and friends, and his hope for the future depends upon the progress of the race, which involves the sequence of birth, marriage and death and the leadership of godlike men such as Hallam. Natural imagery is the most important reference system in the poem, for our response to it can be guaranteed, and Tennyson employs it particularly to provide a correlative for the poet's emotional state. He remarks in section v that 'words, like Nature, half reveal / And half conceal the Soul within'. Words which image nature can go far towards revealing the inner condition of the poet.

VIII

IMAGERY: FIGURES OF SPEECH

THERE are very many ways of forming figurative connections between words, and even more systems by which to categorize them. The most important figures—simile, metaphor and symbol—seem to function primarily as devices for bringing together two ideas or groups of ideas: a literal element commonly called the 'tenor' and a figurative, the 'vehicle'. An example may help us to see just what is involved.

Section 1 of *In Memoriam* begins, 'Be near me when my light is low', and this is a useful case to take because the Lincoln manuscript shows that Tennyson first thought of writing 'the pulse' instead of 'my light'. The general sense of the line is something like 'be near me when I am feeling despondent', but Tennyson's metaphor employs the notion of a candle or lantern burning down as the vehicle for the poet's state of mind. This causes several effects which 'the pulse' would not.

1. It makes an attractive picture.

2. It produces a clearer and more extended thought, for whilst we would probably imagine the pulse as remaining steady, the flame (and the poet's life) will soon begin to flicker and will shortly be extinguished altogether.

3. It brings in a group of strong associations which 'light' carries in our culture—it is suggestive of truth, virtue, spiritual reality, faith, activity, warmth, vitality and the good things of life in general and, indeed, of life itself.

4. Notice also that it does not 'stand for' 'pulse'; that is by no means the first replacement word which occurs to people. No direct substitution is possible—the image stands for the whole complex of ideas I have mentioned and is far more inclusive than any of them.

5. Finally, as the reader may recall from Chapter VI, 'my light' relates this opening line to the close of the section, where the poet envisages 'on the low dark verge of life / The twilight of eternal day'. The difference between the poet's present depression and the glory of heaven is conveyed by the enlarging of the image of light— and this 'the pulse' could not have expressed.

This brief analysis has thrown up several points, some more important than others. The attractive picture is nice to have, but obviously not an essential of figurative language. The fact that 'light' stands for no single specified idea is not an invariable feature, for if Tennyson had written 'when my pulse is (like) a light burning low' all the other aspects would nevertheless have remained. The relationship between the first and last lines of the section which is created by the images is again not an essential of figurative language, though it is often the case that an evocative image is more open to such development. The other two points (2 and 3) identify the most basic results of bringing two groups of ideas together: a gain in the clarity and extent of the thought, and the inclusion of additional associations and impressions. These two are the fundamental effects of simile, metaphor and symbol.[1]

One may regard all figures as being primarily images of thought or of impression (to use Foakes' terms), but it is rare to find one which contains no hint of the other. Tennyson uses many images of impression; they are mostly drawn from nature and, as I argued in the previous chapter, were useful to the nineteenth-century poet because they carried dependable value connotations. The poet says of Hallam, 'Thy leaf has perish'd in the green' (lxxv), and the image adds suggestions of freshness, springtime and natural fertility to the thought of Hallam cut down in his prime. Again, the poet concludes his offer of his second friendship in lxxxv:

> Ah, take the imperfect gift I bring,
>   Knowing the primrose yet is dear,
>   The primrose of the later year,
> As not unlike to that of Spring.

The point about his first and second friendships has already been spelt out: the image bathes it in associations of delicate natural beauty. At the beginning of the poem the poet's loss of control is indicated by the line, 'I sit within a helmless bark' (iv); at the end he is 'like a statue solid-set, / And moulded in colossal calm' (Epilogue). Hallam, towards the opening, is 'thy dark freight' (x); towards the close he is a 'happy star' (cxxvii). The principal function of all these

---

[1] Cf. Nowottny, *The Language Poets Use*, chapter 3; C. Day Lewis, *The Poetic Image* (London, 1947); Murry, *The Problem of Style*, pp. 75–6; I. A. Richards, *The Philosophy of Rhetoric* (New York, 1936), chapters 5 and 6; Max Black, *Models and Metaphors* (New York, 1962), chapter 3; and Foakes, *The Romantic Assertion*, pp. 32–4.

figures is to suggest the connotations we are to attach to people or events, the emotional weight which we should place upon them.

Tennyson's exploitation of the impressionistic aspects of an image does not prevent him from including an element of thought also— indeed, some such element is usually essential if the suggestiveness is to be controlled. In section iv the poet says, 'Break, thou deep vase of chilling tears, / That grief hath shaken into frost!' Here the reader is required to bring with him all the unpleasant associations of frost and its destructive potentialities, but the metaphor is also quite precise. The link with the poet's heart (which has just been mentioned) is made by the verb 'break', which can refer to both hearts and vases, and by the dead metaphor of being shaken with grief, which also works in both cases. The rest of the meaning depends upon the fact that water will remain liquid at temperatures below freezing point until it is moved; then it turns to ice, expands, and so breaks its container. This rigorous intellectual organization is evident again in a related use of the same image:

> 'My sudden frost was sudden gain,
>   And gave all ripeness to the grain,
> It might have drawn from after-heat'.   (lxxxi)

Hallam's death brought the poet's love to a rapid maturity. A further fact about frost is that is can cause an overnight ripening, and this is in turn utilized to give a different twist to the image according to the poet's later state of mind. In the first instance the harmful potentialities of frost were evoked, in the second frost is linked in contrary fashion with ripeness. In both cases the metaphor has an important intellectual content, for Tennyson has played upon the precise facts about the operation of frost to particularize his meaning on each occasion.

It is not true, as some have supposed, that Tennyson is content to fall back on evocative images which give us a nice feeling without any controlling intellectual tautness. Section xix compares the poet's grief to the effect of the Severn tides on the river Wye:

> There twice a day the Severn fills;
>   The salt sea-water passes by,
>   And hushes half the babbling Wye,
> And makes a silence in the hills.

> The Wye is hush'd nor moved along,
>   And hush'd my deepest grief of all,
>   When fill'd with tears that cannot fall,
> I brim with sorrow drowning song.

> The tide flows down, the wave again
>   Is vocal in its wooded walls;
>   My deeper anguish also falls,
> And I can speak a little then.

Here we have a close-fitting analogy, precise at every point: the Wye only babbles along when it is not overwhelmed by the influx from the Severn, and the poet can only speak when the full flood of his grief is not upon him. Moreover, the evocative associations of rivers are not, I believe, very operative here. We do not think much of 'waters, rolling from their mountain-springs / With a soft inland murmur' or of 'steep and lofty cliffs' ('Tintern Abbey'); the Wye is not a symbol of the changing pattern of existence or of the journey through life or eternity. The Wye is appropriate here (apart from its wetness) largely because it makes most noise when it is least full: the most prominent aspect of the figure is the exact—almost diagrammatic—model which it affords for the poet's two states of mind and the relationship between them. This image of thought is quite different from the common notion of nineteenth-century imagery—it is like a metaphysical conceit.

The reader may be surprised that I have not distinguished metaphor and simile, but I am inclined to agree with Middleton Murry that 'it seems impossible to regard metaphors and similes as different in any essential property: metaphor is compressed simile'.[2] The form of the simile is more explicit, but as far as I can see there is only one thing which metaphor is able to do and simile not, namely leave the referent unstated (as 'pulse' or whatever is unstated in section l), but this is by no means always the way in which the metaphor is used and the relation between the two parts of a simile may be sufficiently unexplicit to present the reader with the same kind of challenge. I am not suggesting that metaphor is merely a matter of comparison; I accept that the tenor and vehicle modify each other and that 'interaction' is usually a better word to describe what happens. But metaphor may function primarily as a comparison, and simile, despite its appearance of an analogy, may really constitute an interaction as vital

---

[2] *John Clare and Other Studies* (London, 1950), p. 87. Cf. Foakes, *The Romantic Assertion*, p. 23.

as that found in metaphor. The forms which metaphor and simile may take are legion, and details of wording are so important that it is almost impossible to lay down general criteria. Discussions of the issue are sometimes distorted by taking account only of very simple examples, but the briefest figure can prove complex. In section ix the poet asks that the ship will be untroubled by storms in the night 'till Phosphor, bright / As our pure love, thro' early light / Shall glimmer on the dewy decks'. The simile 'as our pure love' adds little to our knowledge about the brightness of Phosphor, for the quality of their love is as yet hardly defined, and stars are themselves generally taken as emblems of brilliance. I suggest that this simile functions almost in reverse: it is primarily the poet's love which is to watch over the ship and keep it safe, and Phosphor, which could literally shine above, is an indirect way of introducing it. The image is most significant for its amplification of our notion of the love of the poet and his friend, which is only obliquely the subject of the section. It invests it with the symbolic connotations of Phosphor, traditionally the star of love, thus establishing a link which runs right through *In Memoriam*. This simile certainly involves interaction rather than simple comparison.

It is true that simile may easily become over explicit and lengthy— Tennyson sometimes falls into this trap, specially in the domestic sections—but this may also happen with metaphor, as perhaps it does in the representation of discussion at Cambridge in terms of archery in section lxxxvii and in the metaphor of Love as 'Lord and King', with couriers, a court, a guard and a sentinel, which runs through the three stanzas of section cxxvi. It does not follow at all that simile is necessarily less intense, compressed or vital than metaphor. The example at the end of section xcvi defied Bradley's powers of interpretation:[3] the poet says he knew a person, evidently Hallam, who fought through his doubts,

> And Power was with him in the night,
> Which makes the darkness and the light,
> And dwells not in the light alone,
>
> But in the darkness and the cloud,
>   *As* over Sinai's peaks of old,
>   While Israel made their gods of gold,
> Altho' the trumpet blew so loud.

[3] A. C. Bradley, *A Commentary on Tennyson's In Memoriam*, 3rd edn. (London, 1910).

K

The point of the section is to show the poet resolving to trust in the vision of the preceding section xcv. His trance was 'cancell'd, stricken thro' with doubt', but he feels he must defeat this doubt and, like Hallam, have faith in the ultimate order of things. The simile in the last three lines alludes to *Exodus* xix and xx, where the Lord appears to Moses and gives him the Law. The poet too has experienced a revelation; it mixed the dim lights of East and West, even as the Power in this section dwells not in the light alone. When Moses returned from the mountain he found that the Israelites had made themselves a golden calf, and the poet's society is similarly tempted by materialism. Like Moses with the tablets, he now has a new charter for his time, and we see him revealing it in the rest of the poem: the message for the nineteenth century is like that for the Israelites—'Ring out the narrowing lust of gold' (cvi). This simile challenges us to perceive its relevance and, when we think, we find that it has a deep and complex application to the poet's situation.

The distinction between simile and metaphor is further confused in Tennyson's case by his habit of sliding from one to the other.

> From art, from nature, from the schools,
>   Let random influences glance,
>   Like light in many a shiver'd lance
> That breaks about the dappled pools.   (xlix)

The comparison is between the influences on the poet's mind and light broken on the surface of a pool. Within this is the metaphor of the fragmented lance, which adds detail and concreteness to our picture of the light. It is because the form of the simile makes the stanza quite clear in outline that Tennyson is able to have a figure within a figure—only because we have firmly grasped the basic simile can we be expected to take a metaphor in the middle of it. Once the simile has been established, Tennyson goes on to use it as if it were a metaphor:

> The lightest wave of thought shall lisp,
>   The fancy's tenderest eddy wreathe,
>   The slightest air of song shall breathe
> To make the sullen surface crisp.

The simile has turned into a metaphor whose provenance it is. In 'wave', 'eddy' and 'surface crisp' the pool-mind image is kept alive, giving cohesion to the section and bringing back to full life the moribund metaphors in 'air' and 'breathe'. These are usual language for a song, but when the surface crisps we think of them as terms for a breeze as well.

> And look thy look, and go thy way,
>   But blame not thou the winds that make
>   The seeming-wanton ripple break,
>   The tender-pencil'd shadow play.

The image is now so well established in the section that Tennyson can leave it entirely for the first line and half of this stanza and, though the thought has taken a new tack, we pick it up again at once on its return. And it is still strong enough to contain the metaphorical epithet 'tender-pencil'd'. The final stanza returns again to the literal, but nevertheless contains ambiguous words which suggest the water image:

> Beneath all fancied hopes and fears
>   Ay me, the sorrow deepens down,
>   Whose muffled motions blindly drown
>   The bases of my life in tears.

'Beneath', 'deepens down', 'drown' and 'tears' all refer back more or or less covertly to the simile of the first stanza. 'Tears' at the end gives a major new twist to the image, for the water which before stood for the poet's *mind* now represents his *grief*. From this we must draw the syllogistic conclusion that the poet's sorrow fills his entire mind so that the two become the same thing. The original simile was so well established and has been so persistently maintained that this further elaboration can follow very quietly, but very easily.

Tennyson not only moves freely between simile and metaphor: a major feature of his imagery is a general blending of literal and figurative. This is in fact what is happening in the sections I discussed in the previous chapter where what might be just background description comes to suggest the poet's emotions. In sections vii and xcix, ii and xxxix, lxxxiii and cxv, the literal scenery becomes more or less explicitly a figurative representation of the poet's state of mind. On Hallam's birthday the bitter weather outside is in contrast with the 'solid core of heat' and the 'festal cheer' the family make indoors (cvii). Again, it is no ordinary wind which at the end of section xcv

> Rock'd the full-foliaged elms, and swung
> The heavy-folded rose, and flung
> The lilies to and fro, and said
>
> 'The dawn, the dawn,' and died away.

The breeze in section lxxxvi seems similarly Pentecostal; time and again Tennyson exemplifies the tendency which Wimsatt has observed in Romantic nature imagery, namely a 'blurring of literal and figurative'. Wimsatt says, of a sonnet by Coleridge, 'Both tenor and vehicle, furthermore, are wrought in a parallel process out of the same material. The river landscape is both the occasion of reminiscence and the source of the metaphors by which reminiscence is described'.[4] The imagery may start off as background scenery, but by the end of the poem it has taken on some more figurative import.

We find just this effect in the section about the Wye (xix) and in the calm and storm of sections xi and xv. In the latter the poet consciously considers the weather's appropriateness as an image of his condition:

> The wild unrest that lives in woe
> Would dote and pour on yonder cloud
>
> That rises upward always higher,
>   And onward drags a labouring breast,
>   And topples round the dreary west,
> A looming bastion fringed with fire.

The storm is both the occasion for the writing of the section and a metaphor within it, for it images the wild unrest in the poet's mind. The relationship between literal and figurative is brought to the point of actual identity in the expression 'a labouring breast', for this suggests both the shape of the cloud and the poet's own sorrowing heart. If only the cloud was meant, '*its* labouring breast' would be a more natural expression; if only the poet, 'my' would make it clear. The way Tennyson has put it allows us to believe that both are referred to, and the two items in the section—the storm and the poet's mood—come together in one phrase. The distinction between tenor and vehicle breaks down and the poet's mind and external phenomena are fused utterly.

Thinking about the dependence of Tennyson and the Romantic poets upon experience for their beliefs makes one realize that this

---

[4] William Kurtz Wimsatt, *The Verbal Icon* (Lexington, 1954), pp. 114, 109.

blurring of literal and figurative is only to be expected. The sections of *In Memoriam* form a series of experiences, and it is natural that on a number of occasions the scenery should be mentioned; this done, the obvious way of continuing is to draw upon that 'background' for figurative images. Quite often, of course, the situation is itself the impulse for the experience—in the sections about spring, for instance, or section lxxxvi—and then its further employment in figures describing the poet's condition is most appropriate. Section lxxii is stimulated by a combination of the weather and the fact that it is the anniversary of Hallam's death, and the one becomes an image for the other:

> Lift as thou may'st thy burthen'd brows
>   Thro' clouds that drench the morning star,
>   And whirl the ungarner'd sheaf afar,
> And sow the sky with flying boughs.

The determined reversal of the creative power of nature in the last line—this is a destructive sowing—was discussed in Chapter III. Notice also the obscuring of the morning star, Phosphor, by the hostile clouds: the day, burdened (as in the last line of the section) with shame, is seen as the extinguisher of love. The landscape is more than an incidental accompaniment of the day: it becomes responsible for the death of the poet's friend who, like the 'ungarner'd sheaf', was removed before his potentialities could be fulfilled.

The result of this tendency to blur the literal and figurative is of the utmost importance for the way in which we read nineteenth-century poetry. Wimsatt contrasts the Metaphysicals, and explains, 'The interest derives not from our being aware of disparity where likeness is firmly insisted on, but in an opposite activity of discerning the design which is latent in the multiform sensuous picture'.[5] The appeal of this kind of poetry resides in the delicate interactions between words which might at first sight appear to be doing little or just presenting an evocative picture. The language may not seem extraordinary initially, but a carefully woven pattern of interrelations between the literal and figurative may be perceived, for the small details of the language combine to form a finely textured structure. All this is very like the more general point which I have been making about Tennyson's poetry throughout this study. His

[5] *The Verbal Icon*, p. 110.

language is characteristically unobtrusive, but a closer examination often reveals subtle and complex connections.

In *In Memoriam* Tennyson frequently intensifies this fluidity of literal and figurative elements by using words which could belong to either. This was the case in section xlix with 'beneath' and 'deepen down' which could refer to both water and the mind, and with 'air' and 'breathe' which work equally well for water and the poet's song. We have come across many examples already—the 'labouring breast' (xv) could belong to the poet or the cloud; and 'Break, thou deep vase of chilling tears, / That grief hath shaken into frost' (iv) contains two words which can refer to hearts as well as vases. This kind of exceptionally close-knit figure is almost incredibly common in *In Memoriam*. It is usually assumed that there will be literal terms and figurative ones—tenor and vehicle—in any metaphor or simile, but Tennyson manages to include words which are both: 'And all the bugle breezes blew / Reveillée to the waking morn' (lxviii). Both bugles (figurative) and breezes (literal) *blow*. Or section xvii: 'my prayer / Was as the whisper of an air / To breathe thee over lonely seas'—the identification of the prayer and the wind is completed by the ambiguity of 'whisper—air—breathe'.

> So that still garden of the souls
> In many a figured leaf enrolls
> The total world since life began.   (xliii)

Books as well as plants have leaves. The image starts as a garden in which departed souls are flowers closed up for the night, but at some point it begins to sound like the book of life—is it at 'figured'? or 'figured leaf'? or not until 'enrolls'? and it never quite stops being a garden anyway. At the close of the section the poet imagines that love might rewaken 'at the spiritual prime', and again levels of meaning coalesce—that glorious moment will occur when the souls have reached their greatest excellence, and it will be like the opening of flowers at dawn. 'Prime' is both tenor and vehicle.

This close texture in which literal and figurative merge is furthered by Tennyson's preference for adjectives which can refer to both physical and mental conditions. In 'Be near me when my light is low', the adjective readily fits the light as well as the pulse, faith, powers of endurance, or whatever the literal term would be. The same is true in the sunset when the poet feels 'A spectral doubt which makes me *cold*' (xli), in 'Risest thou thus, *dim* dawn, again' (lxxii and xcix), where both the bad visibility and the poet's gloom and incomprehension are in question, and in the dawn at the end of section vii, for the street is 'bald' and the day 'blank', and the poet feels bleak and destitute. In section xi the distinctions between the calmness of the day, Hallam and the poet are focused by the application of the same adjective to all three; 'The wild unrest' of section xv is found in the storm as well as the poet; and the girl in love with one of higher rank lives 'In that dark house where she was born' (lx). The dark house is the world, darkened for the poet by Hallam's absence (we think of section vii), and the adjective suggests the poet's emotional response as well as the appearance of the building. The frequency with which Tennyson manages to achieve this striking kind of indeterminacy between literal and figurative is quite extraordinary. It is of great value in encouraging the reader to move freely between the poet's mind and the landscape which so often reflects it; and it adds to the sense of a delicately precise design which I have repeatedly remarked as characteristic of the structure of Tennyson's language.

The next step on from this blending of tenor and vehicle is the disappearance of the tenor altogether. This is what happens in section vii where, as I pointed out in the previous chapter, the poet finds himself alone at Hallam's house and describes the weather. There is no overt connection between the landscape and the poet's state of mind, but the intensity of the writing and the structure of the section make us think of his mood as the implied tenor. The word we now need is 'symbol'. This term is much abused; I believe it is in place when there is no (or hardly any) tenor but we nevertheless feel (from the way language is used) that something more than the object itself is in question. Moreover, the idea symbolized must not be immediately translatable into other terms; if there is available a simple equivalent expression then we have not symbolism, but allegory. The context promotes the symbol to our attention, but its significance cannot be pinned down to one, neatly limited notion.[6]

Occasionally in *In Memoriam* we find allegorical images though one suspects that they are actually failed symbols. They seem clumsy and contrived and lack the depth or breadth of meaning we expect from symbol. When we read,

[6] Cf. Nowottny, *The Language Poets Use*, pp. 174–86; Robin Skelton, *The Poetic Pattern* (London, 1956), pp. 92–3; and Reuben A. Brower, *The Fields of Light* (New York, 1951), pp. 44–5.

> I found an angel of the night;
> The voice was low, the look was bright;
> He look'd upon my crown and smiled,   (lxix)

we find it all too easy to say, Oh, the angel is Hallam and he is pleased that the poet is still working at his elegies. Something of the same is true of section ciii, which is unfortunate because it is important in the scheme of the poem. Nevertheless, Tennyson was by no means antagonistic to multiple meanings in his writing. His son records how he would say that poetry is 'like shot-silk with many glancing colours', and when questioned as to whether the three Queens who accompany Arthur on his last voyage are Faith, Hope and Charity, he replied:

> They mean that and they do not. They are three of the noblest women. They are also those three Graces, but they are much more. I hate to be tied down to say, '*This* means that,' because the thought within the image is much more than any one interpretation'.[7]

(One feels time and again that Tennyson was not very fortunate in his questioners.)

In section xxxv the poet imagines that he might receive incontrovertible evidence that existence ceases with death; he would reply,

> 'Yet even here,
> But for one hour, O Love, I strive
> To keep so sweet a thing alive:'
> But I should turn mine ears and hear
>
> The moanings of the homeless sea,
> The sound of streams that swift or slow
> Draw down Æonian hills, and sow
> The dust of continents to be.

The water image is clearly of significance, but it is not explained. A voice might say, then he would reply, then comes this image, and in the next stanza Love concedes the argument. The meaning of the symbol is partly a matter of the huge perspective of time which will make the poet's love appear insignificant; but then it is also to do with the neutrality or even destuctiveness of nature which wears away the most permanent-seeming objects. The sea here is an image of death too—because of its earlier association with Hallam's re-

---

[7] Hallam Tennyson, *Memoir*, II, 127.

mains, because of the use of the words 'moaning', 'homeless' and 'dust', and because of its connotations in our culture: we might, for instance, relate the 'streams' to Lethe, particularly in view of the phrase 'forgetful shore' in the next stanza. All these things worry the poet, and his anxiety is shown by his evident involvement with the symbol. The notions suggested by the image are in fact refuted by the end of the section, but the symbol is such a forceful form that our lasting impression is of the third stanza (as we can see from the frequency with which it is quoted out of context).

I believe it is not sufficient for us to say 'water symbol', mention Jung, and assume that we have demonstrated great poetic quality; neither would we be troubling with Tennyson's language in this way if he had merely thrown in some lines about water whenever he felt things were getting a bit flat. In section xxxv he does not simply present us with the sea and leave us to get on with it, but brings out quite specifically the areas of meaning he requires; we do not, I believe, think of life after death (as in section ciii) or of the toil of everyday life (as in 'The Lotos-Eaters') or of the challenge of the unknown (as in 'Ulysses'). There are three controls on the meaning of a symbol: the precise wording of it and its context, its traditional associations, and the connotations it has gathered during the poem so far.

In section xxxvi the poet is thinking of the power of the Gospels,

> Which he may read that binds the sheaf,
>   Or builds the house, or digs the grave,
>   And those wild eyes that watch the wave
> In roarings round the coral reef.

Superficially the poet is confident, but 'the homeless sea' of the previous section is still in our ears and when we look closely at this account we find suggestions of gloom and alarm which confirm our doubt. The parallel clauses which evoke the whole process of life in the first two lines conclude with the grave, the eyes are 'wild' and the wave is roaring round the reef so that we may think of the threat to sailors or of the turmoil raging just beyond any small island of peace we might construct for ourselves. These hints, perhaps by themselves rather dubious, combine with the effect of the imagery in the previous section to create a symbol of menace and despondency. The sea appears so overpowering that we cannot really feel very optimistic about the ability of the Scriptures to defeat it. All this is suggested without any help whatsoever from explicit statement; we have a vehicle whose tenor is completely absent.

Previous uses of an image are very important agents for investing it with symbolic connotations, and *In Memoriam*, as many commentators have observed, is notable for the recurrence of a few groups of images. The hand, the path, water, dawn, stars, and several others, appear again and again, and are the principal binding force in the poem. They are part of the process I have often remarked whereby the poet, in order to chart his developing attitude, measures it against recurring external objects and events. He redefines his position by making us compare his current use of an image with its previous appearances—the change in the poet's response to the natural cycle (described in the previous chapter) functions in a very similar way, but it seems best to consider as recurring images only fairly specific repetitions of an object. We can see the alteration in the poet's outlook very clearly by comparing the treatment of the sea, say in section ciii (where it carries the poet out beyond death to rejoin Hallam), with the homeless moanings of xxxv.

By way of an example of the manner in which recurring images point up the poet's developing attitude and gather symbolic connotations with each appearance, I propose to consider circles and bounds, for they have been relatively neglected.[8] There are about forty such images in *In Memoriam* and several of them stand out because of the use of strange diction. In section xi is 'mingle with the bounding main', where *N.E.D.* cites Tennyson as the first user of 'bounding' in this sense after Shakespeare and Burns; 'this round of green' (xxxiv) has Tennyson as the only user with Milton and Carlyle; 'the links that bound / Thy changes' (xli) employs a sense which is only in occasional use; and 'orb into the perfect star' (xxiv) contains the only occurrence of this verb given by the dictionary. One naturally wonders why Tennyson should be preoccupied with the image of the circle to the extent of having to invent or revive words for it. In several ways it seems to correspond to the structure of *In Memoriam*. The poem begins, as Tennyson said, with a death and ends with a marriage, and this implies a cyclic view of the generations of human life whereby the child whose birth is foreseen in the Epilogue somehow makes up for the loss of Hallam. Then, the whole technique of employing recurring images whose connotations change

---

[8] The exception is J. G. Taaffe, 'Circle Imagery in Tennyson's *In Memoriam*', *Victorian Poetry*, I (1963), 123–31, but his account is very different from that presented here.

with the poet's development seems related to the idea of circularity; the poet returns to the same image, apparently from an impulse to specify and delimit the precise nature of his experience. And one might even go so far as to say that the *abba* rhyme scheme suggests a circle.

At the beginning of *In Memoriam* the circle is to the poet something which shuts him in: the limits of his experience are firmly bounded and he is confined to the physical universe. The 'bounding main' of section xi, the circles of the sky through which the dove-poet's mind moves in xii and the ship in xvii, and the four sets of church bells which surround him in section xxviii all show the poet frustrated and imprisoned by physical limits. This corresponds to the fact that Hallam is—depending upon how one looks at it—either above the material world (a spirit) or entirely merged with it (a corpse). In either event, the poet is cut off from his friend by the boundaries of earthly existence: only the yew tree has its roots 'wrapt about the bones' (ii) and in section xxxiv he fears that life may be confined to 'This round of green'. Like natural imagery, the circle is occasionally used with pleasant connotations towards the start of the poem, but in a backward-looking context. The poet wonders whether

> the past will always win
> A glory from its being far;
> And orb into the perfect star
> We saw not, when we moved therein? (xxiv)

The first hopeful occasion comes in section xxx, when the family are 'in a circle hand-in-hand', and it seems that

> With gather'd power, yet the same,
> Pierces the keen seraphic flame
> From orb to orb, from veil to veil.

Hallam is lost to the family circle, but in their exhilaration they claim that the personality continues the same in its progress through eternity. Nevertheless, the poet has no means of making contact with Hallam, for their orbits are separate:

> But thou art turn'd to something strange,
> And I have lost the links that bound
> Thy changes; here upon the ground,
> No more partaker of thy change. (xli)

In section xlvii he fears that a person may 'move his rounds' and after death remerge in 'the general soul'; he rejects this view, but is still left with the present difficulty of bridging the gulf between his circle and Hallam's. His friend is now 'mixing with his proper sphere' (lx), 'With all the circle of the wise' (lxi); yet, despite their separation, Hallam may still watch him:

> So mayst thou watch me where I weep,
>   As, unto vaster motions bound,
>   The circuits of thine orbit round
> A higher height, a deeper deep.   (lxiii)

Only gradually, as time brings him more peace of mind, does the poet's attitude to life—and to time itself—begin to change. He begins to speak of it, not as a closed system from which there is no escape, but as a cycle, an onward moving progression which might mean advances for mankind: in section lxxxv he imagines that Hallam was shown in heaven 'All knowledge that the sons of flesh / Shall gather in the cycled times'. Eventually he gains full confidence in the effects of time as when, for instance, he rejects the human circle of the dance for the 'measured arcs', 'The closing cycle rich in good' (cv), or when he speaks of time as a beneficent force in his life, expecting delight a hundredfold for 'every kiss of toothed wheels, / And all the courses of the suns' (cxvii). All these later uses of the image draw resonance from our recollection of the poet's former attitude. The recurrence makes us strongly aware of the change which has taken place and enriches the language with a significance beyond normal usage. The familiar imagery has something of the same effect as a tune (in itself perhaps unexceptional) which brings back personal memories of earlier days.

The main cause of the poet's eventual satisfaction with time and existence in general is the mystical experience of section xcv, for this solves the poet's problem of how to leap the distance between the circles of his life and Hallam's:

> The living soul was flash'd on mine,
>
> And mine in this was wound, and whirl'd
>   About empyreal heights of thought,
>   And came on that which is, and caught
> The deep pulsations of the world,

Æonian music measuring out
The steps of Time—the shocks of Chance—
The blows of Death.

The trance is itself described in terms of circles, suggesting that the poet at last manages to see all creation as part of one vast, harmonious movement. The limits of the physical world, which had so inhibited the poet, are transcended, and the circles which had been separate and distinct coalesce into one. He feels that the whole of existence is included in one great orb: there are no boundaries dividing the living from the dead, the material from the spiritual. This interpretation is almost entirely dependent upon our awareness of earlier uses of imagery of circles and bounds; without this, the significance of the vision is barely apparent. The language is invested with associations which go far beyond the normal meanings of the words. The image is further reinforced, as I pointed out in the previous chapter, by authority derived from Dante's description of Paradise: the poet has been liberated from the prison of his earthly circle and whirled into one of the most exalted models of ideal universal order in European literature. But its relation to the rest of *In Memoriam* is the principal source of the power of the image. It is the vehicle for a tenor which is no narrower than the poet's whole experience: it is unexpressed at this point, but deeply embedded in the whole poem. The poet has been cabined, cribbed and confined by circles and bounds until this moment, but now he is wound and whirled, like Dante, in unison with the deep pulsations of the world. In the last lines of the section the dim lights of East and West 'broaden into *boundless* day'.

In section cxxii the poet remembers his mystical experience, and the same image is employed as he asks

To feel once more, in placid awe,
The strong imagination roll
A sphere of stars about my soul,
In all her motion one with law.

The last sections of the poem are bursting with circle imagery, which is celebrated with delight as all the circles fuse into one. The poet is in Love's court on earth and sleeps 'Encompass'd by his faithful guard' (cxxvi); those without such strength will be overwhelmed by disaster,

> And compass'd by the fires of Hell;
>   While thou, dear spirit, happy star,
>   O'erlook'st the tumult from afar,
> And smilest, knowing all is well.   (cxxvii)

The poet's assurance that all his circles are now one is given most forcibly in section cxxx: 'The voice is on the rolling air', 'I prosper, circled with thy voice'. So finally in the Epilogue we are told,

>   And, star and system rolling past,
>   A soul shall draw from out the vast
>   And strike his being into bounds.

The whole cyclic process is continuing, both in nature and amongst humankind, as a new personality takes the bounds of its individuality beneath the over-arching framework of a total harmonious system. All limits can now be transcended, both in the present through mystical experience and in the future by mankind as it moves towards the crowning race.

Recurring images gain symbolic force in *In Memoriam* because with each use they pick up further connotations which then remain with them. Thus whatever the explicit tenor may be (and there need not be one—the image may be apparently literal), the symbol is a vehicle for the poet's accumulated experience. This technique is developed by Tennyson to a degree almost unprecedented in English literature (Blake is the principal antecedent). It is by no means prominent in *Paradise Lost* or *The Prelude*, and it comes to the fore in the novel at just about the same time. The method figures in Shakespeare, of course, but one of the most remarkable facts in the history of criticism is that commentators did not notice it until the twentieth century—that is, until it became common in modern literature. The creation of symbols by the use of recurring images became essential to Tennyson because of the way in which the action of *In Memoriam* is located in the poet's mind. The poem is set in the present, and the early sections are presented entirely without any certain premonition of the eventual resolution. The continual change in the poet's position means that we cannot say at any point: I see, water means God (or even the womb); the images change with the poet's outlook, and therefore build up a mass of varied and often contradictory associations.

The effectiveness of recurring images is tied to the problem raised in the previous chapter, of how Tennyson was to evoke the value connotations he required in a world where established beliefs on fundamental issues were already disintegrating. *In Memoriam* questions the whole basis of traditional doctrine, and obviously conventional religious imagery cannot alone suffice when one is declaring that we know no essential truths and that all is 'Behind the veil, behind the veil' (lvi). The principal difficulty is that no image can be made, by itself, to imply an intellectually coherent system—in the way, say, that the baby in the manger implies the Crucifixion. The sea, for instance, is a very potent image, but though by calling it 'unplumb'd, salt, estranging' Arnold could get it to signify the lack of contact between people, it would not simultaneously (had he wished it) have suggested closer union after death, the neutrality of nature, or even the melancholy, long, withdrawing roar of faith, unless he had added fairly pointed indications that this was what he wanted it to do. Recurring images in a long poem answer this problem, for they enable the poet to build his own scheme as he goes along. 'Star and system rolling past' in the Epilogue means Hallam, love, the oneness of creation, the poet's assurance that all will be well, the onward development of the race and the possibility of breaking out of the circle of earthly existence and communicating with the dead; yet it is in external form a completely literal statement.

It is fascinating to watch the operation of such a powerful system of symbols in the sections towards the end of the poem. The first two stanzas of section cxxi describe a sunset, or, rather, the moment after sunset:

> Sad Hesper o'er the buried sun
> And ready, thou, to die with him,
> Thou watchest all things ever dim
> And dimmer, and a glory done:
>
> The team is loosen'd from the wain,
> The boat is drawn upon the shore;
> Thou listenest to the closing door,
> And life is darken'd in the brain.

Things are coming to a standstill at the end of the day. The sun has gone, the waggoner has released his horses, the fisherman has left his boat, cottage doors are closing for the night and men and women are going to sleep. The lines are also about the close of a human life, however. This meaning comes partly from such words as 'buried' and 'die' and partly from the last line quoted, which gives the impression of a final extinction; but it arises also from the associations which sunset has in our culture and in the rest of the poem. Within *In Memoriam* darkness has been repeatedly linked to death—we think at once of the 'thousand years of gloom' of the yew tree (ii), of the 'Dark house' where the poet failed to find his friend (vii) and of the 'jaws of vacant darkness' where we are said to 'cease' in section xxxiv. In section cxxi, however, death does not seem frightening. This is because of the peaceful movement of the verse, clauses fitting into lines and stresses falling in the expected places, and because of the gentle tone of the images themselves. Life is running down very gradually, slipping away; things are almost imperceptibly coming to a rest. We have this feeling from 'dim / And dimmer' (where the first word looks initially like a verb), from the fact that Hesper is 'ready' to die, and from the tenses of the verbs in the second stanza, which suggest that the team is at this very moment being loosened, the boat being drawn up, the door actually in the process of closing.

This peaceful view of death also comes to us from the recent uses of the images: in section lxxxvi the evening air fanned the poet with new life and streamed on 'To where in yonder orient star / A hundred spirits whisper "Peace" ', and at the end of xcv 'East and West . . . Mixt their dim lights'. The evening imagery of section cxxi reminds us of how death was seen in the early part of the poem as a grim shadow, but is itself an instance of the poet's new outlook. The image of the boat drawn upon the shore is also relevant, for water has also often been linked with death in *In Memoriam*. Here our memory of the ship which carried Hallam's body towards the beginning of the poem will be subordinated to the more recent 'little shallop' of ciii, in which the poet glided out to meet the 'great ship' bearing Hallam and himself toward 'a crimson cloud'.

Most important in these two stanzas is Hesper, the evening star, Venus, or love which, though sad, is ready to die with the sun. Venus has been used as love at various points in the poem—in section ix it was associated with Hallam's dead body; in xlvi the poet hoped that love would be a 'brooding star' from marge to marge of eternity; in lxxii, on the 'dim dawn', clouds drenched the morning star; in lxxxvi the spirits in the orient star whispered 'Peace'; and in lxxxix Hesper concluded a happy memory of life with Hallam when they returned 'Before the crimson-circled star / Had fall'n into her father's grave'. In section cxxi Hesper (love and Hallam) watches over the close of life with complete equanimity and, moreover, is ready itself to die. This shows the poet's full confidence in the natural order: love is calmly dying because it is the end of day—in the due course of things. Furthermore, as we go on to the next two stanzas we find that Venus does not die for ever, but rises again next morning:

> Bright Phosphor, fresher for the night,
>> By thee the world's great work is heard
>> Beginning, and the wakeful bird;
> Behind thee comes the greater light:

> The market boat is on the stream,
>> And voices hail it from the brink;
>> Thou hear'st the village hammer clink,
> And see'st the moving of the team.

The dawn has no longer the connotations of the 'blank day' which broke in section vii or of the dim dawns of the sections on the death anniversary. Now it is the triumphant dawn of the end of section xcv and of cv, where the poet wants

> No dance, no motion, save alone
> What lightens in the lucid east

> Of rising worlds by yonder wood.
>> Long sleeps the summer in the seed;
>> Run out your measured arcs, and lead
> The closing cycle rich in good.

But these stanzas carry with them the memory of all the dawns in the poem, pleasant and unpleasant, thus recalling the whole of the poet's struggle. This section therefore appears not as an over-confident assertion, but as the resolution towards which the poet has worked during the various experiences of two years, including the visionary dawn of section xcv. Hesper dies, but Phosphor rises as a precursor of 'the greater light', and though this must logically be the same sun which set the previous night, the circumlocution allows us to believe that the reference is to a new world after death, more wonderful than

L

that on earth. The movement from night to day described in this section reflects the poet's faith in the survival of love, and it is also a microcosm of the natural cycle with which he is now in harmony. 'The world's great work' implies the poet's confidence in the affairs of men and in humanity as 'The herald of a higher race', and thus these lines are made to symbolize all the poet's concerns in *In Memoriam*. The endurance of love, the natural order and the future of mankind are brought together under the benediction of the star of love.

In the final stanza the poet affirms that evening and morning are essentially the same, as Venus is the one planet:

> Sweet Hesper-Phosphor, double name
> For what is one, the first, the last,
> Thou, like my present and my past,
> Thy place is changed; thou art the same.

This ending strongly recalls the last stanza of xcv, where East and West mixed their dim lights, and also the following section:

> And Power was with him in the night,
> Which makes the darkness and the light,
> And dwells not in the light alone,
>
> But in the darkness and the cloud.   (xcvi)

The light/dark conflict in *In Memoriam* is not dismissed by a claim that all is light and there is no darkness, but resolved by an insistence that there is that which offers man an overall purpose whether he is in sorrow or in joy. That is why Hesper and Phosphor are declared to be one in cxxi: the poet has demonstrated to himself that love is the Alpha and Omega which conquers time, change and death.

I have heard it suggested that the only weakness here is the further equation, 'like my present and my past', but this does in fact follow from the premises of the imagery. The first four stanzas show love surviving death—and this is either the poet's death in the future, which will be followed by a new dawning in love, or Hallam's death in the past. The latter meaning gives the section the implication that Hallam's loss did not cause the final death of love, for after the night Phosphor returns. The poet has passed through the dark night in the course of *In Memoriam* and his new-awakened confidence is like the dawning of a new day. Similarly we see that in section vii there was no real return of light with the dawn, but in the partner section cxix the poet says,

> I see
> Betwixt the black fronts long-withdrawn
> A light-blue lane of early dawn,
> And think of early days and thee.

The poet's present and past are identical like Hesper and Phosphor because the friendship of Hallam and himself has been and is the guiding light of his life. The imagery, supported by earlier uses, symbolizes the survival of love both in the poet's life and beyond his death—and all with the minimum of explicit statement.

At this point it might be well to recapitulate. The principal functions of figures of speech are to extend and clarify thought and to add associations; and Tennyson's practice is by no means restricted to the latter. Any true understanding of his imagery is threatened by the danger of assuming that because he often generates great evocative power his images are necessarily vague and uncontrolled—just thrown at the reader who is left to write the poem for himself by indulgent self-abandonment to beauties of sight and sound. On the contrary, the use of such imagery imposed upon Tennyson the task of carefully limiting the associations to those required on the individual occasion, and this he usually succeeds in doing by the most rigorous attention to the detail of the linguistic environment.

Tennyson's language shows a strong tendency to slide between the literal and the figurative, for the external situation often becomes material for metaphor and simile. The process is accentuated by his remarkable facility in finding words which could be regarded as either tenor or vehicle, and is in accord with the closely worked structure which has been demonstrated in other aspects of his language. The blurring of the literal and figurative leads to symbolism, where an image, unsupported by explicit indications, comes to suggest a wide and relatively loosely defined area of meaning. The significance of a symbol is dependent upon its traditional associations, the precise linguistic context and the connotations it has gathered during the poem. Tennyson's heavy employment of recurring images enables him to invest certain objects with deep symbolic implications and so construct for himself an entire system of images which makes it possible for a few words to evoke the whole of the poet's developing experience.

The move towards symbolism in *In Memoriam* is very much of a piece with the use of natural imagery to suggest mood (which I considered in the previous chapter) and with the tendency of Tennyson's clause structure towards a condition of no syntax (Chapter VI). *In Memoriam*, markedly more than most previous poetry, aspires to express directly the mind of the poet. External objects are pertinent mainly in so far as they throw light upon his thoughts and feelings, syntax inclines towards the immediate recording of sense data unsifted by the patterns of logic, and images are made to carry a rich significance without the assistance of explicit linking devices. The poet does not pause to explain his meaning; we have to follow the workings of his mind and interpret the relevance for him of the images upon which he bestows so much attention. The action of *In Memoriam* is located in the poet's mind, for he finds his values in subjective experience. The symbol proclaims its significance solely through the importance which he evidently attaches to it, and thus compels us to intuit his immediate and complex mental responses as they develop. Tennyson found reason and dogma insufficient guides to belief and created linguistic structures which would present directly his characteristic and preferred pattern of thought.

IX

SOUND: BACKGROUND, THOUGHT AND EVOCATION

BACKGROUND, thought and evocation are the three stages in which I propose to consider Tennyson's use of sound in *In Memoriam*. First I will describe its effect on the general texture of the verse, then some examples of the employment of sound to support and clarify argument, and finally the contribution of this aspect of language to the communication of states of feeling.

Tennyson's interest in the sound of his poetry is well known; if anything, it has received exaggerated attention at the expense of other features, yet there has been no full and detailed analysis. Little evidence is available for deciding whether Tennyson makes more use of sound than other poets, but Ants Oras has counted the occurrences of assonance and alliteration in Spenser and Milton,[1] and comparison with *In Memoriam* seems to indicate that Tennyson uses assonance as much as these poets, and alliteration quite a lot more. We should not assume that there is anything simple about these devices, or that any kinds of repetition were welcome to Tennyson. He remarked, 'People sometimes say how "studiedly alliterative" Tennyson's verse is. Why, when I spout my lines first, they come out so alliteratively that I have sometimes no end of trouble to get rid of the alliteration'.[2] There comes a point when sound repetitions are ridiculous, and at a number of places in the manuscripts we can observe Tennyson taking care over this. He wrote, 'To *b*lack and *b*rown on *b*rother *b*rows' (Trial Edition), but changed it to 'kindred brows' (lxxix); and 'A night-long present of the *past* / In which we *paced* thro' summer France' (Trial Edition) became 'In which we went thro' summer France' (lxxi). In both cases we catch Tennyson in the act of removing an absurd excess from his sound patterning: there is clearly a limit beyond which it is not useful for the poet to go, unless he is aiming at a humorous effect.

It seems best for most purposes to take into account, as Oras does, only stressed syllables. The role of sound in poetry is by no means

---

[1] In *Sound and Poetry*, ed. Northrop Frye (New York, 1957).
[2] Hallam Tennyson, *Memoir*, II, 15.

fully understood, and it is safer to concentrate upon the more prominent manifestations. This policy also enables one to avoid difficulties which otherwise arise from the tendency in speech to reduce unstressed vowels to [ə] (the final sound in 'china') and generally to slur weak syllables. (Phonetic symbols are enclosed within square brackets; Appendix B contains a table illustrating their use.) Another major problem is the differences in pronunciation between the various parts of the English-speaking world. It is known that Tennyson retained a Lincolnshire accent but, on the other hand, he wrote for the educated British public, and I therefore propose to assume English Received Pronunciation in my analyses.

We may approach the general phonic background of *In Memoriam* by dividing effects of sound into the horizontal and the vertical. Horizontal patterns (which I shall consider first) occur within the line; vertical patterns have their most evident effect over several lines. Though I had long been conscious of the operation of sound in Tennyson's verse, I was amazed, on close inspection, by the high degree of organization. The number of horizontal patterns of assonance possible is strictly limited (as a rule there are only four syllables available), yet Tennyson sometimes manages to involve all four—most commonly in an *abab* formation:

As h*i*s unl*i*keness f*i*tted m*i*ne   (lxxix)

And p*a*rt it, g*i*ving h*a*lf to h*i*m.   (xxv)

We can see such a pattern in the making in section xl, where the line 'She *e*nters *o*ther r*e*alms of l*o*ve' originally read, 'She enters novel realms of love' (Trial Edition). The next most common horizontal assonantal pattern is *abba*:

Nor *a*ny w*a*nt-beg*o*tten r*e*st   (xxvii)

For ch*a*nges wr*ou*ght on f*o*rm and f*a*ce.   (lxxxii)

The Harvard manuscript has three versions of a line from section ix written over each other. The final version establishes an *abba* pattern, 'So dr*a*w him h*o*me to th*o*se that m*ou*rn', whereas the earlier attempts began, 'Draw thy dear freight' and 'Convoy thy charge'. Tennyson told Rawnsley that the line he was most glad to have written was 'The m*e*llow *ou*zel fl*u*ted in the *e*lm',[3] and this line has an *abba* assonantal pattern. Finally, there is *aabb*:

---

[3] H. D. Rawnsley, *Memories of the Tennysons* (Glasgow, 1900), p. 101.

> As drop by drop the water falls   (lviii)

> Be sometimes lovely like a bride.   (lix)

These symmetrical patterns occur surprisingly frequently. They carry horizontal assonance to its limit, and seem the more remarkable when we remember that rhyme is also involved and that there are many other examples where vowels are closely related though not identical. The effect is often further complicated by alliteration. Occasionally the consonants co-occur with the vowels, reinforcing the simple design:

> The *lips* of that Evange*list*;   (xxxi)

but more often they run counter:

> Or crush her, like a vice of blood.   (iii)

Here the vowel pattern is *abba*, but the consonants are in counter-point, for [k] appears only in the first two stressed syllables, [l] only in the second and fourth, and the closely related fricatives [s] and [ʃ] only in the third and first syllables. All three pairs of alliterating consonants oppose the pattern of the vowels: they make every connection but the one established by the assonance.

Sound patterns may consist entirely of alliteration, which is more common than assonance—presumably because there are more opportunities for it. There are usually only four stressed vowels in a line, but each of them can have several consonants on either side of it. This fact would also explain why alliteration is rarely exactly balanced—'His *heavy-sh*otted *h*ammock-*sh*roud' (from section vi) is exceptional. It is also rather cumbrous, and Tennyson much prefers the interweaving effect of a reversal in the order of the consonants or of their position in the syllable:

> And *st*ill as va*st*er grew the shore   (ciii)

> But I re*m*ain'*d*, whose hopes were *d*i*m*,
>   Whose *l*ife, whose *th*oughts were *l*ittle wor*th*   (lxxxv)

> When the blood *creeps*, and the nerve*s prick*.   (l)

In the first example [st] is placed first at the beginning and then at the end of the stress; in the second, [m] and [d] recur in reverse order, and though [l] twice holds the same position in the syllable, [θ] is first initial and then final; and in the third example, if we allow for the close relationship of the sounds [s] and [z], the consonants [k, r, p, s-z] occur at the end of the line in exactly the opposite order to that in which they appeared in the middle. Horizontal patterns (to summarize) sometimes consist of vowel patterns which involve all the stressed syllables, and more frequently of consonant patterns, which are usually more subtle. The horizontal examples are fairly obvious, and Tennyson more often selects vertical correspondences. Though less obtrusive, they take us to the heart of the characteristic sound of *In Memoriam*. They are handled with the greatest delicacy, and show quite incredible skill on Tennyson's part.

My first example is the fourth stanza of section lii; the stressed vowels are abstracted on the right:

> 'So fret not, like an idle girl,   [e ai ai ə:
>   That life is dash'd with flecks of sin.   ai æ e i
>   Abide: thy wealth is gather'd in,   ai e æ i
>   When Time hath sunder'd shell from pearl.' ai ʌ e ə:]

Apart from the rhymes, twelve vowels are stressed: [ai] occurs in each line (twice in the first), [e] in each line, [æ] in each of the centre lines, and [ʌ], the only vowel not used more than once, in the last line. Looking at the alliteration, we might begin with the second line, whose stressed consonants may be transcribed:

> [lf dʃt flks sn].

This series accounts for almost every stressed consonant in the stanza, with the following exceptions: [g] occurs in the first and third lines; [θ] and [ð] occur in the third line ('weal*th*, ga*th*er'd') but are similar and may be taken together; [m] is in line four, but is closely related to [n]; [b] and [p] (lines three and four) are also similar; and [r] and [w] occur once each. Allowing for the sounds that are closely related, we find that though there are 36 stressed consonants in the stanza, only about a dozen different ones are involved. The ratio of vowels is similar.

Vertical patterns almost always run over one stanza only. Section lxvi provides a further example:

> The shade by which my life was crost,   [ei i ai ɔ
>   Which makes a desert in the mind,   ei e   ai
>   Has made me kindly with my kind,   ei ai   ai
>   And like to him whose sight is lost.   ai i ai ɔ]

If we except the rhyme vowels (one of which coincides with one of the vowels in the remaining pattern), we find [ai] in lines 1, 3 and 4 (twice); [ei] in lines 1, 2, and 3; and [i] in the first and last, with one occurrence of [e] left over. Turning to the consonants, the first line runs:

[ʃd wtʃ lf krst].

Only [f] does not reappear: the line contains every other consonant in the stanza (taking [ʃ, s, z], together) except [r], [h] and [w], which occur once each, and [m] and [n] which are frequent in the other three lines. Once again the sound structure of the stanza is highly patterned, but in a very subtle way. It is not a matter of obvious repetition of one or two vowels or consonants, but of limitation to a relatively large group of sounds which is, however, hardly at any point overstepped.

One more example may make it plain that deliberate artistry is involved here. A comparison of the first reading of section xxix in the Trinity manuscript with the final version shows that horizontal patterning was sacrificed for vertical in a most decisive way. Here is the eventual complete stanza:

> With such compelling cause to grieve
> As daily vexes household peace,
> And chains regret to his decease,
> How dare we keep our Christmas-eve.

Now follows the draft version:

> My sister with such cause to grieve
> As that which drains our days of peace
> And fetters thought to his decease—
> How dare we keep our Christmas-Eve?

The difference between the assonantal patterns in the two versions is not particularly great, but the revision does tend to spread them vertically. We lose the [ei] repeat from the second line, but we have instead one in the second and one in the third; [ɔ:] now comes only once; one of the three [i] sounds disappears; but we find three occurrences of [e] instead of one. The alliteration shows more clearly the additional patterning which the change brings about. The horizontal [d] linkage is lost from the second line, but *every one* of the stressed consonants in the replacement words is repeated in the surrounding, unchanged words. In the deleted parts, on the other hand, there were five consonants which had no partner in the stanza. Moreover, in the draft version there were two consonants outside the words subsequently altered which were not repeated, but after the revision all these are paired. To sum up, in the early stanza there were seven consonants which appeared only once and eight which were repeated, whereas in the revised stanza none is used only once, and eleven occur two or more times.

Vertical patterns are the most important feature of the sound level of the language of *In Memoriam*. The stanzas I have chosen are more extreme than most of the poem, but the general tendency they exemplify is present throughout. The technique consists of drawing almost exclusively upon a group of vowels and consonants, each item of which is used between two and four times. This is in strong contrast to the effect Oras observed in Spenser's poetry. There a couple of consonants are taken up and used repeatedly both horizontally and vertically, often in pairs and at the beginnings of words (where they are most prominent). Tennyson's repetitions are from within a larger group of sounds, but he uses fewer vowels and consonants from outside that group. The result is less overall variety of sounds, but also less concentration on one or two. At the same time, Tennyson often confines his patterns to the vertical direction, where they are far less obvious; on the whole his verse does not impress the reader with the pyrotechnical effect which Oras demonstrates in Spenser. I think it will be agreed that the stanzas chosen to illustrate vertical patterns are not at all among those which one would turn to as virtuoso pieces. The patterns do not demand attention, but they work just the same, surreptitiously controlling the range of sounds we absorb.

The most apparent effect of sound patterning of this kind is the continuous smooth flow which is characteristic of so much of Tennyson's writing. Within a stanza we return to the same sound several times, instead of being surprised with something new. It is well known that Tennyson wished to avoid clashing sibilants in his verse[4]—in the Trial Edition is the line, 'That crash'd the glass and smote the floor', but this finally became, 'That crash'd the glass and *beat* the floor '(lxxxvii). The avoidance of harsh sibilants combines with the vertical patterns to produce a pervasive mellifluous sound

[4] See Hallam Tennyson, *Memoir*, II, 14 and 286, and Knowles, 'Aspects of Tennyson', p. 182.

base in the poem—we can see the same effect being created when we notice that in about one in twelve stanzas all four rhyme words assonate. This mellifluous sound seems perfectly appropriate to the elegiac subject of *In Memoriam*. We move gently through the succession of words, compelled to slacken the pace of reading by the return of the sound upon itself, aware always that the language is claiming unusual significance by its high degree of structure. I will return to the point in the next chapter, for rhythm also contributes to the subdued and weighty tone which permeates *In Memoriam*.

Tennyson's frequent use of sound patterning and preference for vertical effects fits exactly with other 'classical' aspects of his language. On the one hand, it is unobtrusive and rarely forces its way to the reader's attention; on the other, it is highly wrought and gives the poem a persistent air of artificiality. We observed the same paradox in the syntax of *In Memoriam*. Tennyson does not often (or only in the sections at highest tension) do things with sound which would be completely unexpected in prose; yet, at the same time, the sound is *never* quite the same as in ordinary language, and in fact seems distinct from any other in English. At all times the sound is arranged so as to make us conscious that it is, after all, a poem which we are reading, even though we may be unable to say just where this impression derives from. In *In Memoriam* Tennyson has a basic sound which is entirely his own and which rarely fails him. It continues throughout, whatever the changes on the other levels of language and theme. It thus functions as a major factor in the unity of the poem; there must be high and low points, but the basic stylization of sound continues throughout.

For some readers the assiduously maintained ordering of sounds will seem irritating and perhaps soporific, but it makes its own contribution to poetic structure, for it is a powerful agent in the poem's unique atmosphere, and provides an ever varying background for its meaning. As Wordsworth said of rhythm in the Preface to *Lyrical Ballads*, sound patterns give the mind pleasure 'from the perception of similitude in dissimilitude'. As the thoughts and feelings expressed change from line to line and section to section, the sound organization remains constant in nature, though its surface varies continuously. This, however, is the least of the claims that can be made for the use of sound in *In Memoriam*. A result of the background of which I have been speaking is the creation in the reader of that state of excited receptivity which seems necessary in poetry as a jumping-off point for more adventurous effects. It is to such effects that I turn now.

'I think myself [sound's] most important mode of action is to connect two words by similarity of sound so that you are made to think of their possible connections'.[5] Discussion of Tennyson's expressive use of sound is often limited to rather obvious onomatopoeia— innumerable bees in immemorial elms, and so on. In *In Memoriam* we find little of this, but a lot of the more subtle usage referred to by Professor Empson. On occasion it works quite simply, as in one line of section v: 'In words, like weeds, I'll wrap me o'er'. The simile declares that words and weeds are alike, and sound supports the contention.

The effect occurs wholesale in the last stanza of section xviii:

> That *dies* not, but en*dures* with pain,
> And slowly *form*s the *firm*er mind,
> Treasuring the look it cannot find,
> The *word*s that are not *heard* again.

In the first line the contrast between the poet's alternative courses, to die or to endure, is pointed up by the similarity in sound; in the second the connection between 'forms' and 'firmer' seems to suggest his determination to hold on to a balanced outlook; but in the fourth line the hyperbolic intensity of the sound echo in 'words' and 'heard' helps to communicate the poet's yearning for his friend's voice. This section is important because the ship carrying Hallam's remains has at last arrived, and it can no longer serve as a focus for the poet's grief. The attitude he adopts at this point must be crucial, and the emphasis deriving from the repetitions of sound helps to make it clearer. In the first two lines the sound linkages stress the poet's resolution to embrace a calmer state of mind, but in the last we are made to understand that he is still fundamentally backward looking.

Sound follows the stages of the poet's thought even more precisely in this example from the Prologue:

> Forgive these wild and wandering cries,
> Confusions of a wasted youth;
> Forgive them where they fail in truth,
> And in thy wisdom make me wise.

---

[5] Empson, *Seven Types of Ambiguity*, p. 12; cf. Sebeok (ed.), *Style in Language*, pp. 371–2.

There are several sound linkages here which emphasize the connections made by meaning. We may notice the assonance of 'wild' and 'cries' and of 'Confusions' and 'youth', the alliteration of 'Confusions' and 'fail', and the double relationship of 'wasted youth' and 'fail in truth'. But the main movement concerns [w], which is set firmly in our minds by 'wild and wandering'. This phrase is summed up and evaluated in the next line by 'wasted', but by the end of the stanza there is a further transition to 'wisdom-wise'. The early uses of the consonant are superseded, even as the poet's former folly may be replaced by a greater sagacity. At each stage of the argument we find [w]; it charts the movement of ideas from the poet's past to his prayer for the future.

The most prominent sound connections are made by rhyme, which occupies the most conspicuous syllables in the stanza. Tennyson's rhymes are often far more than a compelled adherence to the demands of the stanza form, for he manages to fill them with words of key importance to the thought: in section lvi he asks 'shall man',

> Who trusted God was love indeed
> And love Creation's final law—
> Tho' Nature, red in tooth and claw
> With ravine, shriek'd against his creed—
>
> Who loved, who suffer'd countless ills,
> Who battled for the True, the Just,
> Be blown about the desert dust,
> Or seal'd within the iron hills?

In the first stanza 'law' and 'claw' are juxtaposed, the first representing an ordered state of affairs, the second the bestiality which opposes it; the second pair of middle lines contrasts one of man's highest ideals with the futile dust to which he must come ('trust' and 'dust' in xxxv are similar). The outer rhymes of this stanza set the thousand natural shocks that flesh is heir to against the rigidly unsympathetic 'iron hills'; and in the first stanza one may even claim that the rhyme releases the underlying meaning 'in deed', so as to oppose man's theory about God with his actions in the world.

There are very many examples of this meaningful use of rhyme—we think of 'strife' and 'life' in section l, or 'grope' and 'hope' in lv. Tennyson uses several times the combination 'breath—death', which contains, at first sight at least, an absolute opposition. But when the poet is most pessimistic they are represented as not really distinct for life and death seem all one to Nature: 'I bring to life, I bring to death: / The spirit does but mean the breath' (lvi). The difference is wiped out in another way in section lxviii: 'Sleep, Death's twin-brother, times my breath; / Sleep, Death's twin-brother, knows not Death'. Sleep enables the poet to escape from reality, prefiguring the exaltation to a higher plane of being which the vision ultimately brings. In the second half of the poem the group of meanings around 'breath-death' undergoes a major change, for 'breath' comes to signify the accession of a new, more spiritual life, rather than just the intake of air which maintains physical existence. In section lxxxvi the wind is asked to blow

> The fever from my cheek, and sigh
> The full new life that feeds thy breath
> Throughout my frame, till Doubt and Death,
> Ill brethren, let the fancy fly . . .

By the agency of this higher breath, death can be overcome. So, in section cxxii, he desires that his blood

> Be quicken'd with a livelier breath,
> And like an inconsiderate boy,
> As in the former flash of joy,
> I slip the thoughts of life and death.

The rhyme emphasizes the key terms in the poet's position, and binds together—in different ways according to his state of mind—the paradoxically related constituents of his thought.

The power of sound to suggest or reinforce connections between words may be illustrated once more from section xix. The tidal movement of the Severn in the Wye is compared to fluctuations in the poet's grief, and the key words in the section are '*fill*' and '*fall*'. When the river 'fills' (line 5) the Wye is silent: so is the poet, 'When fill'd with tears that cannot fall' (11). But as the tide flows down again, the poet's 'deeper anguish also falls' (15), and he, like the water, is vocal. The words 'fill' and 'fall' are important for three movements which criss-cross each other in this section:

1. By their similar sounds the two words reinforce the metaphor linking the poet and the river—they are, in fact, examples of the blurring of literal and figurative elements which I discussed in the previous chapter. The alliteration makes these key terms more

prominent; 'fall' is never actually used of the water, but since it obviously could be and it is connected with 'fill', we tend to transfer it so that it applies to both. Thus we are made to link the poet and the river indirectly in a way which supports the more overt combination created by the metaphor.

2. The two words sound similar, but in fact they signify opposing states in the river and the poet. When they are filled there is no falling, and *vice versa*. In this case the sound link points up a contrast; it does not run parallel with the first movement, but intersects with it repeatedly, for both poet and river both fill and fall.

3. By their repetition over eleven lines the two words point up the temporal progression in the argument. In stanzas two and three we are told about when the river/poet is filled and water is not falling; in stanza four further information about what happens when falling does occur is added. The alliteration runs through both these accounts, binding them together and yet strengthening our sense of their difference. This again cuts across movement one, for first we learn about poet and river when they are full, and then when they fall; and it cuts across movement two because first there is filling and no falling, and then there is falling and no filling.

The sound link, then, functions here in three ways: it strengthens the metaphor, highlights the key aspects of the poet's two contrasting states of mind, and marks out the sequence in which it is all presented. At each [f, l] alliteration all three movements intersect, and each of them takes a step in its own direction. Yet all directions are ultimately the same, for the whole process is fully worked out by the end of the section. None of the movements I have been describing was created by sound—they could each work fairly well without the added linkage. But it is sound which unites the three in one structure over and above the theme of the section—in fact, it creates the kind of delicately inter-related texture which was advanced in the previous chapter as a feature of Tennyson's imagery. Sound is capable of much more than the euphonious background which is sometimes taken as Tennyson's sole aim, although it should not be forgotten that the persistent basic patterning alerts the reader to the more individual effects I have been examining.

I believe that the effects which I have so far claimed for sound in *In Memoriam* are, in principle at least, quite acceptable. Associations with states of feeling founded upon qualities supposedly adherent in the sounds themselves are more controversial—the familiar argument points out that although little, tiddly, miniature, diminutive, trivial, and so on contain high front vowels and suggest smallness, 'big' also constains such a vowel. Nevertheless, one of the distinctive excellences which Hallam claimed for Tennyson's poetry was the 'exquisite modulation of harmonious words and cadences to the swell and fall of the feelings expressed'; indeed, he went so far as to assert that Dante and Petrarch 'produce two-thirds of their effect by *sound*', which alone is able to render 'innumerable shades of fine emotion in the human heart'.[6] And it does seem that there is a difference—which is not entirely a matter of meaning—between the Harvard manuscript 'dripping' and the published 'drizzling' in the lines, 'And ghastly thro' the drizzling rain / On the bald street breaks the blank day' (vii). The less abrupt (or so it seems) sound, in conjunction with 'ghastly' and 'street', is more suggestive of the poet's desolate feelings.

I think that there is a connection between some sounds and some meanings. It seems that, within a given speech community (in a hot country drizzle would be very welcome), people have become accustomed to regard certain combinations of sounds as warm, hard, fluid and so on. There may be no logical basis to the practice in semantics or phonology, but it is something that happens. It is disputable how far these associations can operate without the support of meaning, but the issue is not very important in a study of poetic language. Perhaps we would not find [zl] depressing outside the word 'drizzle', but the mutual reinforcement, whereby we think the scene gloomy, then notice the sound, then think it even more gloomy, is a perfectly valid procedure—and, I would say, basic to the way poetic structure functions in many of its aspects. Thus it is beside the point that there are exceptions to any 'rule' we might attempt to construct for the relations between sound and meaning: as Whorf says, we probably only perceive such links when the connection is appropriate.[7] The pattern-making faculty, which causes us to fail to notice a misprint when the word remains generally clear, promotes to our attention only those features which are relevant and ignores those which add nothing to our final overall impression.

[6] Motter, *The Writings of Arthur Hallam*, pp. 191, 194.
[7] Benjamin Lee Whorf, *Language, Thought and Reality*, ed. John B. Carroll (paperback, Cambridge, Mass., 1964), p. 267. For full discussion of the whole issue, cf. Dell Hymes in *Language and Style*, ed. Sebeok, pp. 110–16, and J. R. Firth, 'Modes of Meaning', *Essays and Studies*, new series, IV (1951), 123.

If we grant that sound—in propitious circumstances—may evoke meanings, we are nevertheless left with the problem of identifying which sounds are responsible for an effect. It may well be pointless to claim that a passage contains a significant amount of [n] or [t] when these consonants are probably the most common in the language,[8] though one might also argue that when reading (and particularly, perhaps, when reading poetry) one is most acutely conscious of the immediate context, and a lot of [n] is felt absolutely as just that. The safest method is to work through comparisons, for then it should be possible to isolate significant differences without becoming involved in vast statistical surveys.

I described in Chapter VII how Tennyson uses natural imagery to communicate the poet's mood, and we might expect that the delicately evocative agency of sound would be of great assistance in the task of rendering concrete the emotions. In section lxxii the dim dawn is a correlative for the poet's distraction on the anniversary of Hallam's death:

> And howlest, issuing out of night,
> With blasts that blow the poplar white,
> And lash with storm the streaming pane?

The blustering violence of the storm is suggested by the repetition of the heavy and clashing consonant clusters [st] and [bl] and the hostile-seeming sibilants. Here are the equivalent lines from the second anniversary (xcix):

> So loud with voices of the birds,
> So thick with lowings of the herds,
> Day, when I lost the flower of men.

The initial clusters have almost gone, and there is a big contrast in the proportions of voiced and unvoiced consonants among the plosives and fricatives in stressed syllables (these terms are illustrated in Appendix B). In lxxii there are two voiced and sixteen unvoiced; in xcix there are eight voiced and seven unvoiced (and that is without counting 'of' in the first two lines, where it is only weakly stressed). This difference seems to be felt in a contrast between a roughness and a mellowness of tone in the two passages: the second anniversary murmurs to the poet 'A song that slights the coming care', and is by no means so discordant in mood.

[8] Cf. Sebeok (ed.), *Style in Language*, pp. 344–5.

M

The manuscripts sometimes provide useful comparative material—consider the first stanza of section lxxxvi, where the poet begins to invoke the breeze which breathes new life into him:

> Sweet after showers, *ambrosial* air,
>> That rollest from the gorgeous gloom
>> Of evening over brake and bloom
> And meadow.

If Tennyson had left 'delicious' (Lincoln manuscript) in the first line, the balance of our impressions would be tipped towards the sibilants of 'Sweet' and 'showers' and the high front vowels of 'Sweet' and 'evening'. 'Ambrosial' establishes the dominance of the full, rounded sound of voiced consonants and back vowels by giving support to phrases like 'gorgeous gloom' and 'brake and bloom'. These seem to express better the fruitfulness of the experience and the deep satisfaction it brings.

The mood is again happy at the end of section lxxi, but this scene is recalled from the past in a dream and is gentler in tone than the immediate experience of the previous example. Hallam and the poet walked

> Beside the river's wooded reach,
>> The fortress, and the mountain ridge,
>> The cataract flashing from the bridge,
> The breaker breaking on the beach.

Syntax and rhythm evidently contribute to the equilibrium of the description, but the gentle sound transitions are also important. The earlier version in the Trinity manuscript shows Tennyson moving towards this: the middle two lines once ran,

> The meadow set with summer flags,
> The cataract clashing from the crags.

The rough clusters of [kl], [gz] and [kr] give way in the published version to the milder sounds in 'flashing' and 'bridge'. The change in rhyme words is also valuable, for it brings about a very near identity in all four rhymes. Their vowels are the short and long manifestations of the same basic sound, their initial consonants are all made up of [b] and [r], and their final consonants are the two affricates, voiced and unvoiced. It seems almost unnecessary to detail the sounds which unite to such an obviously euphonious effect. This could not be the

scene of an unpleasant experience; all elements in the language combine to suggest flawless contentment.

In the first part of this chapter I showed that Tennyson is usually
concerned to create mellifluous sound patterns, but a corollary is
that he is able to make a greater effect with jarring sounds when they
are appropriate for the poet's mood. Section cvii is a particularly
effective example of this, for the first part describes a winter's day,
cold and bleak:

> Fiercely flies
> The blast of North and East, and ice
> Makes daggers at the sharpen'd eaves,
>
> And bristles all the brakes and thorns
> To yon hard crescent, as she hangs
> Above the wood which grides and clangs
> Its leafless ribs and iron horns
>
> Together, in the drifts that pass
> To darken on the rolling brine
> That breaks the coast.

We hear a succession of harsh, grating sounds, unvoiced plosives and
fricatives, often in ugly clusters such as [st, ks, fts]. Only towards the
close of the extract does the tone begin to mellow, as the poet's
imagination moves away from the immediate external scene to the
ocean (which is no longer a focus of alarm in the poem). His mood is
becoming calmer, and he turns to the events inside the room, where
all is warm and cheerful round the blazing fire. The contrast is
expressed in the sound:

> But fetch the wine,
> Arrange the board and brim the glass;
>
> Bring in great logs and let them lie,
> To make a solid core of heat;
> Be cheerful-minded, talk and treat
> Of all things ev'n as he were by.

The vowels are not of markedly different types, but the distribu-
tion of consonants shows a majority of unvoiced plosives and fricatives (which I take to have the colder and bleaker sound) in the
earlier part of the first passage, and a predominance of the softest and

warmest consonants, continuants and non-fricatives ([m, n, w, r, l]) in the second passage. The difference would not, perhaps, be significant did the meaning not suggest it, but much depends also upon the exact placing of the sounds. The proportion of clusters is higher in the earlier passage and they more often involve unvoiced consonants, and this seems to add to the prominence of the rasping sounds; conversely, [l] in the fourth line from the end is highlighted by its frequency within a few syllables. The warmth of the family circle—even as if Hallam were there—despite the uncompromising rigour of nature, is the point of the section; the vivid account of the weather sets off the poet's mood of contentment. The expressiveness of sound combines with carefully chosen descriptive detail to provide a powerful objectification of the poet's feelings.

I hope to have shown that Tennyson is as skilful at suggesting mood by the use of sound as he is with other types of sound-meaning relationship. This aspect of language is one with few secure guidelines laid down by previous criticism, and we do not really know very much about the relationship between sound and sense. Tennyson in bursts of inspiration wrote lines where we suspect the importance of sound, but we can only plod clumsily along in the rear of his intuitive feel for the appropriate language.

X

RHYTHM: NORMS AND VARIATIONS

In 1857 Coventry Patmore wrote an article in which he asserted that certain rhythmic forms are intrinsically solemn or high spirited. Tennyson in a letter contradicted each of Patmore's statements in turn by altering his examples so that they display the opposite qualities.[1] The incident forms a useful introduction to this chapter, for it shows Tennyson's skill and interest in the topic, but at the same time warns us of the dangers of rash assumptions about the properties of rhythm.

Any study of the subject must first of all recognize the distinction between metre and rhythm. *Metre* is a stress pattern which we abstract from the whole poem and which we feel is there, underneath, throughout; *rhythm* is the sequence of stresses exhibited by any particular passage as a result of the interaction between metre and the stresses the words would receive in prose.[2] The nature of the English language obliges us to stress (partly according to their context) some words and not others. When this requirement is in line with the demands of the metre, then metre and rhythm coincide; but very often they conflict, and as we read we are conscious of the pull between the two systems.

Just what rhythm consists of—what stress *is*—has not been fully explained.[3] It seems that a number of factors are involved in our identification of a 'di-dum' rhythm in such a line as 'And faintly trust the larger hope' (lv). Indeed, properly speaking we should not use the term 'stress' at all for this phenomenon, but since it is traditional in literary criticism and not likely here to lead to confusion I propose to retain it. Linguists have suggested, moreover, that we should recognize not just 'di-dum', but three or four degrees of stress in English. At first sight this would seem to overturn completely more traditional attitudes to metrics, but English metre in fact requires us to perceive only the distinction between stressed and unstressed: it

---

[1] Hallam Tennyson, *Memoir*, I, 469–70.
[2] See Sebeok (ed.), *Style in Language*, pp. 178–81; John Thompson, *The Founding of English Metre* (London, 1961), p. 6; and Seymour Chatman, *A Theory of Meter* (The Hague, 1965), pp. 95–6.
[3] For a full discussion see Chatman, *A Theory of Meter*.

depends, as Wimsatt and Beardsley point out, 'not on any kind of absolute, or very strong stress, but merely on a relative degree of stress—on a certain moreness of stress in certain positions'.[4] Thus a 'stressed' syllable in one line may, when measured on a sound spectrograph, be physically weaker than an 'unstressed' syllable in another line, but the first item of interest is whether the syllable which occurs where we expect 'dum' is stronger than the syllables on either side of it, where we expect 'di'. If it is, then the metre is confirmed; if not, the metre is violated. The strength of the syllables in themselves (and the question is complicated because the context is important) must also be influential at some level of our awareness, but at the moment it does not seem possible to say very much about the nature of this influence.

The functions of metre and its interactions with speech rhythms are also in dispute. It is generally agreed that a writer may gain expressive effects by counterpointing the two—we experience a 'dum' where we expected a 'di' and the syllable is thrown into prominence (as with sound, our interpretation of such an event will be by no means independent of meaning). I argued in Chapter I that the essential feature of poetic language is the degree of structuring it exhibits over and above the semantic and syntactic congruity which we expect in ordinary language. Metre is one way of creating such intensity of patterning, for it superimposes on the usual sequence of sounds a whole additional system of correspondences which forms complex and varying relationships with other elements in the structure. But the pull between metre and rhythm may also have value in itself. Thus Wimsatt and Beardsley write that it produces 'contours of tension so special as perhaps better not translated into any other kind of meaning but simply regarded as shapes of energy', Thompson claims that in metre we enjoy the experience of language imitating and perfecting itself, and Abercrombie insists that when reading poetry we undergo contractions of the breathing muscles which arouse 'phonetic empathy' with the writer.[5]

It is also often suggested that metre and rhythm excite the reader into a particularly receptive condition where he is the more ready to

[4] W. K. Wimsatt, Jr., and Monroe C. Beardsley, 'The Concept of Metre', *PMLA*, LXXIV (1959), p. 591; and see the discussion in Sebeok (ed.), *Style in Language*, pp. 197–209.
[5] Wimsatt and Beardsley, 'The Concept of Metre', p. 597; Thompson, *The Founding of English Metre*, pp. 9–12; and David Abercrombie, *Studies in Linguistics and Phonetics* (London, 1965), pp. 17–20.

perceive the densely worked fabric of poetic structure; they set poetry apart from other linguistic events and promote in us a state of readiness for whatever heightened uses of language the poem may exhibit in its other elements.[6]

With these considerations in mind I propose first to attempt to identify the norms of the rhythm of *In Memoriam*, with a view to assessing their contribution to the characteristic tone of the poem and arriving at a position where we can recognize variations from the norm; then I will consider some examples of such variations.

I distinguish three dominant features in the rhythm of *In Memoriam*: its smoothness, its slowness, and its characteristic cadence.

The iambic four-stress line constitutes the basic metre of *In Memoriam*; it is grouped into stanzas of four lines rhyming in an *abba* sequence. When we have said this we have only just begun, however. One factor of interest is how frequently the norm is confirmed or violated. With this in mind I examined 400 lines (more than an eighth of the poem); the most striking result was the large proportion of lines which confirmed the metre. Half the lines contained four stresses, and in 160 cases they fell in complete accord with the metre:

> My lóve invólves the lóve befóre;
> My lóve is váster pássion nów;
> Tho' míx'd with Gód and Náture thóu,
> I seém to lóve thee móre and móre.   (cxxx)

As Wimsatt and Beardsley point out, some deviations are so frequent as to hardly count as such, and amongst these we must include stress on the first syllable of the line instead of the second, and stress on both the first two sylllables. Even more common (131 occurrences) was the three stress line which was regular except for a weakness where there should be a stress:

> Thou stándest in the rísing sún.   (cxxx)

Here, as Wimsatt and Beardsley again suggest, we are still very close to the metre, for the strength of the regular organization is such that we are inclined to absorb 'in' into the metrical system by weighting it more heavily than we would in prose, because it is in a position

---

[6] Cf. Chatman, *A Theory of Meter*, pp. 210–11; Middleton Murry, *The Problem of Style*, pp. 110–11; and Reuben A. Brower, *The Fields of Light* (New York 1951), p. 58.

where we expect a stress—'The precise measurement tilts and juggles the little accents into place, establishing their occurrence as a regular part of all that is going on'.[7] Taking together all these patterns which are on or close to the metre gives a total of 82 per cent of the lines, a high degree of regularity.

This closeness of many lines to the metre helps to give *In Memoriam* a smooth-flowing rhythm, but the use of pauses is also important. Taking the pause as signified by a punctuation mark, I found that only 126 of the 400 lines considered contained an internal pause, and a quarter of the stanzas had no pause at all other than at line ends. The pause, then, is not generally a strong disruptive influence. When it does occur, moroever, it very often comes between feet rather than in the middle of them; quite frequently it is in the exact centre of the line:

> Far off thou art, but ever nigh;
> I have thee still, and I rejoice.   (cxxx)

We can see that this smoothness was Tennyson's deliberate aim from the fact that the early editions used a large number of exclamation marks, which were later removed and replaced by the weaker comma. Pauses at the ends of lines, on the other hand, occur in three-quarters of the sample:

> Thy voice is on the rolling air;
> I hear thee where the waters run;
> Thou standest in the rising sun,
> And in the setting thou art fair.   (cxxx)

As a result, the line is usually relatively self-contained from a syntactic point of view, and the rhythm is not disturbed by run-ons. The significance of this feature can best be seen in comparison with one of the few wholesale violations of the practice:

> And gathering freshlier overhead,
> Rock'd the full-foliaged elms, and swung
> The heavy-folded rose, and flung
> The lilies to and fro, and said . . .   (xcv)

In general the *In Memoriam* line moves smoothly through its eight syllables and then comes to rest before starting again on a very similar movement. This close adherence to a smooth basic metrical

---

[7] 'The Concept of Metre', p. 592. Cf. Chatman, *A Theory of Meter*, pp. 97, 125–6 and 139.

pattern is what we should expect when we have seen that Tennyson avoids startling the reader in so many other features of his language. These findings are generally similar to those of Pyre, who remarked in Tennyson's revisions of his early poetry 'his consistent standardizing of language and verse, while securing with the simpler and more conventional means an augmentation of the stylistic and metrical effect at which he had originally aimed'.[8]

The second feature of the rhythm which I distinguish is the slow and weighty reading which *In Memoriam* usually seems to demand. W. P. Ker observed how in 'Mariana' and Tennyson's subsequent poetry 'the short line is here made weighty and solemn, nearly the equal of the heroic line.'[9] This results in part from the persistent sound patterning which I discussed in the previous chapter, for it makes us linger on the syllables to obtain the full value of their relations with each other. The fact that many lines are close to the metre is also relevant, for it makes them fall with a ponderous regularity, avoiding the effect of an unusual line like 'Púll sídeways, and the dáisy clóse' (lxxii), where the first two stresses hurry in before expected, and we therefore skip over the three light syllables that follow them.

The most important item tending towards a slow rhythm is probably the high proportion of monosyllables. The following figures will make clear this predominance: out of 720 lines, 107 had 8 monosyllables; 264 had 6; 310 had 5, 4 and 3; 26 had 2; and 13 had one or none. In fact, just over half the lines contained six or eight monosyllables (this is what we might expect in view of the tendency, discussed in Chapter III, towards simple diction). A line of monosyllables is likely to contain more stresses than one of polysyllables. Northrop Frye remarks: 'We notice that the slower the rhythm is, the more stressed monosyllables there are, and in so heavily stressed a language as English, the longer Latin words have the effect of lightening the rhythm by a series of unstressed syllables'.[10] Out of 400 lines of *In Memoriam* about half had four stresses and another 60 had five or six: the high number of stresses makes us read more slowly (compare the Shakespearean blank verse line, which characteristically contains *fewer* stresses than the metrical five). It also seems to be the case that monosyllables tend to employ more consonants than an equivalent number of polysyllables, and words

---

[8] *The Formation of Tennyson's Style*, p. 86.   [9] *Collected Essays*, I, 264.
[10] Frye (ed.) *Sound and Poetry*, p. xviii; cf. Chatman, *A Theory of Meter*, pp. 123–4.

containing groups of consonants take longer to say than those without. There is interesting confirmatory evidence for this in Oras' count of consonant clusters in Spenser and Milton,[11] for Tennyson has 12 per cent more of them. Here, then, is a further factor in the slow rhythm of *In Memoriam*.

Both the smoothness and the slowness seem perfectly appropriate to their elegiac subject—remembering that they are only the norms providing the dominant atmosphere, and Tennyson is able to reverse them when the sense requires. They also contribute to a character-istic cadence in *In Memoriam*, a kind of dying fall. Wimsatt and Beardsley have noticed this, and they suggest a further cause:

> Maybe some of the languor and soft drag of Tennyson's verse, for instance, comes sometimes from the interplay between the rising iambic motion of the line and the falling trochaic character of a series of important words.[12]

There seems to be a lot in this. Comparison with *Paradise Lost*, *An Essay on Criticism* and *The Prelude* shows that *In Memoriam* has many more instances of two-syllabled words spanning feet as opposed to being contained in them. Sometimes a whole line will have this arrangement of word and stress: 'The wizard lightnings deeply glow' (cxxii). The foot comes to a peak on its second syllable, but when a word runs over into the next foot the reader, instead of start-ing the metrical movement completely afresh, must drop away from the peak as he finishes the word—which therefore seems to trail off, so contributing to the characteristic dying fall.

Another relevant factor can be seen by following Professor Oras in *Sound and Poetry*. He counted the consonant clusters in a selection from Spenser and Milton, and compared the two poets from the point of view of whether such clusters occurred more often at the begin-nings or ends of stressed syllables, and, correspondingly, whether stressed syllables predominantly began or ended with vowels. Finding that Spenser preferred to begin syllables with consonants and end them with vowels, whilst Milton was the opposite, Oras concluded:

> The contrast, reduced to its essentials, then, is: in Spenser, a vigorous initial consonantal effect followed by weakened consonantism or none—decresendo; in Milton, an unobtrusive beginning followed by a strong consonantal finale—crescendo.[13]

11 In Frye (ed.), *Sound and Poetry*, p. 111; cf. Chatman, *A Theory of Meter*, pp. 198–9.
12 'The Concept of Metre', p. 597.
13 In Frye (ed.), *Sound and Poetry*, p. 112.

In Memoriam proves to be very close to Spenser in this matter, in spite of the fact that Tennyson does not make two syllables out of words like 'crowned' as Spenser does, but allows a consonant cluster in such cases. This 'decrescendo' is surely related to the dying fall which I have identified. Plosive consonants in particular cut off the sound with a definite abruptness at the end of a syllable, whereas an open vowel may be prolonged as we choose, so that the word fades away, as it were, into the distance. Oras goes on to observe that 'the two methods are even more sharply contrasted in the line endings of the two poets' (p. 114), and this is true of Tennyson also: I found that of 720 final syllables, 186 began with clusters and 172 ended; 43 began with vowels and 166 ended. (The number of initial clusters may not seem significantly greater than the number of final ones but, as Oras says, the latter are more common in English.)

The tendency to begin stressed syllables with consonant clusters and end them with vowels contributes to *In Memoriam*'s characteristic cadence. The intensification of this feature at the ends of lines goes with the frequency with which end-stopping occurs (three-quarters of the lines), for this usually makes the reading voice drop, again producing a dying fall. The result of this combination is similar to that noticed by Graham Hough in 'Tears, Idle Tears':

> the end-sounds of the lines are not purely fortuitous; they are all
> either open vowels, or consonants or groups of consonants that can
> be prolonged in reading. The result is that each line is self-contained
> —yet does not end with a snap, but trails away, suggesting a passage
> into some infinite beyond.[14]

The effect cannot be quite the same in *In Memoriam* because rhyme is employed, but the fading out of syllables is a marked feature of line ends. It is also noticeable that whatever Tennyson does with stress and pause during the early part of the line, all is usually back to rights by the end (I found stress on the seventh syllable only three times in 400 lines; final stress failed only seven times).

The final feature which I have been able to identify as contributing to the dying fall is the *abba* rhyme scheme. I propose to discuss the *In Memoriam* stanza in full in a moment, and will therefore leave this point for now with Pyre's excellent description of the effect of the delayed fourth rhyme, 'which falls with a dimmed and mournful

---

[14] In Killham, *Critical Essays on the Poetry of Tennyson*, p. 188; the point is endorsed by Spitzer, in Killham, p. 195.

echo of the first, giving the entire rhyme music the effect of being conceived in a minor key, harmonising admirably with the tone of combined sadness and austerity.'[15] All these factors are involved in the creation of the dominant tone of *In Memoriam*, a tone which is exactly suited to its elegiac theme.

In general, then, the rhythm of *In Memoriam* stays close to the metre, and is distinguished by the slowness and smoothness of its movement. These factors and others contribute to a characteristic dying fall in the line, producing an elegiac tone. The fairly close adherence to metre is completely in accord with two of the persistent classical features of the poem's language, its superficial unremarkability and its stylization. On the one hand, the rhythm does not repeatedly startle the reader by violent disjunctions; on the other, its adherence to a regular pattern distinct from that of ordinary speech reminds the reader incessantly that what he is reading is an artifact. Seymour Chatman has shown[16] that in Donne's Satires II and IV and Pope's reworking of them, some 32 per cent of the Metaphysical Poet's lines are on or near the metre, whereas the corresponding figure for Pope is around 90 per cent. The 82 per cent I found for Tennyson is obviously much closer to the Enlightenment poet.

Yet to me the rhythm of *In Memoriam* rarely seems too monotonous, though I realize that it does to other people. This is plainly a matter of taste and, as Chatman points out,[17] the degree of regularity required has varied from period to period of English poetry. Tennyson's practice seems to have been in somewhat reluctant accord with Victorian theory; he observed, 'In a blank verse you can have from three up to eight beats; but if you vary the beats unusually, your ordinary newspaper critic sets up a howl'.[18] W. J. Fox, in a largely approving review of the 1830 volume, protested against Tennyson's 'irregulatities of measure':

> There are few variations of effect which a skilful artist cannot produce, if he will but take the pains,—without deviating from that regularity of measure which is one of the original elements of poetical enjoyment; made so by the tendency of the human frame to periodical movements; and the continued sacrifice of which is but ill compensated to the disappointed ear by any occasional, and not

[15] *The Formation of Tennyson's Style*, p. 186.
[16] In Sebeok (ed.), *Style in Language*, pp. 164–5.
[17] *A Theory of Meter*, p. 207.
[18] Hallam Tennyson, *Memoir*, II, 14.

otherwise attainable correspondence between the movement of a
verse and the sense which it is intended to convey.[19]

These quotations suggest a general swing, of the kind I posited in
Chapter II, back to classical qualities in poetry. The emphasis is on
order rather than expressiveness, on what is generally desirable
rather than on individual peculiarities.

Poetry which stays close to the metre will not be conspicuously
diverse, but it may nevertheless contain plenty of variety. We should
distinguish, as do Wimsatt and Beardsley, between deviations, which
occur relatively infrequently and which often stand in a special relation to the meaning of the line, and the constant tension between
metre and the actual stress the words call for.[20] The minutest of
differences between degrees of stress and pause interact with the
metre, which admits only the distinction 'stressed/unstressed'. The
following lines never really contradict the metre, but they vary from
it in many different ways:

> Thy voice is on the rolling air;
>   I hear thee where the waters run;
>   Thou standest in the rising sun,
> And in the setting thou art fair.   (cxxx)

Each line has a weak foot, but though in the first three it is the
second ('on', 'where' and 'in'), line two seems to fail perceptibly less
than the other two on this point. Line four, on the other hand, is
weak in the first foot, so that it seems to form a fully rounded conclusion to the stanza, although the syntax is also very important here.
If we look at the syllables which should be weak according to the
requirements of the metre, we again find subtle differences. Both
'thee' in the second line and 'art' in the fourth seem in themselves
more deserving of stress than the prepositions I have already mentioned, and the result is a complex shuffling on the reader's part
between the claims of the metre and the prose sense. Or, looking at
the line ends, although there is a pause at each, the difference between
the semi-colons and the comma followed by 'And' causes us to
move over the line gaps in quite distinct ways. Although the stanza
generally confirms the metre, it does not follow it slavishly—and
this kind of delicate variation persists throughout *In Memoriam*.

[19] John D. Jump (ed.), *Tennyson, The Critical Heritage* (London, 1967), p. 32.
[20] 'The Concept of Metre', p. 596.

Before considering more spectacular deviations from the norm, I wish to say something about Tennyson's use of the *abba* rhyming stanza. It is well known that, though Tennyson thought he had invented this unusual form, it had in fact already been employed by seventeenth-century poets. The stanza is not only rare in itself; it is also remarkable to find such a simple structure used continuously in a long poem. Paul Goodman has described the strange effect this can cause:

> As the same pattern is repeated again and again, its succession to itself becomes more and more probable . . . the probability may seem, in a strange way, to be transmitted to the progressing action or the ongoing thought, with a powerful increase of feeling, conviction, necessity; the utterance that is causing the effect is not noticed, the inevitability seems to belong to the incidents or the reasoning; the effect is hypnotic. Perhaps the condition for this kind of success is that with the long series of stanzas there is also a strong progression in the other parts and a great fulness and variety, so that the monotony cannot be heard.[21]

In *In Memoriam* the repetition of the same stanza is complicated by the added division into sections. In a sense these provide another repeating element, but the differences in their lengths and in the kinds of experience they contain provide an element of variety.

Nearly all the stanzas are closed off from what follows by some kind of pause, most often a semi-colon or a full stop. The effect when Tennyson allows one to run on is thus considerable, as in this example from section xlvii:

> That each, who seems a separate whole,
>   Should move his rounds, and fusing all
>   The skirts of self again, should fall
> Remerging in the general Soul,
>
> Is faith as vague as all unsweet.

Here the entire predicate of the main clause is withheld till the start of the second stanza, and the firmness with which the poet dismisses the possibility that the personality should be extinguished comes over very strongly. For the most part, though, each stanza is an entity, and the problem of differentiation to avoid monotony and gain the benefits talked of by Goodman remains. One factor which acts in this direction is the sound patterning, which is almost always confined within the stanza:

[21] Paul Goodman, *The Structure of Literature* (Chicago, 1954), p. 198.

I leave thy praises unexpress'd	[i: ei ʌ e
In verse that brings myself relief,	ə: i e i:
And by the measure of my grief	ai e i:
I leave thy greatness to be guess'd;	i: ei e

What practice howsoe'er expert	æ au eə ɔ:
In fitting aptest words to things,	i æ ə: i
Or voice the richest-toned that sings,	ɔi i ou i
Hath power to give thee as thou wert?	au i æ ə:]

In the first of these stanzas from section lxxv the dominant vowels are [i:] and [e], but neither of them appears in the second. In the second stanza [æ:], [ə] and [i] dominate, but only the second two of these appear in the first stanza, and only once each. In fact, they are the only two occasions where the stanzas have a vowel in common. This is Tennyson's usual practice in *In Memoriam*—in section xxviii, for instance, [i] is used a great deal in the first stanza, but it hardly appears at all after that.

The use of a different group of sounds in each stanza is one way of alleviating monotony; another is to break down the shape of the stanza itself so that the element of repetition is not so great. The preference for vertical patterns of sound tends in this direction, for it encourages us to make links across the lines so that we become less aware of their *abba* relationship. This tendency is especially strong when the same sound is placed at corresponding points in non-rhyming lines—

> Come stepping lightly down the plank,
> And beckoning unto those they know   (xiv)

> Expecting still his advent home;
> And ever met him on his way.   (vi)

The most radical place in which to attack the problem is, of course, in the rhymes, and it is surprising how often Tennyson makes two different rhymes sound alike in some way. Here are some varying examples from section cxxii; the only common method not seen here is identity of the final consonants:

> And yearn'd to burst the folded gloom,
> To bare the eternal heavens again

> If thou wert with me, and the grave
>   Divide us not, be with me now,
>   And enter in at breast and brow
>
> Be quicken'd with a livelier *b*reath
>   And like an inconsiderate *b*oy
>
> And all the breeze of Fancy *blow*s,
>   And every dew-drop paints a *bow*,
>   The wizard lightnings deeply *glow*,
>   And every thought breaks out a *rose*.

All through the poem we find this tendency of the *abba* rhyme scheme to turn into some less rigid system because of the counterbalancing effect of assonance and alliteration.

The movement of the syntax in relation to the shape of the stanza is obviously of great importance. The principal danger point is the central two lines, for if they appear too much like a rhyming couplet they must emphasize the form of the stanza, whilst at the same time threatening to dislocate it by splitting off the last line from the rest. Parallelism is more often found contradicting the stanza structure than confirming it:

> The seasons bring the flower again,
>   And bring the firstling to the flock   (ii)
>
> Was drown'd in passing thro' the ford,
>   Or kill'd in falling from his horse   (vi)
>
> And one is glad; her note is gay,
>   For now her little ones have ranged;
>   And one is sad, her note is changed,
> Because her brood is stol'n away.   (xxi)

Parallel syntax is used so extensively in *In Memoriam* that did it not run against the stanza in most cases it would become clumsily over-emphatic.

Tennyson often prevents the central lines from achieving the strength and independence of a couplet by his use of pause. In 100 stanzas I found that the most frequent arrangement of end-stopping was all four lines stopped (31), but next came lines 2 and 4 (22) and then 1, 2 and 4; all these operate in the direction of preventing the central couplet from closing itself. There are many examples of

Tennyson removing punctuation from the third line in his revisions
(mostly after publication—there is very little punctuation in the
manuscripts):

> O thou, new-year, delaying long,
>   Delayest the sorrow in my blood,
>   That longs to burst a frozen bud
> And flood a fresher throat with song.   (lxxxiii)

This is perhaps the most important single feature of Tennyson's use
of the stanza. Pyre observed its frequency, and commented on the
'characteristic hurry on the second of the enclosed rhymes' which it
causes:

> Thus as the rhyme of the fourth verse is diminished by remoteness
> from its mate, that of the third line is frequently diminished by the
> movement of the sense, a striking subtlety of correspondence which
> has much to do with the quality of the stanza as Tennyson uses it.[22]

This treatment of the stanza seems to have a major part in the
characteristic tone of the poem which I was discussing earlier. The
hurry over the third line is followed by the return to the rhyme of the
first line, producing a kind of quiet satisfaction at having returned to
base after a sally forth; there is little of the triumphal sense of difficult
achievement engendered by the longer stanzas poets have used.

Thinking rather more impressionistically, one might regard the
In Memoriam stanza as a microcosm of two related structural principles of the poem—the cycle and the parallel. The poet's attitude is
given in relation to the seasonal cycle of nature, and parallel syntax,
linked sections and recurring images (one of them the circle) all
show the poet trying to define and redefine his evolving experience
by putting it in a parallel form or returning to a situation or image
in order to re-examine his relation to it. These movements are inherent in the stanza, for the first and last lines encircle the central,
parallel lines. In any event, Tennyson's treatment of the pattern of the
stanza is like his other uses of sound and rhythm: the basic idea is
very simple and often repeated without much obvious variety. When
we look closer, however, we find that there is a subtle wearing away
of the normal outline so that nuances of many kinds provide a
continually changing pattern amidst the apparent uniformity.

The failure of our expectations is often more important than success.
Verse in which we constantly get exactly what we are ready for and

22 *The Formation of Tennyson's Style*, p. 187.

N

no more, instead of something which we can and must take up and incorporate as another stage in a total developing response is merely toilsome and tedious.[23]

Tennyson, as I have shown repeatedly, often satisfies the reader's general expectations, but it must be true that the more regular the background is, the more outstanding are departures from it. The early part of my discussion of rhythm should have shown that there are a great many factors which may be involved in deviations from the rhythmic norm; in an effort to cover as many of them as possible I will make three analyses, two of them comparing sections and a third studying more closely the movement within a section. By this means I hope to demonstrate the facility with which Tennyson adapts the smoothness and slowness of his basic rhythm and employs unusual stress patterns to suit the thought and feeling of individual sections.

Section cxxix is interesting in the pauses it uses. The first stanza has a high number of pauses within lines; the second and third stanzas are quite remarkable in this respect:

> Known and unknown; human, divine;
> Sweet human hand and lips and eye;
> Dear heavenly friend that canst not die,
> Mine, mine, for ever, ever mine;

> Strange friend, past, present, and to be;
> Loved deeplier, darklier understood;
> Behold, I dream a dream of good,
> And mingle all the world with thee.

These lines begin with a rare pause pattern, but the fourth and fifth lines quoted are almost unparalleled in the poem. It is very unusual to have three pauses within a line at all, and hardly anywhere else do they occur so determinedly off the beat. One result is that we feel the poet insistently itemizing various entities which are normally considered irreconcilable. We are made aware of the separateness, the incompatibility of human and divine, past, present and to be, in order that the proclaiming of the one-ness of them all shall be the more forceful. This occurs in the last line, which returns to the smooth rhythm we have come to expect. The irregularities in rhythm help bring out the sense of these stanzas, then, but they also communi-

[23] I. A. Richards, *Principles of Literary Criticism*, 2nd edn. (London, 1926), p. 140.

cate the poet's excitement at the reconciliation of opposites he has achieved. This is specially true of the line, 'Mine, mine, for ever, ever mine'; the point can be demonstrated by comparison with the version in the Trial Edition, 'My friend, for ever, ever mine!', which lacks completely the ecstasy expressed by the break in the first foot of the final reading.

With section cxxix we may compare lxxxvi, 'Sweet after showers, ambrosial air', which I also discussed in Chapter IV. Here pause is interesting through its absence. Tennyson said that the section must be read in one breath, and he put this requirement into the language itself by writing sixteen lines with only five pauses at the ends of lines and just another seven within them. After the comma at the end of the first line we sweep without check over the next two and a half lines; then we take off again, but the disregard for the normal rhythm of *In Memoriam* is shown once more as we cross the stanza boundary unimpeded—and this happens at the ends of the next two stanzas as well. The effectiveness of this can again be demonstrated by comparison with the Trial Edition, where we find semi-colons instead of the commas after 'meadow' (line 4) and 'ripples' (8) and commas instead of the present lack of punctuation after 'evening', 'brake' and 'bloom' (3) and after 'below' (5). If one tries to read the section with this punctuation the effect is quite different. In section cxxix the use of pauses breaks up the words into separate items for our individual consideration; here it allows them all to run together in an impressive sweep which mirrors the movement of the in-spiriting breeze. In both sections the elegiac tone is modified in order to reflect the poet's excitement, but by varying his exploitation of pause Tennyson is able to individualize the two moods.

In the previous chapter I discussed the sounds in some lines from sections lxxii and xcix, and it will be interesting to consider them again in respect of their rhythm. They exhibit a complete contrast in the reading speeds they demand. The despair of lxxii, where the poet condemns the day (and by implication the whole of nature) as responsible for Hallam's death, is reflected in its heavy and violent rhythm; section xcix, on the other hand, is almost light-hearted in tone. The earlier section usually has four or more stresses to the line, rarely less, whilst the later one never has more than four (except in the opening line), and most often has three. I have argued that more monosyllables tend to mean slower pace, and whilst section lxxii has the usual proportion of short words, xcix has only half the number we would expect—in the following stanza there are two bisyllabic words in each line:

> Who wakenest with thy balmy breath
> To myriads on the genial earth,
> Memories of bridal, or of birth,
> And unto myriads more, of death.

We notice also in this stanza that 'wakenest', 'myriads', 'genial' and 'memories' hover between having two and three syllables. The metre makes us take them as bi-syllabic, and we must therefore hurry over them. Section xcix contains several more words of this kind, and we can see their effectiveness in comparison with the Lincoln manuscript: 'swoll'n' was first written as 'wild', and the line 'Who *murmurest* in the *foliaged* eaves' originally read, 'Who risest not as one that grieves'. The words I have remarked must be hurried if the metre is to be satisfied.

I also suggested earlier that heavy consonant clusters slow our reading, and here too the sections vary from the average in the appropriate directions. The contrast is intensified by the way section lxxii repeats the same cluster initially in the syllable, making it more prominent. I quoted from the first stanza in connection with this phenomenon in Chapter IX, but it is evident throughout— [bl], [st(r)], [kl] and [kr] all appear several times, and other consonants are also combined with [l] and [r] to produce lines such as 'Which sicken'd every living bloom, / And blurr'd the spendour of the sun', and 'Lift as thou may'st thy burthen'd brows / Thro' clouds that drench the morning star'. There is nothing comparable in section xcix.

The other principal feature of the contrast concerns rare stress patterns. There are hardly any in section xcix, but section lxxii, where we might expect the poet's powerful feelings to disjoint the normal rhythm, is completely different. The destructiveness of the storm is figured in:

> With thy quíck téars that máke the róse
> Púll sídeways, and the dáisy clóse
> Her crímson frínges to the shówer.

The heavy, unexpected emphasis on 'thy quick tears' seems to represent the force of the rain. We take the rest of the line to recover, but the sense hovers over the line end, and then the second line again throws us: just as we have turned the corner we are shaken by the successive stresses in 'Pull sideways'. After this the swing of the first line is nearly mirrored as we regain our balance with 'the daisy close'. The violence inflicted by the storm on the tender plants is reflected in the disjunction of the rhythm. There are several more examples of the emphatic use of rare rhythmic patterns in the section, specially through surprising stress on the third syllable. This helps the strong sense we have of the force of the blow received by the poet in the line, 'When the dark hand struck down thro' time', or the way we believe the poet really means it with all his being when he puts from him the sun, and the light and life it usually represents:

> Clímb thy thíck nóon, disástrous dáy;
> Tóuch thy dúll góal of jóyless gráy,
> And híde thy sháme benéath the gróund.

The first line quoted springs off from an initial stress, but is slowed abruptly by the adjacent stresses on 'thick noon'; and then, to emphasize the poet's strength of feeling, the second line takes a similar pattern. In the final line we seem to sink back—exhausted, one might say—into the familiar iambics.

The four sections I have considered show how the background rhythm is abandoned to display the more effectively a particular mood or thought, both through the overall tone of a section and in individual lines. My final analysis will treat more closely the use of the norm and departures from it in section liv. Rhythm interacts with syntax as well as meaning, and I wish to consider this too. I will look at rhythm in relation to the scheme of the section, and follow it through trying to bring out the effect of its movement from line to line. I stress the section as follows (the single accent is a crude indicator, but subtler distinctions are best dealt with in discussion):

> Oh yét we trúst that sómehow góod
>   Will be the fínal góal of íll,
>   To pángs of náture, síns of wíll,
> Defécts[24] of dóubt, and táints of blóod;   4
>
> That nóthing wálks with áimless féet;
>   That nót óne lífe shall be destróy'd,
>   Or cást as rúbbish to the vóid,
> When Gód hath máde the píle complète;   8

[24] *N.E.D.* stresses the word this way, so it is presumably right for Tennyson.

That nót a wórm is clóven in váin;
That nót a móth with váin desíre
Is shrívell'd in a frúitless fíre,
Or bút subsérves anóther's gáin.   12

Behóld, we knów nót ánything;
I cán but trúst that góod shall fáll
At lást—fár óff—at lást, to áll,
And évery wínter chánge to spríng.   16

So rúns my dréam: but whát am Í?
An ínfant crýing in the níght:
An ínfant crýing for the líght:
And with nó lánguage but a crý.   20

Earlier versions of this section reveal several interesting alterations. The most pronounced is the omission of an additional stanza
between lines 12 and 13, where the Trinity manuscript reads:

For hope at awful distance set
Oft whispers of a kindlier plan
Tho never prophet came to man
Of such a revelation yet.

Tennyson very possibly thought that this stanza could be read as
suggesting more uncertainty about Christianity than he subsequently
felt—or was prepared to admit. Secondly, the shift in pronouns
from 'we' (lines 1 and 13) to 'I' (lines 14 and 17), which shows the
poet moving from an attempt to speak for everyone to a more
desperate statement of his own position, is absent in Trinity, which
uses 'I' all the way through. Thirdly, the Trinity manuscript reads,
for line 14, 'But that I would that good should fall', and the main
effect of this is that the parallel with the opening line is less marked.
Fourthly, 'Behold' (13) was followed by an exclamation mark in the
Trial Edition; its removal, resulting in a slight relaxation of the
rhythm, is in accord with Tennyson's practice in many similar cases.
And finally, the first line once had commas on either side of 'somehow' (Lincoln and Trinity manuscripts).

This last alteration may lead us into a detailed discussion of the
section. The removal of this punctuation is quite significant, for as
the first stanza now stands, its opening runs swiftly through to the
end of the second line, aided by the unusual lack of stress in the

first syllables of the second line. This opening gains almost epigram-matic point from the opposition of 'good' and 'ill' at the line ends. But compared with the heavy emphasis of the third and fourth lines, the first two lines sound insufficiently considered and their optimism seems too easy. These last two lines of the first stanza have their stresses squarely on the regular iambic beat, and gain great strength from their complete parallelism. The sample of 100 stanzas showed few others with pauses so evenly distributed in two suc-cessive lines. Moreover, there is a spurious parallel between 'goal of ill' and the three succeeding phrases, although, logically, 'pangs of nature, sins of will, / Defects of doubt' are all expansions of 'ill'. The two parts of the stanza are thereby held together and their bearing on each other is emphasized, despite the differences in rhythm. The effect is of an uneasily asserted 'good' outweighed by a powerful mass of 'ill', for the parallel syntax is linked to the rhythm so that each reinforces the other.

The next two stanzas go together, for they consist of a series of grammatical complements of the verb 'trust'. It is important to notice the extent to which all these clauses are in parallel:

subject (a negative)	verb (often passive)	adjunct (suggesting vainness)
That nothing	walks	with aimless feet
That not one life	shall be destroy'd	
	Or cast	as rubbish
		to the void
		When God hath made the pile complete
That not a worm	is cloven	in vain
That not a moth		with vain desire
	Is shrivell'd	in a fruitless fire
	Or but subserves	direct object: another's gain.

The rhythm of these two stanzas is not, for the most part, very striking if we consider it in isolation. Only the second line (6) has a rare stress pattern, and its function is to establish firmly 'not one', which grammatically governs the rest of the stanza. The remainder of these eight lines alternates between the commoner three and four stress patterns, working almost symbolically in the case of 'shrivell'd', and returning to the four stress line for an emphatic close to each stanza.

Over against all this is the syntactic sequence outlined in the table above. All these clauses take up 'ill' (line 2), and tentatively deny it; repeatedly they begin with 'that' or 'or', producing a blatant list effect which makes plain the persistence of the poet's worries. Each clause begins with some sort of negative; this is followed by a verb, which in most cases is passive, suggesting the inability of life to control its own end; and finally, as a rule, comes a phrase (grammatically an adjunct), which expresses vainness or fruitlessness. Yet there is really only one clause whose syntax accords absolutely with this description ('That not a worm is cloven in vain'); the others all vary in some way or other, and this means that syntax and rhythm do not work quite together. In lines 6 and 7, for example, the rhythm is nearly the same, but one has the structure, *subject—verb*, the other, *verb—adjunct—adjunct*; or, in lines 9 and 10, a similar rhythm is counterpointed with the two structures, *subject—verb—adjunct* and *subject—adjunct*. This is despite the considerable sense of parallelism which the repetitions of 'That not' and 'Or' encourage, and despite the end-stopping which fails only once (such a high proportion without medial pause is unusual), and which gives the lines a strong air of finality and completeness.

Syntax and rhythm, then, do not work quite together, although this is not a section of pyrotechnical disjunction, like lxxii or the end of xcv. The two lines which are outside the obvious pattern of the clauses are the last of each stanza (lines 8 and 12). They have in common an appearance of being positive. 'When God hath made the pile complete' seems purposive, and includes God as the actor—but the overall sense is not confident, for the poet has no certainty with which to look forward to the end of the world, and 'pile' is a very material word to use of human souls. The other line hopes that even a moth should not die fruitlessly, 'Or but subserve another's gain'. 'Gain' contrasts with 'vain', its partner in rhyme, but in context is no more cheerful. This line presents the last of the poet's demands, which have been steadily becoming more extravagant, and so less likely to be granted—he finally claims that it is not enough for the death of a moth to help something else, but there must be some more direct benefit. Thus the line which in form is quite

positive is really the most pessimistic, for it makes an almost impossible demand. And yet, like line 8, it receives the most regular of
stresses, and firmly closes its stanza.

With the opening of the fourth stanza there is a change of direction. After 'Behold' comes the first medial pause since the half lines
of the first stanza, and it acts as a jumping-off point for the rest of the
line. The remaining six syllables are very unusual, for the [n] alliteration, the displacement of 'not' and the word 'anything' makes us stress:

> Behóld, we knów nót ánything.

The rhythm gives maximum emphasis to this line, which picks up
the thought of the opening of the section and, indeed, of the Prologue
('We have but faith: we cannot know'). The stresses on this line
were unique in the 100 stanza sample, and the lack of stress on the
last syllable is especially rare; it is very appropriate here, of course, for
it is 'nothing' which is being expressed. But above all, the poet's
feeling of inadequacy and uncertainty comes through—as it does in
the rest of the stanza. The semi-colon after 'anything' is followed
by an entirely separate statement, so that the line 13 stands on its
own as a despairing gasp. This is far more effective than the Trinity
reading—'anything / But that I would that good should fall'—which
does not convey the same sense of a hopeless and abrupt throwing-up
of the hands. 'I can but trust that good shall fall' also has a clearer
connection with line 1, 'Oh yet we trust that somehow good'; the
expression is even less hopeful now, and line 15 is broken into
four parts by punctuation—a massive disjunction by the standards
of *In Memoriam*—suspending the sense for three pessimistic qualifying phrases: 'At last—far off—at last, to all'. The poet's hope for
good is at its most tentative—but yet the pauses correspond with the
feet, which are almost straightforwardly regular. The effect of the
disjointed iambs is of a series of attempts to get started, all failing; in
stress the line is similar to its predecessor, but in rhythm it denies all
that the other said. The last line of the stanza—'And every winter
change to spring'—is rhythmically just like line 14, and, indeed,
simply restates its meaning in more evocative terms. 'At last—far
off—at last, to all' comes between the two regular lines, qualifying
them both by its disjunction. This simultaneous presence of order
and instability may be seen as an epitome of the action of the section,
which sets out to assert what we trust, but in fact gives us more of
the poet's doubts.

The first line of the last stanza, 'So runs my dream: but what am I?', breaks into two parts, the first summing up the section so far, the second leading on to the rest of the stanza by its rhetorical question. The first, recapitulatory part suggests the incompleteness of the poet's attainment by consisting of just half a line—it is like a despairing gasp. We should notice that the poet has now shifted from 'we' (lines 1 and 13) to 'I': it seems as if he loses the comforting sense of solidarity with the rest of humankind at the moment when he most needs it. The first half of this line is linked to the second and to the rest of the stanza, across all the variations in rhythm and syntax, by a subtle continuation in the imagery, for the poet's 'dream' is taken up in his definition of himself in the next line as 'An infant crying in the night'. The regular stress of line 17 seems to be a preparation for the deviation of the following lines; the second and third lines are not unusual, being three stress lines which are like the four stress standard except for a weak foot, but the degree to which parallel syntax (and strongly parallel at that) works with the rhythm is exceptional. In fact, the lines are almost identical in every way, and the effect of this is to throw into relief the items which differ, namely 'in the night' and 'for the light'. These represent the opposing poles of 'ill' and 'good' which have run right through the section, and we see that although the poet has circled round these ideas he has been unable to make any progress. After four stanzas of more or less intellectual discussion the poet breaks down to a cry for guidance in an uncertain existence. But although 'night' and 'light' are so strongly opposed, both lines amount nevertheless to much the same thing—to be in the night is to be lacking light, and *vice versa*.

The last line is linked to the others because it takes up 'cry', but now the stress is most unusual:

> And with nó lánguage but a crý.

This line is rare in almost every way—in its lack of stress for the first two syllables, in its stress on the third syllable, and in the fact that these irregularities are not accompanied by an otherwise large number of stresses (stress on the third syllable most often occurs in five or six stress lines). In fact, in the four hundred lines it occurred on only one other occasion. The metre is now completely disjointed, and threatens to collapse like the poet's world. Once again, Tennyson does not use his effects crudely, for this line is held to the rest of the stanza by the sounds [ai, n, l], but the greatest disjunction is at the point where the poet's despair is greatest. He has no language but a cry, and his ineffectuality is represented by the dislocation of the rhythm in this line.

We might see this statement as reflecting on the whole of *In Memoriam* which, after all, is written in language. In many ways the poem is simply a cry: it consists of a series of short sections whose sequence is governed by the development of the poet's subjective experience. Yet *In Memoriam* is by no means the entirely unstudied song of the linnet: life may be in disorder, but art is not. Though rhythm, like the other aspects of language I have discussed, often functions as an intensifier of the poet's mood and thought, it is also meticulously controlled so that we always feel a contrasting classical quality. We have observed these features all through this study of *In Memoriam*; in my final chapter I want to discuss briefly what happens to some of them in subsequent poetry.

XI

IN MEMORIAM AND THE LANGUAGE OF MODERN POETRY

What hope is here for modern rhyme
To him, who turns a musing eye
On songs, and deeds, and lives, that lie
Foreshorten'd in the tract of time?   (lxxvii)

THE reader who has followed with sympathy my explorations into the structure of the language of *In Memoriam* may admire, as I do, the subtlety and complexity of the interactions which Tennyson creates. Yet, as I have indicated at various points, critical opinion has not always been approving. This is doubtless due in part to the fact that not all Tennyson's poetry is as good as *In Memoriam*; but then, such inconsistencies are to be found in the work of all poets. At the risk of seeming impertinent, I would like to suggest that critical attitudes to Tennyson have been formed almost entirely by people whose parents were Victorians. Sir Harold Nicolson claimed, at the start of his highly influential study published in 1923, that it was becoming possible to see the Victorians in perspective, that the details which had obscured the general outline had faded and the principal landmarks become evident. But notice the kinds of reaction to this state of affairs which he envisaged:

> The individual emotions aroused by this change of aspect will vary according to temperament. For some the immensities of the Victorian background will but emphasise what they regard as the complacent futilities of the foreground; others, again, will feel a stirring of indignation at the thought of so vast an opportunity having fallen to a generation seemingly so ignorant, so optimistic and so insincere. And there will be some who, from the troubled waters of our insecure age, will look back wistfully at what may appear to them as the simple serenities, the sun-lit confidence, the firm dry land which formed the heritage of that abundant epoch.[1]

One could hardly call these responses detached—complacent futilities, sun-lit confidence, wistfulness, stirrings of indignation; it is *Look Back in Anger* thirty years before!

[1] Nicolson, *Tennyson*, pp. 1–2.

To a younger commentator, who may be aroused and yet irritated by the apparently uncomplicated heroics of the Spanish Civil War— or even of the Campaign for Nuclear Disarmament—Tennyson's period is no more, and no less, personally significant than Chaucer's. There will still be prejudices, but they will be of a different character, and it should be possible to take some tentative steps towards a new perspective. Some such reaction against the art of the previous age as Nicolson describes seems to be an indispensible condition for the achievement of an individual voice in the new generation. Nevertheless, it also appears to be the case that a movement is rarely as different from its predecessors as its theorists may like to claim. In Chapter II I suggested some relationships between *In Memoriam* and Enlightenment and Romantic thought; by way of conclusion I wish to point out that there are elements of continuity as well as contrasts in the language of nineteenth- and twentieth-century English poetry (to include American works would be hopelessly ambitious), and that the seeds at least of later developments can be found in *In Memoriam*. Such a purpose must inevitably produce partial and over-generalized results, but they may nevertheless prove suggestive.

Of course, the differences between Tennyson's use of language and, say, Eliot's are very marked. An attempt to place in context Nicolson's comments on his contemporaries does not make the feelings he describes any less influential, and in such a climate of opinion we would not expect poetry to remain the same. The changes for the most part involve the qualities which in Chapter II I called 'classical'—the claim to speak for the whole of mankind, the cultivation of unobtrusive nuances rather than broad or startling effects, and the persistent stylization of language which makes us always aware of the artificiality of *In Memoriam*. The twentieth-century poet is always conscious that any opinion may be his alone; he may well use abrupt contrasts to express his alarm, his frustration, or his sense of the fragmentation in society; and he is liable to reject self-conscious artifice as insincere and 'rhetorical'—metre, syntactical inversions[2] and poetic diction are all questioned or completely abandoned.

> Why should not old men be mad?
> Some have known a likely lad

[2] For a general discussion of factors influencing the syntax of modern poetry, see William E. Baker, *Syntax in English Poetry, 1870–1930* (Berkeley and Los Angeles, 1967), chapter five.

> That had a sound fly-fisher's wrist
> Turn to a drunken journalist;
> A girl that knew all Dante once
> Live to bear children to a dunce;
> A Helen of social welfare dream,
> Climb on a wagonette to scream.

Yeats' poem rhymes, though not always fully, and has vestiges of a metre, but its diction is completely colloquial and its syntax largely straightforward. Unusual and unexpected juxtapositions (Helen of Troy and old age pensions) convey the strength of the poet's disappointment at the failing of the old aristocratic ideals. Though the first line may give the impression that a general statement is intended, the poem immediately becomes highly personal in its allusions; despite some more inclusive remarks in the second sentence, Yeats can really be sure of only his own feelings, and in the last line he relinquishes the claim to speak for others: 'Know why *an* old man should be mad.'

Tennyson believed that progress was possible if man could 'Move upward, working out the beast, / And let the ape and tiger die' (cxviii); but in *The Waste Land* we find 'hooded hordes swarming / Over endless plains', in his last poem Wilfred Owen prophesies that 'None will break ranks, though nations trek from progress', and Yeats' rough beast slouches towards Bethlehem for the horrific Second Coming. In such circumstances we should hardly expect poets to be able to identify hopes and ideals held in common by our civilization or delicately to balance their phrases and rhythms as Pope and Tennyson had done. These manifestations would suggest at least some confidence in the sanity of the ultimate order of things. Tennyson's *Maud* closes with the hero's regeneration through war:

> And hail once more to the banner of battle unroll'd!
> Tho' many a light shall darken, and many shall weep
> For those that are crush'd in the clash of jarring claims,
> Yet God's just wrath shall be wreak'd on a giant liar.

The exclamation and repetition in the syntax, the heavy alliteration, the archaisms and the grandiloquent tones which allow the speaker to wave aside individual suffering all proclaim Tennyson's conviction that such simple solutions are viable. In the First World War Owen saw and heard

the blood
Come gargling from the froth-corrupted lungs,
Obscene as cancer, bitter as the cud
Of vile, incurable sores on innocent tongues.

When our forebears all believed that 'Dulce et decorum est pro patria mori' they dignified the notion by retaining the ancient expression of it. Tennyson, in that tradition, employed elevated language as his hero went off to fight in the Crimea, but Owen, conscious of his alienation from the aspirations of many of his countrymen, draws his diction and syntax from ordinary language and communicates his horror through the violence of his imagery. The old certainties become, as Owen says, the old lies, and the classical tones characteristic of *In Memoriam* lose their point. It is no longer feasible that one man should speak for a nation so divided, let alone the race; delicate nuances seem insufficiently dramatic to express the deep perplexities of modern life; and rhetoric of all kinds—with its traditional assumptions about what is valuable and what worthless, its assurance, which seems to imply that all shall eventually be well and, above all, its tone of confidence in the worth of human endeavour—seems meretricious. It is dismissed in this period by Pound as 'perdamnable' and by T. E. Hulme as 'divorced from any real vision', and Yeats declares that 'We make out of the quarrel with others, rhetoric, but of the quarrel with ourselves, poetry'.[3]

Irony becomes the dominant mode in twentieth-century poetry—not the Popean variety, which makes its affirmation by striking off against unacceptable values and so achieves unison with prevailing cultural norms, but an irony which is simply destructive, or in which the assertion is either minor or personal and idiosyncratic. Yeats, the earliest major poet whom we call modern, resisted the negative impulse of his age, not because he did not feel it, but because he thought that 'if I affirm that such and such is so, the more complete the affirmation, the more complete the proof, and even when incomplete, it remains valid within some limit. I must kill scepticism in myself...'[4] Inconsistencies did not matter to Yeats; the point was that one should always be reaching towards some kind of positive statement, however uncertain, for human nature demands

[3] Ezra Pound, in *Poets on Poetry*, ed. Charles Norman (New York, 1962), p. 329; T. E. Hulme, 'Notes on Language and Style', *The Criterion*, III (1925), 487; Yeats, *Selected Criticism*, ed. Norman Jeffares (London, 1964), p. 170.
[4] Quoted by Richard Ellmann, *The Identity of Yeats* (paperback, London, 1964), p. 239.

that we strive to transcend incompleteness. This position is never-theless far from Tennyson's devotion to his belief which, though no more than a hope, was most fervently held.

The irony of Eliot's early poetry seems to me almost entirely pessimistic and destructive (and I must insist that I do not regard these terms as constituting adverse criticism).

> The host with someone indistinct
> Converses at the door apart,
> The nightingales are singing near
> The Convent of the Sacred Heart,
>
> And sang within the bloody wood
> When Agamemnon cried aloud,
> And let their liquid siftings fall
> To stain the stiff dishonoured shroud.

'Sweeney Among the Nightingales' juxtaposes the brothel-keeper with the Christian shrine, the murder of the victor of Troy by his adulterous relatives, and the droppings of the bird which, in *In Memoriam*, 'Rings Eden thro' the budded quicks' (lxxxviii). One might maintain that the ironic treatment of the traditionally lofty images serves to place the squalor of modern life, but the disillusion-ment and the distaste for sex—and indeed, for humanity—are so violent as to leave us with no positive values at all. I find the same features in *The Waste Land*. It is not very helpful just to be told that one is lacking is spiritual values, and the aversion to sex unbalances the presentation to the extent that, although we know of Eliot's respect for 'objectivity', it becomes hard to see the poem as any more impersonal than *In Memoriam*. We may also notice that the irony is by no means always gentle or subtle—outside the typist's window are 'perilously spread / Her drying combinations touched by the sun's last rays'. Eliot evidently does not intend to permit any reader to continue in the 'complacent futilities' attributed by Nicolson's contemporaries to the Victorians.

Other poets retain in their language the restraint and unobtrusive-ness of *In Memoriam*, but not the stylization or the confidence.

> About suffering they were never wrong,
> The Old Masters: how well they understood
> Its human position; how it takes place
> While someone else is eating or opening a window or just walking
>   dully along.

In Auden's '*Musée des Beaux Arts*' the irony is in the theme itself, and the whole subject is presented in just that casual manner in which suffering is said to occur. The diction and syntax are yet again those of ordinary language—almost to the point of bravado. But this is not the gentle tone of Tennyson when he writes, for instance,

> But in my spirit will I dwell,
> And dream my dream, and hold it true;
> For tho' my lips may breathe adieu,
> I cannot think the thing farewell.   (cxxiii)

The poet is here undertaking a major statement of the principle upon which he bases his whole existence, and the quiet intonation, though tinged with a note of defiance in the face of scepticism, embodies his inner assurance. The unassuming language of Auden's poem is right because the subject makes no pretensions to grandeur or even to originality—the Old Masters have already expressed it very well. The tone is almost apologetic; it seems to be saying, This is just an odd idea I thought I would mention, nothing special—I am not Prince Hamlet . . . A lot of modern poetry is like this. A small incident gives rise to a small moral and it seems that to venture further is too risky—hence, perhaps, the death of the long poem.

Twentieth-century English poetry, then, tends towards the negative, or towards the small or personal affirmation; the more common mode is a tentative irony which eschews large statements. It does not seem extravagant to relate the developments in sensibility I have described to the disappearance of the classical qualities Tennyson cultivated in *In Memoriam*. The claim to speak for all men becomes invalid, the sensitive restraint becomes inadequate or the vehicle for relatively unambitious reflections, and the stylization becomes irrelevant. But these features represent only one side of the linnet and artifact dichotomy which I have distinguished in Tennyson's creative impulse. The other is the Romantic, with its opposition to rationalism and science, its dependence upon subjective and even mystical experience, and its desire to employ only such forms as are dictated by the subject matter. These aspects of Tennyson's approach are not rejected, but are taken up with even greater enthusiasm by the Symbolist and Imagist movements of the later nineteenth and early twentieth centuries. Frank Kermode and Marshall McLuhan have already argued impressively for this continuity,[5] but

---

[5] Frank Kermode, *Romantic Image* (London, 1957); and McLuhan's two articles in Killham, *Critical Essays*.

O

it is worth examining again in the specific context of the language of
In Memoriam.

For Arthur Symons, the publicizer of Symbolism in England, the
writings of Gérard de Nerval, Villiers de L'Isle-Adam, Rimbaud,
Verlaine, Laforgue, Mallarmé and Huysmans were essentially a
reaction against materialism, 'an attempt to spiritualize literature'. He
declared that Symbolism consisted in

> this revolt against exteriority, against rhetoric, against a materialistic
> tradition; in this endeavour to disengage the ultimate essence, the
> soul, of whatever exists and can be realised by the consciousness; in
> this dutiful waiting upon every symbol by which the soul of things
> can be made visible. . . .[6]

Tennyson too hated materialism; Symbolism is a more extreme
statement of his position. The Symbolist locates reality exclusively in
his own mind, thus carrying much further the concentration on
individual experience which I have pointed out in *In Memoriam*
and earlier Romantic poetry. The elements in Tennyson's approach
which are discarded are those we should expect—rhetoric, the concern with social issues and mankind in general, the long poem.
Symons observes that Verlaine admired *In Memoriam*—'Only, with
Verlaine, the thing itself, the affection or regret, is everything; there
is no room for meditation over destiny, or search for a problematical
consolation'.[7] To seize the essence of a mood is the Symbolist's one
endeavour; he is not interested in circumstances, opinions, analysis
of motive or consequence, but in evoking the quality of an immediate experience. A long poem is therefore a contradiction in terms.
On the last point, Symons conveniently phrases his belief so that it
fits in neatly with my argument on *In Memoriam*: 'no long poem was
ever written; the finest long poem in the world being but a series of
short poems linked together with prose'.[8] Tennyson can be seen as
approaching an awareness of this doctrine in the way he explicitly
builds *In Memoriam* out of a series of short poems, for he establishes
a distinct split between the sections at the highest tension, each embodying one moment when the poet's immediate and unalloyed

---

[6] Arthur Symons, *The Symbolist Movement in Literature*, 2nd edn. (London, 1911),
pp. 8–9. For further discussion see Wilson, *Axel's Castle*, and C. M. Bowra, *The Heritage
of Symbolism* (London, 1943).
[7] *The Symbolist Movement in Literature*, p. 93.
[8] *The Symbolist Movement in Literature*, p. 134.

emotions break through, and the others leading up to and away from them.

Tennyson's dependence upon mystical experience also relates him to the Symbolists—who revered Blake above all other poets. But, again, the Symbolists went further. For them all experience was ultimately supernatural in character—there was no disjunction between the world of the senses and the world of ideal beauty which they wished to capture in their verse. Many Symbolists, including Yeats, involved themselves in spiritualism or magic, thus setting themselves at the furthest remove from the methods of scientific enquiry. They placed at the centre of their ontology a mode of experience which had been for Tennyson only intermittent. Hence the title of the movement: 'they attempted', says Bowra, 'to convey a supernatural experience in the language of visible things, and therefore almost every word is a symbol and is used not for its common purpose but for the associations which it evokes of a reality beyond the senses'.[9] The danger in this approach is of poetry becoming so inward-looking as to be inaccessible to most or all readers. For many people, obscurity is the most obvious feature of modern poetry and its language. The neo-classical aspirations in Tennyson's writing preserve him from this fate; indeed, he seems at times to be making a last desperate attempt to write for the whole culture, and there is no doubt that this impulsion sometimes leads him into vulgarity. Yet he did succeed, and he was the last to do so, for later English authors seem suddenly to abandon as hopeless any such pretensions. Then, in revulsion against the apparent compromises of their predecessors, they swing completely to the opposite extreme, and poetry becomes the preserve of a very select few.

The most significant result for poetic language of the Symbolist determination to view every object as an emblem of a transcendent beauty is the extensive use of the symbol, as I defined it in Chapter VIII. The image represents ideas and feelings which cannot be neatly rendered in other terms and whose literal referent is left unstated. Now this procedure is decked out in the fully self-conscious theories of Mallarmé, for whom literal and figurative are simply not distinct. He rejects as 'brutal' any ordering of images by direct thought—Symons translates:

> To be instituted, a relation between images, exact; and that therefrom should detach itself a third aspect, fusible and clear, offered to the

[9] *The Heritage of Symbolism*, p. 5.

divination. Abolished, the pretension, aesthetically an error, despite its dominion over almost all the masterpieces, to enclose within the subtle paper other than, for example, the horror of the forest, or the silent thunder afloat in the leaves; not the intrinsic, dense wood of the trees.[10]

I have shown how Tennyson feels his way towards this position through the blurring of the literal and figurative, leading to the disappearance of the literal element. He is nearest to the Symbolists in a section like cxxi, 'Sad Hesper', which I discussed at the end of Chapter VIII. The poet describes the boat drawn upon the shore, the wakeful bird and the movements of the sun, and we understand that the reality of love and eternal life is his ultimate theme. In the last stanza he resorts to the literal and states explicitly a part of his thought, and we can see that he is still held by rationalist assumptions. But the impulse towards the Symbolist aesthetic is there too.

In England, the Pre-Raphaelites were writing poetry which in many ways approximates to Symbolist theories—Rosetti's 'The Woodspurge' describes a walk in the countryside in a time of grief, and concludes with a defence of the moment in and for itself:

> My eyes, wide open, had the run
> Of some ten weeds to fix upon;
> Among those few, out of the sun,
> The woodspurge flowered, three cups in one.
>
> From perfect grief there need not be
> Wisdom or even memory:
> One thing then learnt remains to me,—
> The woodspurge has a cup of three.

But the major exponent of Symbolism in English is the early Yeats, to whom Symons dedicated his book.

> I went out to the hazel wood,
> Because a fire was in my head,
> And cut and peeled a hazel wand,
> And hooked a berry to a thread;
> And when white moths were on the wing,
> And moth-like stars were flickering out,
> I dropped the berry in a stream
> And caught a little silver trout.

[10] *The Symbolist Movement in Literature*, p. 131.

The fish turns into a 'glimmering girl':

> Though I am old with wandering
> Through hollow lands and hilly lands,
> I will find out where she has gone,
> And kiss her lips and take her hands;
> And walk among long dappled grass,
> And pluck till time and times are done
> The silver apples of the moon,
> The golden apples of the sun.

'The Song of the Wandering Aengus' is more etherial and enigmatic than anything in *In Memoriam*, and the symbolic trout and apples are made more prominently the focus than is usual with Tennyson. What we do find here, and in just the same kind of way as in *In Memoriam*, are two linguistic features which I have already associated with Tennyson's development of the symbol: the use of incidental landscape to evoke mood, and a preference for analogical syntax which is at times almost no syntax at all. The mind of the speaker is the principal concern for both Tennyson and Yeats, and external 'background' objects—here, the moths, stars and long dappled grass—are significant because of their contribution to the atmosphere, and so to our impression of the speaker's emotions. The syntax is also very close to Tennyson's practice. Yeats repeats the same kind of clause, and avoids clauses of condition, cause and result, which would characterize an analytical approach. The syntax is self-effacing, so that we are left to pass through a series of images; we feel that we are experiencing the poet's immediate mental sensations, with the minimum of intervention from any conscious organizing faculty. In these respects Symbolist language is in a direct line from the mode of writing which Tennyson employs in *In Memoriam*. In theory and in practice there is full continuity.

English Symbolism, because of its late appearance, blurs into Imagism—Eliot's *Prufrock* volume shows signs of Laforgue whereas *The Waste Land* was influenced by Pound. The principal differences seem to be that the transcendental justifications are replaced by a concentration on aesthetic effectiveness and psychologically based conceptions of the nature of the mind, and that vague evocation gives way to irony (which we already find in Laforgue) and to a preference for hard, precise diction and images.

The theorist of this development is T. E. Hulme, and the correspondences between his thought and Tennyson's practice as I have described it are very revealing. Hulme, who leans heavily towards a Roman Catholic position, denies completely that man is capable of progress, and here at once we see the break with Tennyson: the faith in mankind is absent. Hulme insists upon the absolute disjunction between three facets of our experience—the inorganic world of the physical sciences, the organic world of biology and related approaches, and the world of religious and ethical values.[11] He represents these three fields as contained within concentric circles, thereby using the very same image as Tennyson in *In Memoriam*. The great achievement for the poet there is to gain the belief that all the circles are one, that all differences of time, space and matter can be transcended in the moment of mystical awareness; but for Hulme, right thinking depends upon keeping the circles separate.

Yet Hulme is really tackling the same problem—the status of the creative imagination in a scientific age. He and Tennyson are both in the same Romantic tradition. To the early nineteenth century it seemed that science had spoilt the rainbow, but there was plenty of scope left for the individual, and rationalist methods could be disregarded. For Tennyson the position was far more serious; he could not avoid the 'brooding over scientific opinion' which Yeats considered so deleterious.[12] Science was as meaningful to him as the gyres were to Yeats (and a good deal more meaningful to his readers). Tennyson was just able to absorb the discoveries of the geologists, but by the time of Yeats and Hulme such inclusiveness had become impossible. The only answer was to deny completely the validity of science and to live entirely within the self—'Only in the fact of consciousness', says Hulme, 'is there a unity in the world'.[13]

But this was basically Tennyson's position too, and when Hulme asserts the value of intuitive as well as analytical thinking,[14] he is only endorsing Tennyson's faith in the heart standing up and answering 'I have felt', and advocating the kind of thought process which Tennyson exemplifies through his analogical syntax. Hulme draws upon Bergson's view of existence as a formless flux upon which,

---

[11] T. E. Hulme, *Speculations* (paperback, London, 1960), pp. 3–11.
[12] 'The Symbolism of Poetry' (1900), William Butler Yeats, *Essays and Introductions* (London, 1961), p. 163.
[13] Hulme, *Speculations*, p. 222.
[14] This is the main argument of 'Notes on Language and Style'. Cf. Baker, *Syntax in English Poetry*, chapter five.

because of the structure of our minds, we impose an artificial order; Tennyson evidently sensed that a form founded on analytical processes could falsify, for *In Memoriam* is built upon the principle of following the poet's consciousness. The issue is imperfectly revealed —imperfectly grasped, no doubt—by Tennyson, but the seeds are there. It is by no means true that Imagist theory and Tennyson's practice in *In Memoriam* are irreconcilably at odds. In his general outlook, his attitude to form, and his syntax Tennyson either anticipates or is recognizably a predecessor of Hulme.

There is no definite evidence of a connection between Hulme's thinking and Eliot's poetry, but the two are certainly not inconsistent. The very striking technique, specially prominent in *The Waste Land*, of baldly juxtaposing images so that the whole poem is pieced together like a mosaic can be related to Hulme's insistence that reality is distorted by the logical connecting processes we have learnt to apply. As I have suggested, Tennyson shows an awareness of this issue in *In Memoriam*. His repetitions of the same syntactic structures verge at times upon the simple effect of a sequence of images ungoverned by any rational procedures. There is little of the violence of Eliot, and the verse form, the inversions and the punctuation distract our attention from the implications of the technique; but consider these lines from section xcv, which I have altered only by moving one or two phrases:

> The brook alone was heard far-off
> And the fluttering urn on the board
> And bats in fragrant skies
> Went round.
>
> And the filmy shapes
> Wheeled or lit, that haunt the dusk with ermine capes
> And woolly breasts and beaded eyes.

Now here is part of 'What the Thunder said':

> A woman drew her long black hair out tight
> And fiddled whisper music on those strings
> And bats with baby faces in the violet light
> Whistled, and beat their wings
> And crawled head downward down a blackened wall
> And upside down in air were towers
> Tolling reminiscent bells, that kept the hours
> And voices singing out of empty cisterns and exhausted wells.

The sequences of relationships between the clauses in the two passages are really very similar. Tennyson's repetitions of structure, which I have called analogical syntax, make the connections between clauses as simple and undemanding as possible, so that we are left to move through a series of images. Eliot makes this the primary rationale of his verse; often the juxtapositions are more jerky than in the lines I have quoted, but fundamentally the method is the same.

The tendency to invest external objects with qualities indicative of the mental state of the speaker is also shared by Tennyson and Eliot. This too can be explained in terms of Hulme's Bergsonian account of the relationship between consciousness and the material world. Imagist theory tends to claim that the natural object should be presented just for itself, but in fact it usually seems the bearer of emotive connotations which we are expected, in Tennysonian fashion, to relate to the theme or the speaker. This is always true in Eliot—what could be more evocative, and in just the same way as sections x and xi of *In Memoriam*, than part IV of *The Waste Land*?—

> Phlebas the Phoenician, a fortnight dead,
> Forgot the cry of gulls, and the deep sea swell
> And the profit and loss.
>   A current under sea
> Picked his bones in whispers. As he rose and fell
> He passed the stages of his age and youth
> Entering the whirlpool.

As in *In Memoriam*, the detail indicates the exact significance: the second line seems to contain both the pathos and the grandeur of life; the whispers of the current suggest the reverence with which we are to regard the event; and the whirlpool may be either that where Phlebas' remains finally disintegrate or the vicissitudes of life. The example may not seem altogether typical of Eliot because the image is natural rather than urban, but exactly the same process is at work when he speaks of 'the dull canal/ On a winter evening round behind the gashouse'.

I have written of the absence of an established and agreed system of images whose connotations could be relied upon; this lack has clearly become much greater since 1850. One answer which Eliot finds is literary allusion, which enables him to draw upon systems which other men have created. Tennyson does this too, though to a much lesser extent. Like Eliot, he employs Dante as a source of spiritual imagery; the pastoral convention serves a similar function in *In Memoriam*, but the myth is doubtless too simple to act as a credible antithesis to twentieth-century conditions. However, the most fundamental and important link between the practice of Tennyson and his successors is the use of recurring images which achieve the status of symbols. This becomes the usual method of creating a coherent and yet evocative system of value-bearing images to which the reader can be referred for an indication of the poet's intellectual and emotional attitude. Yeats (like Blake) evolved an entire mythology which exists, as a rule, in an abstract and private world of its own somewhere above the poem; we must make ourselves sufficiently informed to be able to pluck it down and apply it at the poet's whim. Eliot, with brilliant inspiration, uses in *The Waste Land* the vegetation myths of *The Golden Bough*. Thus he draws upon the symbolic system which *other* societies found significant—societies, that is, which had not suffered the fragmentation of modern western Europe. The very mention of the Hanged God is ironical because it reminds us of the absence of such deep-rooted and generally accepted symbols in our own culture.

In *The Waste Land*, as in *In Memoriam*, the major point to notice is that these symbols are not static: they change their connotations with the development of the experience of the poet. 'I sat upon the shore / Fishing, with the arid plain behind me', which occurs a few lines from the end, is filled with echoes from the rest of the poem—indeed, without them it would be practically meaningless. Both Tennyson and Eliot build up round certain images a strong group of associations which fertilize, and are fertilized by, each successive appearance, so that by the end of the poem a brief mention can recall the whole of the poet's experience. We again find the Romantic elements in Tennyson's use of language persisting into the twentieth century.

The connections I have been making may seem surprising, for it is well-known that Eliot wrote slightingly of Tennyson in this period. He thought him a 'reflective poet. Tennyson and Browning are poets, and they think; but they do not feel their thought as immediately as the odour of a rose.'[15] Yet Arthur Hallam, in his review of Tennyson's 1830 volume, contrasted him with Milton and Wordsworth and linked him with Shelley and Keats, whom he called 'poets

[15] *Selected Prose*, p. 110.

P

of sensation rather than reflection'. He makes his point in terms very like Eliot's:

> So vivid was the delight attending the simple exertions of eye and ear, that it became mingled more and more with their trains of active thought, and tended to absorb their whole being into the energy of sense. Other poets *seek* for images to illustrate their conceptions; these men had no need to seek; they lived in a world of images.[16]

There is a clear similarity in ideas here. I believe that Eliot is the successor to a line of thinking about poetry and language which is gradually clarified and emphasized by the Symbolists and others during the nineteenth century—McLuhan points out that Yeats found Hallam's essay an invaluable key to Symbolism.[17] The qualities in the language of *In Memoriam* which might commend themselves to our insecure century are completely interwoven with forms which we have felt obliged to discard, but in general terms I see a continuity. The anxieties which Tennyson faced have intensified so that his form of resolution is no longer acceptable, and correspondingly certain features of his use of language have been accentuated and others largely abandoned. This makes him a very difficult poet for us, since it is hard to disconnect him completely from our modern sensibility, but impossible to see him as a satisfactory expression of it.

So my investigation into the language of *In Memoriam* ends by coming back to the problem of the strange attraction of Tennyson's writing and modern critical attitudes to it. It is not for me to assess the achievements of this study; I can only restate the objective, which was to add to our understanding of the nature of Tennyson's expertise with language. I began by quoting section xi:

> Calm on the seas, and silver sleep,
>   And waves that sway themselves in rest,
>   And dead calm in that noble breast
> Which heaves but with the heaving deep.

It *is* good; and yet, after all the analysis and speculation, one wonders whether we are really much closer to the essential power of the linguistic structures Tennyson created. Diction, syntax, imagery, sound and rhythm have been examined with a variety of techniques, and

---

[16] Motter (ed.), *The Writings of Arthur Hallam*, p. 186.
[17] Killham, *Critical Essays*, p. 67.

hypotheses have been presented about how different manifestations should be regarded in terms of their relationships to each other, to the themes of the poem, and to the more important currents of nineteenth- and twentieth-century thought. The inner temple of imaginative genius will perhaps always be barred to criticism. We can only endeavour continually to approach a little nearer to the central mystery; the major advances will be infrequent, but most attempts should furnish one or two hints which others will develop.

APPENDIX A

ANALYTICAL AND ANALOGICAL SYNTAX

MY belief that Tennyson's syntax is suited not for rational examination of an idea, but for the giving of successive analogues[1] can be supported by analysis based upon linguistic categories adapted from Dr. Hasan's description.[2] For contrast with *In Memoriam* I propose to use a stanza from Donne's 'A Valediction: of Weeping'; it is one which T. S. Eliot quotes with the comment that it requires 'considerable agility on the part of the reader'.[3] This is an understatement; the lines are very hard to analyse grammatically, but it is to be hoped that my efforts come near enough for the present purpose.

> On a round ball
> A workman that hath copies by, can lay
> An Europe, Afrique, and an Asia,
> And quickly make that, which was nothing, *All*,   4
> So doth each teare,
> Which thee doth weare,
> A globe, yea world by that impression grow,
> Till thy tears mixt with mine doe overflow   8
> This world, by waters sent from thee, my heaven dissolved so.

The sentence, the clause, the group (e.g. the nominal group), the word and the phoneme are all units, and they are ranked in order of inclusiveness. The following diagram represents a syntactical analysis of this stanza at the sentence rank:

B &B   F B

$\longleftarrow \quad \longleftarrow$

$\longrightarrow$

In Dr. Hasan's model, there are basically two kinds of clause: those represented by F are non-presupposing, those by B are dependent or presupposing—that is, they cannot stand by themselves as complete

[1] See above, p. 100.
[2] Ruqaiya Hasan, 'A linguistic study of contrasting features in the style of two contemporary prose writers', unpubl. diss. (Edinburgh, 1964). Dr. Hasan generously commented on an early draft of this appendix, though I should add that the procedures presented here do not in all respects reflect her current thinking.
[3] *Selected Prose*, p. 106.

utterances because their form demands another clause to make them entirely meaningful. The arrows signify the direction and the extent of presupposition.

There are four elements in the Donne sentence. The first clause consists of the first three lines and (though it is an unusual construction) has been taken as presupposing the clause beginning 'So doth' in line 5. Line 4 is the second clause and, since it is linked to the first but not dependent upon it, it is represented by &B. Lines 5–7 make up the third clause, and this is non-presupposing and therefore signified by F. And the last two lines comprise the fourth clause, which is presupposing and represented by B. The positioning of the arrows indicates layering—whilst &B presupposes the initial B, and the final B presupposes F, at another layer the whole complex B &B presupposes the whole complex F B.

The clauses I have described are those which operate at the sentence rank; the other six clauses in the stanza are rank-shifted—that is, they operate within another clause or within a group. Thus 'that hath copies by' (line 2) is a rank-shifted qualifier in the nominal group headed by 'A workman'; 'which was nothing' (line 4) qualifies 'that'; 'which thee doth weare' (line 6) qualifies 'each teare'; 'mixt with mine' (line 8) qualifies 'thy tears'; 'by waters sent from thee' (line 9) qualifies 'this world'; and 'my heaven dissolved so' (line 9) qualifies 'thee'. These six clauses are rank-shifted; by definition they operate at a deeper layer in the structure than the four clauses I considered first.

The account I have just given represents what I take to be the more obvious way of understanding the stanza, but at some points different interpretations are possible. Thus in the last line 'my heaven' might be regarded as in apposition to 'thee', in which case the rank-shifted clause would be 'dissolved so', qualifying 'my heaven'. Or, alternatively, 'my heaven' may be in apposition to 'This world'—the convolutions through which the imagery has passed make this quite possible. These ambiguities further complicate the syntax of the stanza.

Now here is the second sentence of section xvi of *In Memoriam*; it runs from line 2 of the section to the end:

> Can calm despair and wild unrest
> Be tenants of a single breast,
> Or sorrow such a changeling be?

Or doth she only seem to take   5
  The touch of change in calm or storm;
  But knows no more of transient form
In her deep self, than some dead lake

That holds the shadow of a lark   9
  Hung in the shadow of a heaven?
  Or has the shock, so harshly given,
Confused me like the unhappy bark

That strikes by night a craggy shelf,   13
  And staggers blindly ere she sink?
  And stunn'd me from my power to think
And all my knowledge of myself;

And made me that delirious man   17
  Whose fancy fuses old and new,
  And flashes into false and true,
  And mingles all without a plan?

Now follows the analysis at sentence rank:

F   &F   &F   &F   &F   &F   &F
←——←———←———←——←———←

The first clause occupies lines 2 and 3; the second, line 4; the third, lines 5 and 6; the fourth, lines 7–10; the fifth, lines 11–14; the sixth, lines 15–16; and the seventh comprises the whole of the last stanza.

There are nine rank-shifted clauses: 'That holds the shadow of a lark' (line 9) qualifying 'lake'; 'Hung in the shadow of a heaven' (line 10) qualifying 'lark'; 'so harshly given' (line 11) qualifying 'shock'; 'That strikes by night a craggy shelf' and 'And staggers blindly ere she sink' (lines 13–14) both qualifying 'bark', and within the second, 'ere she sink'; and each of the last three lines is a rank-shifted clause qualifying 'man'.

These diagrams reveal very clearly a number of differences, all of which reinforce my claim that Donne's syntax is designed to analyse a situation whereas Tennyson's is devoted to the provision of successive equivalents which redefine an experience in other terms so that we appreciate its nature through a process of analogy. The Tennyson passage contains no dependent clauses—it is entirely paratactic. There are no B clauses to tell us about conditions and results, causes and effects: we find a simple string of linked F clauses.

Secondly, there is no layering—we are not asked to take one complex of clauses and relate it to another, but can follow straight through the series, moving from clause to clause without being required at each step to take account of a whole cluster of constructions. Thirdly, there is no ambiguity in the relationships between the clauses in the Tennyson sentence (though I do not believe that syntactical ambiguity, at least in such simple terms, is a typical contrastive feature in the two authors).

Moreover, we find that Tennyson frequently repeats a structure so that successive clauses often provide an additional way of regarding the same phenomenon. This is true both of the clauses operating at the sentence rank and of the rank-shifted clauses. The latter are paired in 'That strikes by night a craggy shelf / And staggers blindly ere she sink', and they occur in a trio in the last lines: the 'delirious man' is successively redefined as one

> Whose fancy fuses old and new,
> And flashes into false and true,
> And mingles all without a plan?

In the Lincoln manuscript Tennyson can be seen encouraging us to be aware of the kind of syntax he is using, for in his first version of the last line he wrote 'In all his works without a plan'. The final reading is very nearly parallel with the preceding lines, and the nature of the structure he prefers becomes very evident. The redefining process is also highly explicit in the F clauses, which amount to something like, Is it this? or that? or can it be this? or that?—which has done this, and this, and this? At every point Tennyson's syntax presents us with a further way of interpreting the poet's state of mind, whereas Donne, who uses this kind of linkage only once, enters into a complicated analysis of the situation in which our attention is drawn primarily to the logical complexities involved.

These analyses should illustrate the individual character of the syntax, and therefore the thought processes, employed in *In Memoriam*. Tennyson's syntax is suited to redefinition rather than rational examination—we build up our understanding of the poet's experience from a series of impressions with a minimum of conscious logical organization in the syntax. The poet says explicitly that an intuitive approach is superior to rational analysis, and this outlook is embodied in the syntax of *In Memoriam*.

APPENDIX B

PHONETIC SYMBOLS

Vowels

Short:				
	hid	i	hood	u
	head	e	bud	ʌ
	had	æ	sitter	ə
	hod	ɔ		

Long Pure:				
	heed	iː	fool	uː
	hard	aː	heard	əː
	hoard	ɔː		

Dipthongal:				
	fail	ei	peer	iə
	file	ai	pear	eə
	foil	ɔi	poor	uə
	foal	ou	pore	ɔə
	fowl	au		

Consonants

Plosive:

Unvoiced		Voiced	
pin	p	bin	b
tin	t	din	d
kin	k	got	g

Affricate:

Unvoiced		Voiced	
chin	tʃ	gin	dʒ

Continuant (all voiced):

maim	m	ring	ŋ
nigh	n		

Non-fricative (lateral) (voiced):

lame	l

Non-fricative (vowel-like) (all voiced):

win	w	rot	r
yacht	j		

Fricative:	Unvoiced		Voiced	
	fin	f	vie	v
	thin	θ	thy	ð
	sigh	s	zoo	z
	shoe	ʃ	rouge	ʒ
	hot	h		

CHECKLIST OF SECTIONS
DISCUSSED IN SOME DETAIL

(* indicates that a draft version is mentioned)

INDEX

Pope, Alexander, 58, 76, 199; compared to
  Tennyson, 17, 26, 36, 76, 90, 178, 180,
  198
Pound, Ezra, 199, 205
Pre-Raphaelites, the, 204
Prickett, Stephen, 21n., 30
pronouns, 35, 71, 74, 78, 81–3, 99, 190,
  194
public issues, in the Enlightenment and
  Romanticism, 31–3, 37; in *In Memoriam*,
  31–3, 37, 50–1, 64, 109, 112, 116, 118,
  138, 154, 203; in modern poetry,
  197–201, 202, 203
Pyre, J. F. A., 59, 177, 179–80, 185

Raleigh, Sir Walter, 61
rank-shift, 213–15
Rawnsley, H. D., 158
reason, in the Enlightenment and Romanticism, 19–21, 29, 201, 206; in *In
  Memoriam*, 25, 29, 36, 101–2, 104, 156,
  201, 204, 215; and modern poetry, 201,
  206
'redefinition', 29–30, 99–104, 113–14,
  146–7, 185, 215; in other poets, 29–30
Redin, Mats, 76
religious faith, 24–6, 37–8, 42–4, 58, 68–
  70, 85–6, 108–12, 116, 165–6, 190–3,
  200; in the Enlightenment and Romanticism, 18–21, 68–9, 101; and syntax,
  91–4, 101–2; Hallam and Christ, 109–10;
  imagery unsatisfactory, 110–11, 151;
  see also evolutionary resolution, visionary experience
rhetoric: *see* stylization
rhyme, 3, 163, 165–6, 170, 179–80, 183–4,
  185, 192, 198
rhythm and metre, 2, 3, 6, 7, 8, 173–95,
  197; typical movement, 3, 91, 162–3,
  175–81, 186; expressive uses, 6, 152,
  170, 186–95; nature and functions,
  173–5, 181; pause, 176, 179, 181, 182,
  184–5, 186–7, 190–3; and stanza form,
  176, 182–5; and syntax, 176, 181, 184,
  189–95; and sound, 178–80, 188, 193,
  194; Tennyson and Pope, 178, 180;
  Tennyson and Spenser and Milton,
  178–9; Tennyson and Donne, 180; in
  modern poetry, 197, 198
Richards, I. A., 41n., 134n., 185–6
Ricks, Christopher, 15
Riffaterre, Michael, 8, 9n.
Rimbaud, Arthur, 202

Robins, Robert H., 47, 74n.
Romanticism, described, 20–2, 140;
  characteristics in *In Memoriam*, 17–18,
  22–40, 56, 68, 72–3, 90, 101–4, 112–14,
  116, 119–20, 140–1, 195, 197, 201, 202,
  206; and modern poetry, 201–10; *see
  also* experience
Rosetti, Dante Gabriel, 54, 204
Ruskin, John, 127
Ryals, Clyde de L., 109, 120

Saporta, Sol, 4n., 12n.
Sassoon, Sir Siegfried, 76
science, 25, 50–1, 102–4, 115–18, 201, 206;
  in the Enlightenment and Romanticism, 18–21, 206; in other poets, 116–17;
  and modern poetry, 203, 206
Sebeok, Thomas A., 4n., 7n., 9n., 12n.,
  14n., 164n., 168n., 169n., 173n., 174n.,
  180n.
section sequence, 26–9, 30, 106, 182, 195,
  202–3
Sendry, Joseph, 63n.
sex, 113–14, 200
Shakespeare, William, 10, 12–13, 42, 57,
  146, 150, 177
Shelley, Percy Bysshe, 13; compared to
  Tennyson, 29, 63–4, 111, 117, 127, 209
simile, 108, 133–4, 164; and metaphor,
  136–9
Sinclair, J. McH., 11
Skelton, Robin, 143n.
Smith, Edward Elton, 18
sound, 2, 5, 6, 7, 13, 157–72, 198; and
  mental states, 126, 167–72, 188; Tennyson and Spenser and Milton, 157, 162,
  178–9; common patterns, 158–64, 177;
  linking ideas, 164–7; and rhythm, 178–
  80, 188, 193, 194; *see also* rhyme
Spencer, John, 3n., 11, 47n.
Spenser, Edmund, 157, 162, 178–9
Spitzer, Leo, 179n.
Stageburg, Norman C., 11n.
Stankiewitz, Edward, 14n.
stanza form, 6, 91, 147, 175, 182–5, 207;
  and syntax, 36, 91, 125, 152, 184; and
  sound, 163, 165–6, 179–80; 183–4; and
  rhythm, 182, 184–5
Storey, Graham, 90n.
structure, poetic, 5–10, 15, 39, 58, 74,
  163, 168, 174
style, 3–4, 8, 16, 17, 20, 33–4
stylization, in the Enlightenment and